비상은 모두가 즐거운
배움의 길을 만듭니다.

배움이 필요한 모든 이들이 그 한계를 넘어설 수 있도록
비상은 더 넓은 세상을 향한 첫 걸음을 응원합니다.

한국에서의 전형 창출을 넘어 세계 교육의 패러다임을
바꾸겠다는 비상은 모든 이의 혁신적 성장에 기여합니다.

교육 문화의 질서와 유기적 융합을 추구하는 비상은
새로운 미래 세대의 행복한 경험과 성장에 기여합니다.

상상 그 이상 ──────

중학 영어의 모든 것

VISANG

All that

중학영어 **3**-2

구성과 특징

PART I 실력 다지기

All that Grammar

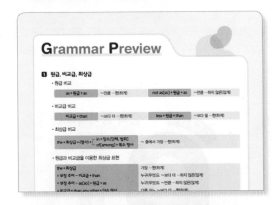

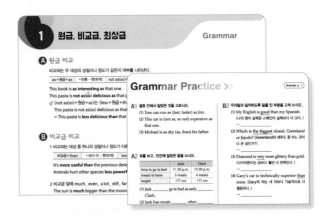

- 단원을 학습하기 전에 꼭 알아야 할 핵심 문법 개념을 소개하는 자기주도적 학습 장치

- 주요 교과서를 철저히 분석하여 구성한 체계적인 문법 목차
- [개념 소개] → [Grammar Practice] → [Grammar Test] 3단계로 구성된 체계적인 문법 학습 시스템
- 출제 빈도가 높은 기출 문항들을 엄선하여 수록한 연습 문제

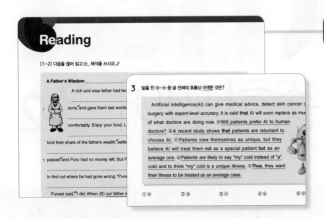

All that Reading

- 재미있고 다양한 소재의 지문 수록
- 교과서 지문을 이용한 끊어 읽기, 해석 연습
- 실제 시험과 유사한 독해 문항 유형을 다양하게 수록

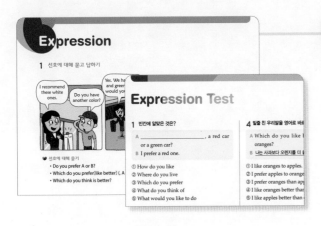

All that Expression

- 주요 교과서에 소개된 의사소통 기능을 엄선하여 소개
- 대화 상황을 재미있는 만화로 생생하게 제시
- 다양한 유형의 기출 문항들을 엄선하여 수록

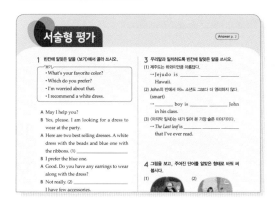

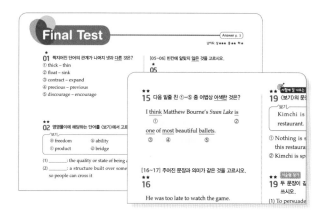

• 문법과 표현을 적용한 서술형 평가 제공
• 학교 서술형 평가 완벽 대비를 위한 다양한 문제 수록

• 실제 시험과 동일한 유형으로 구성된 종합 평가
• 여러 난이도의 문제를 빈출 유형 위주로 수록

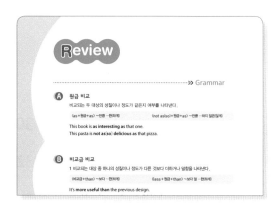

• 단원에서 학습한 문법과 의사소통 기능 복습
• 학습 내용을 도식화하여 신속한 이해 점검 가능

PART II 듣기 실전 모의고사

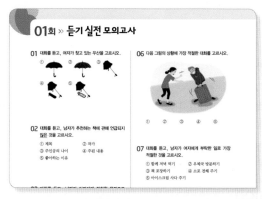

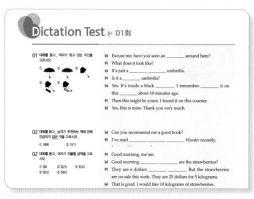

• 시·도 교육청 영어 듣기능력평가를 분석하여 반영한 듣기 실전 모의고사 5회 수록
• 실제 시험과 유사한 분량 및 녹음속도의 듣기 자료를 통해 실전 적응력 향상
• 듣기 능력을 향상시켜줄 Dictation Test 제공

차례

How To Study

* 월간, 주간, 일간 학습 계획을 세운 후 공부하는 습관을 가져 보세요. 무턱대고 공부하는 것보다 훨씬 체계적이고 계획적으로 공부할 수 있어요.
* 먼저, 구체적으로 공부할 분량을 파악한 후에 학습 목표를 세워 보세요. 목표를 세울 때는 막연하거나 장황하지 않게 구체적으로 세우는 것이 중요해요. 그렇게 해야 계획대로 공부할 수 있고 목표한 만큼은 반드시 끝낸다는 마음으로 공부할 수 있어서 효율적이에요.

60일 완성 학습 계획표

Lesson 01 비교 구문

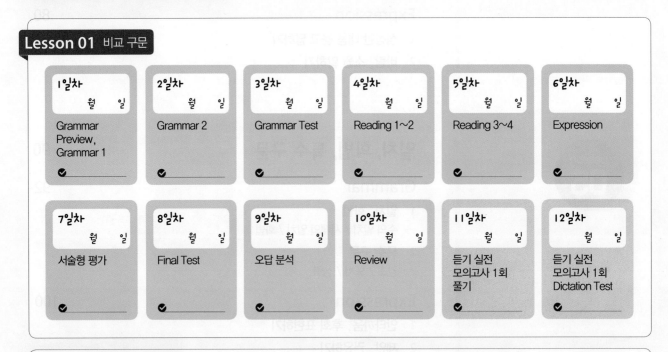

1일차 월 일	2일차 월 일	3일차 월 일	4일차 월 일	5일차 월 일	6일차 월 일
Grammar Preview, Grammar 1	Grammar 2	Grammar Test	Reading 1~2	Reading 3~4	Expression

7일차 월 일	8일차 월 일	9일차 월 일	10일차 월 일	11일차 월 일	12일차 월 일
서술형 평가	Final Test	오답 분석	Review	듣기 실전 모의고사 1회 풀기	듣기 실전 모의고사 1회 Dictation Test

Lesson 02 분사, 분사구문

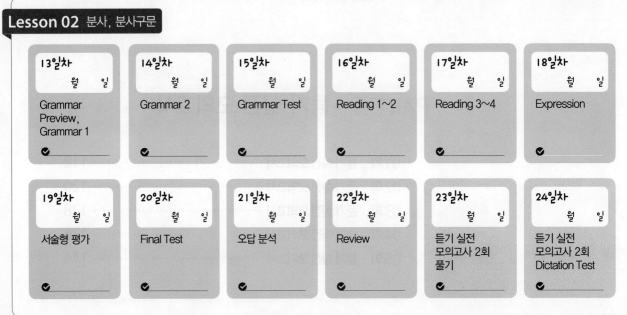

13일차 월 일	14일차 월 일	15일차 월 일	16일차 월 일	17일차 월 일	18일차 월 일
Grammar Preview, Grammar 1	Grammar 2	Grammar Test	Reading 1~2	Reading 3~4	Expression

19일차 월 일	20일차 월 일	21일차 월 일	22일차 월 일	23일차 월 일	24일차 월 일
서술형 평가	Final Test	오답 분석	Review	듣기 실전 모의고사 2회 풀기	듣기 실전 모의고사 2회 Dictation Test

Lesson 03 접속사

25일차 월 일	26일차 월 일	27일차 월 일	28일차 월 일	29일차 월 일	30일차 월 일
Grammar Preview, Grammar 1	Grammar 2	Grammar Test	Reading 1~2	Reading 3~4	Expression
✓	✓	✓	✓	✓	✓

31일차 월 일	32일차 월 일	33일차 월 일	34일차 월 일	35일차 월 일	36일차 월 일
서술형 평가	Final Test	오답 분석	Review	듣기 실전 모의고사 3회 풀기	듣기 실전 모의고사 3회 Dictation Test
✓	✓	✓	✓	✓	✓

Lesson 04 가정법

37일차 월 일	38일차 월 일	39일차 월 일	40일차 월 일	41일차 월 일	42일차 월 일
Grammar Preview, Grammar 1	Grammar 2	Grammar Test	Reading 1~2	Reading 3~4	Expression
✓	✓	✓	✓	✓	✓

43일차 월 일	44일차 월 일	45일차 월 일	46일차 월 일	47일차 월 일	48일차 월 일
서술형 평가	Final Test	오답 분석	Review	듣기 실전 모의고사 4회 풀기	듣기 실전 모의고사 4회 Dictation Test
✓	✓	✓	✓	✓	✓

Lesson 05 일지, 화법, 특수 구문

49일차 월 일	50일차 월 일	51일차 월 일	52일차 월 일	53일차 월 일	54일차 월 일
Grammar Preview, Grammar 1	Grammar 2	Grammar Test	Reading 1~2	Reading 3~4	Expression
✓	✓	✓	✓	✓	✓

55일차 월 일	56일차 월 일	57일차 월 일	58일차 월 일	59일차 월 일	60일차 월 일
서술형 평가	Final Test	오답 분석	Review	듣기 실전 모의고사 5회 풀기	듣기 실전 모의고사 5회 Dictation Test
✓	✓	✓	✓	✓	✓

돌아보는 1학기 차례

PART

I

실력 다지기

Lesson 01

비교 구문

Grammar Preview

1 원급, 비교급, 최상급

• 원급 비교

| as + 원급 + as | ~만큼 …한(하게) | not as[so] + 원급 + as | ~만큼 …하지 않은(않게) |

• 비교급 비교

| 비교급 + than | ~보다 더 …한(하게) | less + 원급 + than | ~보다 덜 …한(하게) |

• 최상급 비교

| the + 최상급 + (명사) + ⌈ in + 장소[단체, 범위] / of[among] + 복수 명사 | ~ 중에서 가장 …한(하게) |

• 원급과 비교급을 이용한 최상급 표현

the + 최상급	가장 …한(하게)
= 부정 주어 ~ 비교급 + than	누구(무엇)도 ~보다 더 …하지 않은(않게)
= 부정 주어 ~ as[so] + 원급 + as	누구(무엇)도 ~만큼 …하지 않은(않게)
= 비교급 + than any other + 단수 명사	다른 어느 ~보다 더 …한(하게)
= 비교급 + than all the other + 복수 명사	다른 모든 ~들보다 더 …한(하게)

2 여러 가지 비교 표현

• 원급을 이용한 표현

as + 원급 + as + possible(주어 + can) 가능한 한 …한(하게)

배수사 + as + 원급 + as ~배만큼 …한(하게)

= 배수사 + 비교급 + than ~보다 ~배 더 …한(하게)

• 비교급을 이용한 표현

비교급 + and + 비교급 점점 더 …한(하게)

the + 비교급(+ 주어 + 동사), the + 비교급(+ 주어 + 동사) ~하면 할수록 더 …하다

no more than (= only) 겨우   no less than (= as much(many) as) ~만큼이나

not more than (= at most) 기껏해야   not less than (= at least) 적어도, 최소한

• 최상급을 이용한 표현

one of the + 최상급 + 복수 명사 가장 …한 것들 중의 하나

the + 최상급(+ that) + 주어 + have ever + 과거분사 지금까지 ~한 것들 중에서 가장 …한

1 원급, 비교급, 최상급

A 원급 비교

비교되는 두 대상의 성질이나 정도가 같은지 여부를 나타낸다.

as+원급+as	~만큼 …한(하게)	not as(so)+원급+as	~만큼 …하지 않은(않게)

This book is **as interesting as** that one.

This pasta is **not as(so) delicious as** that pizza.

cf. 〈not as(so)+원급+as〉는 〈less+원급+than〉으로 바꿔 쓸 수 있다.

This pasta is not as(so) delicious as that pizza.

= This pasta is **less delicious than** that pizza.

B 비교급 비교

1 비교되는 대상 중 하나의 성질이나 정도가 다른 것보다 더하거나 덜함을 나타낸다.

비교급+than	~보다 더 …한(하게)	less+원급+than	~보다 덜 …한(하게)

It's **more useful than** the previous design.

Animals hurt other species **less powerful than** them.

2 비교급 앞에 much, even, a lot, still, far 등을 써서 '훨씬'의 의미를 더한다.

The sun is **much** bigger than the moon.

> **◆ Plus Grammar**
> ┌ senior to (~보다 연상인)
> └ junior to (~보다 연하인)
> ┌ superior to (~보다 월등한)
> └ inferior to (~보다 열등한)
> Mike is **superior to** his brother in English. (Mike는 그의 동생보다 영어 실력이 더 낫다.)

C 최상급 비교

1 셋 이상의 비교 대상 중에서 하나가 '가장 ~하다'의 의미를 나타낸다.

the+최상급+(명사)+ ⎡ in+장소(단체, 범위) ⎣ of(among)+복수 명사	~ 중에서 가장 …한(하게)

Love is **the most valuable** thing **in** the world.

Hilary was **the wisest of all the students**.

cf. 부사의 최상급 앞에는 대개 the를 쓰지 않는다.

Travis behaves **most politely** in the office.

2 원급과 비교급을 이용한 최상급 표현

the+최상급	가장 …한(하게)
= 부정 주어 ~ 비교급+than	누구(무엇)도 ~보다 더 …하지 않은(않게)
= 부정 주어 ~ as(so)+원급+as	누구(무엇)도 ~만큼 …하지 않은(않게)
= 비교급+than any other+단수 명사	다른 어느 ~보다 더 …한(하게)
= 비교급+than all the other+복수 명사	다른 모든 ~들보다 더 …한(하게)

Chris is **the tallest** boy in the class.

= **No (other) boy** in the class is **taller than** Chris.

= **No (other) boy** in the class is **as(so) tall as** Chris.

= Chris is **taller than any other boy** in the class.

= Chris is **taller than all the other boys** in the class.

Grammar Practice >>

Answer p. 1

A1 괄호 안에서 알맞은 것을 고르시오.

(1) Tom can run as (fast, faster) as Jim.

(2) This car is (not as, so not) expensive as that one.

(3) Michael is as shy (as, than) his father.

A2 표를 보고, 빈칸에 알맞은 말을 쓰시오.

	Jack	Clark
time to go to bed	11:30 p.m.	10:00 p.m.
meals to have	3 meals	4 meals
height	177 cm	177 cm

(1) Jack _____ go to bed as early _____ Clark.

(2) Jack has meals _____ often _____ Clark does.

(3) Clark is _____ _____ as Jack.

B1 우리말과 일치하도록 주어진 단어를 이용하여 빈칸에 알맞은 말을 쓰시오.

(1) Helen은 그녀의 남편보다 더 조심스럽게 운전한다. (carefully)
→ Helen drives _____ _____ _____ her husband.

(2) Mandy는 첫 번째 호텔보다 덜 비싼 호텔을 골랐다. (expensive)
→ Mandy chose the hotel _____ _____ than the first one.

(3) 너는 수학에 대해 나보다 훨씬 더 많이 알아. (even)
→ You know _____ _____ about math _____ I do.

(4) Bobby는 그의 남동생보다 3살 많다. (senior)
→ Bobby is three years _____ _____ his brother.

B2 우리말과 일치하도록 밑줄 친 부분을 고쳐 쓰시오.

(1) My English is good than my Spanish.
(나의 영어 실력은 스페인어 실력보다 더 낫다.)
→ _____

(2) Which is the biggest island, Greenland or Jejudo? (Greenland와 제주도 중 어느 것이 더 큰 섬인가?)
→ _____

(3) Diamond is very more glittery than gold.
(다이아몬드는 금보다 훨씬 더 번쩍인다.)
→ _____

(4) Gary's car is technically superior than mine. (Gary의 차는 내 차보다 기술적으로 더 월등하다.)
→ _____

C1 다음 문장들의 의미가 일치하도록 빈칸에 알맞은 말을 쓰시오.

(1) Water is the most useful of all materials.
= Water is more useful than any _____ _____.
= No _____ material is more useful _____ water.

(2) Nothing is as precious as health.
= Health is _____ _____ precious thing _____ all.
= _____ is _____ precious than health.

(3) August is the hottest month in Korea.
= _____ _____ month in Korea is as _____ as August.
= August is hotter than _____ _____ month in Korea.
= August is hotter than _____ the other _____ in Korea.

교과서 어휘 **previous** 이전의 **valuable** 가치 있는 **politely** 공손하게 **meal** 끼니, 식사 **height** 키 **glittery** 번쩍이는 **technically** 기술적으로 **material** 물질 **precious** 귀중한

2 여러 가지 비교 표현   Grammar

D 원급을 이용한 표현

> as + 원급 + as + possible(주어 + can) 가능한 한 …한(하게)
> 배수사 + as + 원급 + as ~배만큼 …한(하게)
> = 배수사 + 비교급 + than ~보다 ~배 더 …한(하게)

◆ **Plus** Grammar

[원급 관용 표현]
as long as: ~하는 한 (시간)
as(so) far as: ~하는 한 (정도)
as good as: ~와 다름없는

Drink milk **as much as possible**.

= Drink milk **as much as you can**.

This room is about **twice as large as** that one.

= This room is about **twice larger than** that one.

E 비교급을 이용한 표현

> 비교급 + and + 비교급 점점 더 …한(하게)
> the + 비교급(+ 주어 + 동사), the + 비교급(+ 주어 + 동사) ~하면 할수록 더 …하다
> no more than (= only) 겨우
> no less than (= as much(many) as) ~만큼이나
> not more than (= at most) 기껏해야
> not less than (= at least) 적어도, 최소한

Your English ability is getting **better and better**.

The higher you climb up a mountain, **the colder** it becomes.

= As you climb up a mountain, it becomes colder.

There is room for **no more than** a bed and a desk.

Write a story of **not less than** 500 words on the subject.

cf. • 〈비교급 + and + 비교급〉 표현에서 단어의 비교급이 〈more + 원급〉의 형태이면
　　　〈more and more + 원급〉의 형태로 쓴다.
　　　The TV show is getting **more and more interesting**.

　　• 〈the + 비교급 + (주어 + 동사), the + 비교급 + (주어 + 동사)〉에서 의미가 통하는
　　　경우에는 주어와 동사를 생략해도 된다.
　　　The more (**you give**), the better (**I like**).

F 최상급을 이용한 표현

> one of the + 최상급 + 복수 명사 가장 …한 것들 중의 하나
> the + 최상급(+ that) + 주어 + have ever + 과거분사 지금까지 ~한 것들 중에서 가장 …한

◆ **Plus** Grammar

[최상급으로 쓰지 않는 형용사]
'절대, 최고' 상태를 뜻하는 perfect,
complete, unique,
favorite 등

The Eiffel Tower is **one of the most famous towers** in the world.

This is **the most beautiful sight that I have ever seen**.

Grammar Practice >

Answer p. 1

D1 괄호 안에서 알맞은 것을 고르시오.

(1) Judy ran away as fast as she (could, would).

(2) My shoes are (two, twice) cheaper than yours.

(3) My dog ran after the thief as fast as (possible, possibly).

(4) Mt. Everest is (three times as, as three times) high as Mt. Baekdu.

D2 밑줄 친 부분을 어법에 맞게 고쳐 쓰시오.

(1) I drove as safely as I possible.
→ _____

(2) Asher ate three as much food as his sister. → _____

(3) This tablet PC is heavier twice than that one. → _____

(4) Alice's father weighs as twice much as her. → _____

E1 두 문장의 의미가 일치하도록 빈칸에 알맞은 말을 쓰시오.

(1) As you go higher, you can see more.
= _____ _____ you go up, _____ _____ you can see.

(2) Olivia has 10,000 won only.
= Olivia has _____ _____ than 10,000 won.

(3) You can enter the competition after practicing for not less than a year.
= You can enter the competition after practicing for a year at _____.

(4) The world keeps getting small gradually.
= The world is getting _____ and _____.

E2 우리말과 일치하도록 빈칸에 알맞은 말을 쓰시오.

(1) I have played tennis for _____ _____ than 2 months. (내가 테니스를 치기 시작한지는 기껏해야 두 달 됐다.)

(2) Penelope was _____ _____ than 23 years old. (Penelope가 23살이나 되었다.)

(3) Luckily, Carl's condition was getting _____ and _____. (다행히도, Carl의 상태는 점점 좋아지고 있었다.)

(4) The _____ you spend, the more you can save. (여러분이 덜 소비할수록, 여러분은 더 저축할 수 있다.)

F1 어법상 어색한 부분을 찾아 바르게 고쳐 쓰시오.

(1) Harry is one of the politest boy in the class. _____ → _____

(2) This soup is more delicious that I have ever had before.
_____ → _____

(3) It was one of the happier moments in her life. _____ → _____

(4) This is the most memorable scene that I ever saw. _____ → _____

F2 주어진 단어를 이용하여 우리말과 일치하도록 빈칸에 알맞은 말을 쓰시오.

(1) Bruce는 지금까지 내가 만났던 중 가장 강한 사람이다. (strong)
→ Bruce is _____.

(2) Beethoven은 가장 유명한 고전 음악 작곡가들 중 한 명이다. (composer)
→ Beethoven is _____ composers of classical music.

교과서 **possible** 가능한 **ability** 능력 **room** 공간 **subject** 주제 **sight** 풍경, 광경 **safely** 안전하게 **weigh** (무게가) ~이다
어휘 **competition** 경쟁, 대회 **gradually** 점차 **memorable** 기억할 만한 **composer** 작곡가

Grammar Test

[01~02] 빈칸에 알맞은 것을 고르시오.

01

If you exercise regularly, you can run as _____ as John.

① fast   ② slowly   ③ faster
④ more fast   ⑤ fastest

02

As time goes by, I got _____ and busier due to my work.

① busy   ② busily   ③ busier
④ more busy   ⑤ busiest

서술형 평가

[03~04] 우리말과 일치하도록 괄호 안의 단어들을 바르게 배열하시오.

03

Judy는 겨우 알파벳 정도만 알았다.

→ Judy knew _____.
(more, the, no, alphabet, than)

04

나는 수학이 영어보다 훨씬 더 쉽다고 생각한다.

→ I think _____ than English. (math, much, easier, is)

05 밑줄 친 ①-⑤ 중 어법상 어색한 것은?

Seoul is one of the largest city in the world.
        ① ②   ③   ④ ⑤

서술형 평가

06 문장들의 의미가 일치하도록 빈칸에 알맞은 말을 쓰시오.

Incheon Bridge is the longest bridge in Korea.

= No other bridge in Korea is _____ _____ _____ Incheon Bridge.
= No other bridge in Korea is _____ _____ Incheon Bridge.
= Incheon Bridge is _____ _____ _____ _____ _____ in Korea.

07 빈칸에 알맞은 것은?

A Mom, I'm home.
B Hi, Adam. Oh, you'd better wash your hands first. Wash your hands for not _____ than 30 seconds.

① more   ② less   ③ harder
④ later   ⑤ earlier

교과서 어휘 **regularly** 규칙적으로 **go by** (시간이) 경과하다 **due to** ~ 때문에 **city** 도시 **bridge** 다리 **wash** 씻다 **second** 초

08 두 문장의 의미가 일치하도록 할 때 빈칸에 알맞은 것은?

Billy is not so diligent as his son.
= Billy is _____ than his son.

① less diligent
② more diligent
③ as diligent as
④ less more diligent
⑤ much more diligent

09 두 문장을 비교하는 문장으로 바꿔 쓸 때 빈칸에 알맞은 말을 쓰시오.

• My sister is 20 kg.
• My mother is 60 kg.

→ My mother is _____ _____ heavier than my sister.

10 의미하는 바가 나머지와 다른 것은?
① Nothing is as important as freedom.
② Freedom is the most important thing.
③ Nothing is not so important as freedom.
④ Nothing is more important than freedom.
⑤ Freedom is more important than anything else.

11 우리말과 일치하도록 빈칸에 알맞은 말을 쓰시오.

우리는 더 많이 가지면 가질수록 점점 더 많이 원한다.

→ _____ _____ we have, _____ _____ we want.

12 밑줄 친 부분 중 어법상 어색한 것은?
① I tried to speak as louder as I can.
② Pigs grow much faster than dogs do.
③ The richer we get, the more worried we are.
④ This product is more expensive than that one.
⑤ Axel is the most intelligent man that I've ever met.

13 표의 내용과 일치하도록 주어진 단어를 이용하여 빈칸에 알맞은 말을 쓰시오.

	Kate	Lisa
키	150 cm	160 cm
몸무게	45 kg	50 kg

(1) Lisa is _____ _____ Kate. (tall)
(2) Kate is _____ _____ _____ Lisa. (heavy)

교과서 diligent 부지런한 son 아들 freedom 자유 loud 크게, 시끄럽게 product 제품 intelligent 명석한
어휘

Reading

[1~2] 다음을 끊어 읽고 ☑, 해석을 쓰시오. ✎

Why We Buy What We Buy

Have you wondered✓why you've bought things✓that you don't even want or need?

3 Let's consider✓what affects us✓when it comes to buying things.

Why do I want to buy✓what my friends bought?

Jeff goes to the shopping center✓and sees ⓐa pair of soccer shoes on display. He recognizes ⓑthe

6 shoes at a glance✓because more than half of the boys on his soccer team wear ⓒthem. Although he

already has many pairs of ⓓsoccer shoes,✓he ends up buying another ⓔnew pair. We can use the

"bandwagon effect"✓to explain Jeff's behavior. A bandwagon is a wagon in a parade✓that encourages

9 people✓to jump aboard and enjoy the music. (A) As more and more people get on the bandwagon,✓

others are more likely to get on or follow it. In this way,✓people tend to buy something✓just because

other people have bought it.

---

1 밑줄 친 ⓐ–ⓔ 중 가리키는 대상이 나머지와 다른 것은?

① ⓐ   ② ⓑ   ③ ⓒ   ④ ⓓ   ⑤ ⓔ

2 밑줄 친 (A)를 다음과 같이 바꿔 쓸 때 빈칸에 알맞은 말을 쓰시오.

→ _____ on the bandwagon, the more likely others are to get on or follow it.

교과서 wonder 궁금해하다 affect 영향을 끼치다 when it comes to ~에 있어서 on display 진열된 at a glance 한눈에
어휘 🎧 end up -ing 결국 ~하다 bandwagon 악대차 encourage ~을 독려하다 aboard 탑승하여 tend to ~하는 경향이 있다

3 다음 글에서 Vespa에 관한 내용과 일치하지 <u>않는</u> 것은?

환경
지구

There are millions of trash floating above the Earth. Most of them are not **bigger than** a pea. But some chunks are **much larger than others**. Among them is a piece of trash called Vespa. It once was a part of a rocket and weighs about 100 kg. It can be dangerous to active satellites and spacecraft. The European Space Agency(ESA) will soon start a project to clean it up. They plan to launch a collector craft, which will grab Vespa floating in space. When the collector goes back to the Earth with Vespa, both of them will burn in Earth's atmosphere.

① 우주를 떠다니는 우주 쓰레기이다.
② 콩만큼의 크기로 매우 작다.
③ 현재 활동 중인 위성이나 우주선에 큰 위험이 된다.
④ 유럽에서 이것을 제거하기 위한 프로젝트를 곧 시작할 것이다.
⑤ 유럽 우주 기구(ESA)의 계획이 성공하면 지구의 대기 중에서 불타 없어질 것이다.

4 주어진 문장 다음에 이어질 (A)–(C)의 순서로 알맞은 것은?

인체

Your body is always trying to keep its temperature **as** close to 37°C **as possible**.

(A) For example, when you feel cold, you start shivering. That's because your body creates heat by contracting and expanding your muscles quickly.

(B) When you feel hot, on the other hand, you begin sweating. Sweat is mainly water and as the water in the sweat evaporates, the body cools down.

(C) However, when the body temperature gets **lower than** 29.5°C or **higher than** 40°C, it threatens your health and can be an emergency situation.

In order to keep the right temperature, your body reacts in various way.

① (A) – (C) – (B)   ② (B) – (A) – (C)   ③ (B) – (C) – (A)
④ (C) – (A) – (B)   ⑤ (C) – (B) – (A)

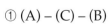

3   **float** 떠다니다, 뜨다   **chunk** 덩어리, 조각   **satellite** 인공위성   **spacecraft** 우주선   **launch** 발사하다   **atmosphere** 대기
4   **shiver** 떨다   **contract** 수축하다   **expand** 이완하다, 확장하다   **evaporate** 증발하다   **cool down** (열기가) 식다   **react** 반응하다

Expression

1 선호에 대해 묻고 답하기

💜 **선호에 대해 묻기**

- Do you prefer A or B?
- Which do you prefer(like better) (, A or B)?
- Which do you think is better?

💜 **선호하는 것 말하기**

- (I think) I'd prefer ....
- I prefer A (to B).
- I like A better (than B).
- I think A is better (than B).

2 걱정 표현하기 / 안심시키기

💜 **걱정 표현하기**

- I'm worried about ....
- I'm worried that ....
- I'm concerned(anxious) about ....

💜 **안심시키기**

- Don't worry. / Cheer up! / Be positive.
- Things will be better.
- (I'm sure) Everything will be OK(fine).
- I'm sure you'll do better next time.
- Don't be frightened(discouraged / disappointed).

Expression Test

Answer p. 2

1 빈칸에 알맞은 것은?

A _____, a red car or a green car?

B I prefer a red one.

① How do you like
② Where do you live
③ Which do you prefer
④ What do you think of
⑤ What would you like to do

서술형 평가

2 빈칸에 들어갈 말을 〈보기〉에서 골라 알맞은 형태로 쓰시오.

┌─보기─────────────────────┐
│ encourage   discourage   better │
└─────────────────────────┘

A I got terrible scores on my final test.

B Don't _____. You will do better next time.

3 다음 중 의도하는 바가 나머지와 다른 것은?
① Be positive.
② Don't worry.
③ I didn't mean it.
④ Everything will be fine.
⑤ I'm sure you'll do better next time.

4 밑줄 친 우리말을 영어로 바르게 옮긴 것은?

A Which do you like better, apples or oranges?

B 나는 사과보다 오렌지를 더 좋아해.

① I like oranges to apples.
② I prefer apples to oranges.
③ I prefer oranges than apples.
④ I like oranges better than apples.
⑤ I like apples better than oranges.

5 빈칸에 알맞은 것은?

A Why the long face?

B Hmm ... My mother has been in hospital since last Tuesday. _____.

① I'm proud of her
② I'm happy about her
③ I'm concerned about her
④ I'm curious about her
⑤ let me introduce her

서술형 평가

6 다음 말에 이어질 대화를 순서대로 바르게 배열하시오.

What's wrong with you? You look worried.

ⓐ If you fail, you have no one to blame but yourself.

ⓑ You had a whole week to study.

ⓒ You know me. I don't start until the last minute.

ⓓ I'm worried about my grades. I didn't study enough for the exam.

_____

1 빈칸에 알맞은 말을 〈보기〉에서 골라 쓰시오.

> 보기
> • What's your favorite color?
> • Which do you prefer?
> • I'm worried about that.
> • I recommend a white dress.

A May I help you?

B Yes, please. I am looking for a dress to wear at the party.

A Here are two best selling dresses. A white dress with the beads and blue one with the ribbons. (1) _____

B I prefer the blue one.

A Good. Do you have any earrings to wear along with the dress?

B Not really. (2) _____ I have few accessories.

A How about these necklace and earrings? They seem to go well with the dress.

B Oh, thanks. I like them.

2 빈칸에 알맞은 말을 〈보기〉에서 골라 쓰시오. (형태 변화 가능)

> 보기
> other   many   interesting   great

(1) A How many books do you have?

   B I don't know. The wall of my living room is full of books so I think I have _____ books than you.

(2) A Who is your favorite singer? Michael Jackson?

   B He is one of the _____ singers of all time. But I like John Lennon.

(3) A Do you like math?

   B Yes. Math is _____ _____ than any _____ subject.

3 우리말과 일치하도록 빈칸에 알맞은 말을 쓰시오.

(1) 제주도는 하와이만큼 아름답다.

   → Jejudo is _____ _____ _____ Hawaii.

(2) John의 반에서 어느 소년도 그보다 더 영리하지 않다. (smart)

   → _____ boy is _____ _____ John in his class.

(3) 〈마지막 잎새〉는 내가 읽어 본 가장 슬픈 이야기이다.

   → *The Last leaf* is _____ _____ _____ that I've ever read.

4 그림을 보고, 주어진 단어를 알맞은 형태로 바꿔 써 봅시다.

(1)   (2)

Scrooge   Samson

(1) The more Scrooge has, _____ _____ he wants. (much)

(2) The _____ Samson's hair gets, _____ _____ powerful he becomes.(short, little)

5 Lucy와 그 자매들에 관한 표를 보고, old와 tall을 이용하여 글을 완성하시오.

	Lucy	Ludia	Lennie
age	15	16	23
height	158 cm	174 cm	162 cm

Lucy has two sisters, Ludia and Lennie. As for the age, Ludia is (1) _____ _____ Lucy. Lennie is (2) _____ _____ than Lucy and Ludia. As for the height, Ludia is (3) _____ _____ of the three. She is (4) _____ _____ than her sisters.

Final Test

Answer p. 3

난이도: 상 ★★★ 중 ★★ 하 ★

★
01 짝지어진 단어의 관계가 나머지 넷과 다른 것은?

① thick – thin
② float – sink
③ contract – expand
④ precious – previous
⑤ discourage – encourage

★★
02 영영풀이에 해당하는 단어를 〈보기〉에서 고르시오.

보기
ⓐ freedom ⓑ ability
ⓒ product ⓓ bridge

(1) _____ : the quality or state of being able
(2) _____ : a structure built over something so people can cross it

★★
03 빈칸에 공통으로 들어갈 말로 알맞은 것은?

· Technology has made it _____ to go to the space.
· Wash your hands as cleanly as _____.

① safe   ② possible   ③ polite
④ valuable   ⑤ intelligent

★
04 의도하는 바가 나머지와 다른 것은?

① Don't be discouraged.
② Things will be better.
③ Everything will be OK.
④ I'm worried about the matter.
⑤ I'm sure you'll do better next time.

[05~06] 빈칸에 알맞지 않은 것을 고르시오.

★
05

A I did my best, but I didn't make it. I'm useless.
B _____

① Don't give up!
② Don't be positive.
③ Things will be better.
④ Look on the bright side.
⑤ I'm sure you'll do better next time.

★★
06

A _____
B I like musicals better than movies.

① Which do you like, musicals or movies?
② Which do you prefer, musicals or movies?
③ I like movies better than musicals, and you?
④ What do you think of musicals and movies?
⑤ Which do you like better, musicals or movies?

★★ 서술형 평가
07 밑줄 친 우리말과 일치하도록 주어진 단어들을 바르게 배열하시오.

A Which do you prefer, going to the movies or going to the mountains?
B 나는 산에 가는 것보다 영화 보러 가는 것을 더 좋아해.
(prefer, the mountains, to, the movies, to, going, I, to, going)

→ _____

교과서 어휘 **thin** 얇은 **sink** 가라앉다 **state** 상태 **structure** 구조물 **space** 우주 **useless** 쓸모없는 **bright** 밝은

[08~11] 빈칸에 알맞은 것을 고르시오.

★
08

The speed of technological development will be _____ faster in the future.

① very   ② less   ③ pretty
④ still   ⑤ more

★★
09

When you eat _____ calories than you use, your body uses stored calories and you lose weight.

① few   ② fewer   ③ little
④ least   ⑤ much

★
10

Joyce draws pictures as _____ as her sister does.

① well   ② better   ③ best
④ the best   ⑤ much better

★★
11

I want to make this drawing as vivid as _____.

① possibly   ② could   ③ possible
④ I could   ⑤ I possible

★★
12 두 문장을 비교하는 문장으로 바꿔 쓸 때 빈칸에 알맞은 것은?

• Sam arrived at 6 o'clock.
• Sally arrived at 5:40.
→ Sally arrived 20 minutes _____ than Sam.

① late   ② later   ③ early
④ earlier   ⑤ earliest

★★ 시험에 잘 나오는 문제
13 의미하는 바가 나머지와 다른 것은?

① Miran is as patient as others in this school.
② No one in this school is as patient as Miran.
③ No one in this school is more patient than Miran.
④ Miran is the most patient girl in this school.
⑤ Miran is more patient than any other girl in this school.

★★ 서술형 평가
14 두 문장이 일치하도록 빈칸에 알맞은 말을 쓰시오.

As Brenda grew older, she became more confident.

= _____ _____ Brenda grew, _____ _____ _____ she became.

교과서 어휘 development 발달, 발전 stored 저장된 lose weight 살이 빠지다 vivid 생생한 arrive 도착하다 patient 참을성 있는
confident 자신감 있는

★★
15 다음 밑줄 친 ①-⑤ 중 어법상 어색한 것은?

I think Matthew Bourne's *Swan Lake* is
　①　　　　　　　　　　　　　②

one of most beautiful ballets.
　③　④　　　　　　⑤

★
16 빈칸에 공통으로 알맞은 말을 쓰시오.

• Kelly is growing taller _____ taller.
• Mr. Mason has become more _____ more discouraged.

★★
17 표의 내용과 일치하지 <u>않는</u> 것은?

name	height(cm)	weight(kg)
Paula	167	60
Andrew	173	65
Jane	175	63

① Andrew is taller than Jane.
② Paula is not so heavy as Jane.
③ Paula is not as tall as Andrew.
④ Jane is the tallest of the three.
⑤ Jane is not heavier than Andrew.

★★ 서술형 평가
18 주어진 단어를 이용하여 두 사람의 소비를 비교하는 문장을 완성하시오.

Kevin spends 25 dollars a month and Joe spends 75 dollars a month.

→ Joe spends _____
　 than Kevin. (three)

★★ 시험에 잘 나오는 문제
19 〈보기〉의 문장과 의미가 같은 것을 <u>모두</u> 고르면?

─보기─
Kimchi is the spiciest food in this restaurant.

① Nothing is spicier than any other foods in this restaurant.
② Kimchi is spicier than any other food in this restaurant.
③ Kimchi is not as spicy as any other food in this restaurant.
④ Nothing is as spicy as kimchi in this restaurant.
⑤ Kimchi is very spicy food in this restaurant.

★
20 밑줄 친 부분 대신 쓸 수 <u>없는</u> 것은?

This apartment is <u>much</u> higher than that building.

① very　　② a lot　　③ far
④ even　　⑤ still

★★ 서술형 평가
21 어법상 <u>어색한</u> 부분을 찾아 바르게 고쳐 쓰시오.

Laura's bicycle is two time as expensive as my.

(1) _____ → _____
(2) _____ → _____

교과서
어휘 🎧　**swan** 백조　**lake** 호수　**ballet** 발레　**discouraged** 낙담한, 낙심한　**spend** 소비하다　**spicy** 매운　**apartment** 아파트

★★★ 서술형 평가

22 주어진 문장의 의미와 일치하도록 빈칸에 알맞은 말을 쓰시오.

> This Japanese lady is the oldest woman in the world.
>
> = _____ other woman in the world is as _____ _____ this Japanese lady.
> = This Japanese lady is _____ _____ all the other _____ in the world.

★★

23 두 문장의 의미가 일치하도록 할 때 빈칸에 알맞은 것은?

> Lois memorized as many as 200 words for that short time.
> = Lois memorized _____ than 200 words for that short time.

① no less
② much more
③ not more
④ not less
⑤ no more

★★ 서술형 평가

24 우리말과 일치하도록 주어진 단어들을 바르게 배열하여 문장을 완성하시오.

> 이것은 지금까지 내가 읽었던 것 중에서 가장 재미있는 책이었다. (most, ever, interesting, book, I, that, read, the, have)

→ This is _____.

★★★

25 다음 글의 내용으로 유추할 수 있는 것은?

> Pointing to a boy who stands outside the store, a shopkeeper says to his customer. "No one is as foolish as the kid. Watch this." The shopkeeper takes out a one-dollar bill and a five-dollar bill, and asks the boy which one he wants. He takes the one-dollar bill. The customer later asks the boy, "Why didn't you take the five-dollar bill?" He replies, "Because the day I choose the five, the game is over. He would not let me stand here again if I chose five rather than one."

① The shopkeeper is rich.
② The boy is wiser than the shopkeeper.
③ The boy is more foolish than other kids.
④ The customer is smarter than the shopkeeper.
⑤ The shopkeeper is kind enough to help the boy.

★★

26 밑줄 친 the finding이 의미하는 내용을 우리말로 간단히 쓰시오.

> The Home Insurance Company asked William LeBaron Jenney to build a taller and safer building than others. One day, Jenney saw his wife put a heavy book on a small birdcage and found that the cage could support the weight. Inspired by the finding, Jenney designed Home Insurance Building's steel skeleton. Built in 1885, it was the first tall building to use steel in its frame and considered one of the world's first skyscrapers.

_____

교과서 **memorize** 외우다 **point to** ~을 가리키다 **shopkeeper** 상점 주인 **customer** 손님 **bill** 지폐 **reply** 답하다 **insurance** 보험
어휘 **birdcage** 새장 **cage** 우리 **support** 지탱하다 **inspire** 고무시키다 **steel** 철 **skeleton** 골격 **skyscraper** 초고층 건물

[27~28] 다음을 읽고, 물음에 답하시오.

Before Christmas, online shopping is ⓐ popular than ever. (①) This is a major time for delivery men. (②) However, the delivery on January 2 is also as ⓑ huge as that on Christmas. (③) So the day is even called as National Returns Day! (④) The delivery service has to deal with millions of the packages on the day. (⑤) The returns cost both businessmen and shoppers a lot, and they need to find a way to sell and buy wisely.

★★★
27 위 글의 흐름으로 보아, 주어진 문장이 들어가기에 알맞은 곳은?

That's because people return or exchange unwanted goods.

①   ②   ③   ④   ⑤

★★
28 위 글의 밑줄 친 ⓐ와 ⓑ의 형태로 알맞은 것은?

	ⓐ	ⓑ
①	more popular	– huge
②	popular	– huger
③	most popular	– hugest
④	popular	– huge
⑤	more popular	– more huge

[29~30] 다음을 읽고, 물음에 답하시오.

Is it possible to play with ice? Ice Music concert is held in northern Sweden. All the musical instruments are made of ice, and the temperature inside the concert hall is about −5°C. The audience should wear very warm clothing, a hat and even gloves. Ice instruments produce a (A) sharp / sharper sound than any other musical instrument. And the sound becomes (B) louder / loudest and sweeter as the instruments are played. That's because ice instruments absorb the vibration, but not as (C) much / more as wood-made instruments.

★★
29 위 글의 제목으로 가장 알맞은 것은?
① How Music Changes by Different Instruments
② How to Make Musical Instruments out of Ice
③ A Unique Music Concert with Ice Instruments
④ The Coolest Concert Hall in the World
⑤ Why Musicians Prefer Ice Instruments

★★★
30 (A)–(C)에서 어법에 맞는 말이 바르게 짝지어진 것은?

	(A)	(B)	(C)
①	sharp	– louder	– much
②	sharp	– loudest	– much
③	sharper	– louder	– more
④	sharper	– loudest	– more
⑤	sharper	– louder	– much

교과서   **major** 중요한   **deal with** ~을 다루다   **cost** ~에게 비용을 부과하다   **businessman** 사업가   **unwanted** 원하지 않는
어휘   **audience** 관객, 관중   **sharp** 날카로운   **absorb** 흡수하다   **vibration** 진동   **wood-made** 나무로 만든, 목조의

A 원급 비교

비교되는 두 대상의 성질이나 정도가 같은지 여부를 나타낸다.

| 〈as+원급+as〉 ~만큼 …한(하게) | 〈not as(so)+원급+as〉 ~만큼 …하지 않은(않게) |

This book is **as interesting as** that one.
This pasta is **not as(so) delicious as** that pizza.

B 비교급 비교

1 비교되는 대상 중 하나의 성질이나 정도가 다른 것보다 더하거나 덜함을 나타낸다.

| 〈비교급+than〉 ~보다 …한(하게) | 〈less+원급+than〉 ~보다 덜 …한(하게) |

It's **more useful than** the previous design.
Animals hurt other species **less powerful than** them.

2 비교급 앞에 much, even, a lot, still, far 등을 써서 '훨씬'의 의미를 더한다.
The sun is **much** bigger than the moon.

C 최상급 비교

셋 이상의 비교 대상 중에서 하나가 '가장 ~하다'의 의미를 나타내는 것을 최상급이라고 한다.
또한 원급과 비교급으로도 최상급을 표현할 수 있다.
Chris is **the tallest** boy in the class. 〈the+최상급〉
= **No (other) boy** in the class is **taller than** Chris. 〈부정 주어 ~ 비교급+than〉
= **No (other) boy** in the class is **as(so) tall as** Chris. 〈부정 주어 ~ as(so)+원급+as〉
= Chris is **taller than any other boy** in the class. 〈비교급+than any other+단수 명사〉
= Chris is **taller than all the other boys** in the class. 〈비교급+than all the other+복수 명사〉

D 원급을 이용한 표현

Drink milk **as much as possible**. 〈as+원급+as+possible(주어+can)〉
= Drink milk **as much as you can**.
This room is about **twice as large as** that one. 〈배수사+as+원급+as = 배수사+비교급+than〉
= This room is about **twice larger than** that one.

E 비교급을 이용한 표현

〈비교급＋and＋비교급〉 점점 더 …핸(하게)
〈the＋비교급(＋주어＋동사), the＋비교급(＋주어＋동사)〉 ~하면 할수록 더 …하다
no more than (= only) 겨우   no less than (= as much(many) as) ~만큼이나
not more than (= at most) 기껏해야   not less than (= at least) 적어도, 최소한

cf. ・〈비교급＋and＋비교급〉에서 단어의 비교급이 〈more＋원급〉 형태이면 〈more and more＋원급〉의 형태로 쓴다.
     ・〈the＋비교급＋(주어＋동사), the＋비교급＋(주어＋동사)〉에서 의미가 통하는 경우에는 주어와 동사를 생략해도 된다.

F 최상급을 이용한 표현

〈one of the＋최상급＋복수 명사〉 가장 …한 것 중의 하나
〈the＋최상급(＋that)＋주어＋have ever＋과거분사〉 지금까지 ~한 것들 중에서 가장 …한

The Eiffel Tower is **one of the most famous towers** in the world.
This is **the most beautiful sight that I have ever seen**.

······································ >> Expression

1 선호에 대해 묻고 답하기

🍫 선호에 대해 묻기
  • Do you prefer A or B?
  • Which do you prefer(like better) (, A or B)?
  • Which do you think is better?

🍫 선호하는 것 말하기
  • (I think) I'd prefer ....
  • I prefer A (to B).
  • I like A better (than B).
  • I think A is better (than B).

2 걱정 표현하기 / 안심시키기

🍫 걱정 표현하기
  • I'm worried about ....
  • I'm worried that ....
  • I'm concerned(anxious) about ....

🍫 안심시키기
  • Don't worry. / Cheer up! / Be positive.
  • Things will be better.
  • (I'm sure) Everything will be OK(fine).
  • I'm sure you'll do better next time.
  • Don't be frightened(discouraged / disappointed).

Lesson 02

분사, 분사구문

Grammar Preview

1 분사

- 분사의 형태와 의미

분사	형태	의미
현재분사	동사원형+ing	능동, 진행
과거분사	동사원형+(e)d / 불규칙 과거분사	수동, 완료

- 분사는 형용사(명사 수식, 보어)처럼 쓰이며, 현재분사와 같은 형태의 동명사는 명사의 역할을 한다.

현재분사	~하고 있는 (진행)	형용사 역할
동명사	~하는 것, ~하기 (용도)	명사 역할

- 분사 형태의 감정 형용사

현재분사	~한 감정을 유발하는	surprising, exciting, interesting, satisfying, tiring 등
과거분사	~한 감정을 느끼는	surprised, excited, interested, satisfied, tired 등

2 분사구문

- 분사구문 만드는 방법

① 접속사 생략	(When) he saw the dog, he got scared.
② 부사절의 주어가 주절과 같으면 부사절의 주어 생략	(he) saw the dog, he got scared.
③ 부사절과 주절의 시제가 같으면 부사절의 동사를 <동사원형+ing>로 바꿈	(Seeing) the dog, he got scared.

- 분사구문의 의미

시간	~할 때, ~하는 동안, ~하기 전에(후에)	양보		~하지만
이유	~하기 때문에, ~하므로	부대 상황	동시 동작	~하면서
조건	~한다면, ~하지 않는다면		연속 상황	~하고 나서

- 주의해야 할 분사구문

독립분사구문	분사구문의 주어가 주절의 주어와 달라서 분사 앞에 주어를 남긴 분사구문
비인칭 독립분사구문	분사구문의 주어가 주절의 주어와 다르지만 일반인이어서 주어를 생략한 분사구문

It being fine, they decided to go on a picnic. (→ As it was fine, ~)
Frankly speaking, Bryan seemed to forget my name.

Ⓐ 분사의 형태와 의미

동사와 형용사의 성질을 모두 가지며, 현재분사와 과거분사 두 종류가 있다.

분사	형태	의미
현재분사	동사원형+ing	능동, 진행
과거분사	동사원형+(e)d / 불규칙 과거분사	수동, 완료

Look at that clown **smiling** at us! 〈능동〉

That little child is **looking** at flying birds. 〈진행〉

This doll was **made** by me. 〈수동〉

My sister has just **finished** her homework. 〈완료〉

> ● **Plus** Grammar
>
> **동사의 일부로 쓰인 분사**
> 현재분사는 진행 시제에, 과거분사는 수동태, 완료 시제에 쓰인다.
> I **was sleeping** on the sofa.
> (나는 소파에서 자고 있었다.)
> This chair **was made** by my father. (이 의자는 나의 아버지에 의해 만들어졌다.)
> I **have just finished** the work.
> (나는 그 일을 막 마쳤다.)

Ⓑ 분사의 역할

1 명사 수식: 분사와 함께 분사를 꾸미는 수식어구가 있으면 분사구를 명사 뒤에 쓴다.

Wash vegetables with **running** water. 〈water 수식〉

Billy will talk about his works **displayed** here. 〈his works 수식〉

2 보어 역할

Sally sat **watching** TV. 〈주격보어〉

Nicole got **surrounded** by books.

I heard Fred **calling** my name. 〈목적격보어〉

I heard my name **called**.

3 현재분사 vs. 동명사

	의미	역할
현재분사	~하고 있는 (진행)	형용사 역할
동명사	~하는 것, ~하기 (용도)	명사 역할

Look at that **waiting** boy. (= a boy who is waiting) 〈현재분사〉

Betty is entering the **waiting** room. (= a room for waiting) 〈동명사〉

> ● **Plus** Grammar
>
> • **현재분사**
> a **sleeping** girl (잠자는 소녀)
> a **walking** bear (걷는 곰)
> a **running** dog (달리는 개)
> • **동명사**
> a **sleeping** bag (침낭)
> a **walking** stick (지팡이)
> **running** shoes (운동화)

Ⓒ 분사 형태의 감정 형용사

'~하게 만들다'라는 뜻을 지닌 동사의 분사는 형용사로 쓰인다.

분사	의미	예
현재분사	~한 감정을 유발하는	surprising, exciting, interesting, satisfying, tiring 등
과거분사	~한 감정을 느끼는	surprised, excited, interested, satisfied, tired 등

Caleb's failure was **surprising**.

I was **surprised** at Caleb's failure.

Grammar Practice >

Answer p. 4

A1 괄호 안에서 알맞은 것을 고르시오.

(1) My father is (fixing, fixed) my radio.

(2) The boy (running, run) after a mouse is my cousin.

(3) I'm sure it is the (stealing, stolen) clock.

(4) It is the present (giving, given) by her.

(5) I was (teaching, taught) to ride a bike by my father.

A2 밑줄 친 단어를 알맞은 형태로 쓰시오.

(1) Hundreds of sheep were <u>sleep</u> in the meadow. _____

(2) The language <u>use</u> in the United States is English. _____

(3) A <u>roll</u> stone gathers no moss. _____

(4) My father fixed the <u>break</u> bike. _____

(5) The airplane has just <u>take</u> off. _____

B1 우리말과 일치하도록 주어진 단어들을 바르게 배열하시오.

(1) 우리는 그가 무대에서 춤추는 것을 보았다.
(him, saw, dancing)
→ We _____ on the stage.

(2) 저 서 있는 고양이를 봐. (cat, that, standing)
→ Look at _____.

(3) 이것은 나에 의해 쓰여진 소설이다. (the novel, by me, written)
→ This is _____.

(4) 편하기 때문에 나는 운동화를 좋아한다.
(running, like, I, shoes)
→ _____ because they are comfortable.

B2 우리말과 일치하도록 주어진 단어들을 이용하여 빈칸에 알맞은 말을 쓰시오.

(1) 떨어지는 바위들을 조심해라. (fall, rocks)
→ Watch out for the _____.

(2) 부상 당한 군인들은 병원으로 후송되었다.
(wound, soldiers)
→ The _____ were carried to the hospital.

(3) 나는 영어로 쓰인 한 통의 편지를 받았다.
(write, a letter, in English)
→ I received _____.

(4) 벤치에 앉아 책을 읽는 소년은 내 사촌이다.
(read a book, the boy)
→ _____ on the bench is my cousin.

C1 밑줄 친 단어를 알맞은 형태로 쓰시오.

(1) I am <u>satisfy</u> with my job. _____

(2) This roller coaster is <u>excite</u>. _____

(3) You look <u>tire</u>. _____

C2 두 문장의 의미가 일치하도록 빈칸에 알맞은 말을 쓰시오.

(1) Reading books interests me.
= I am _____ in reading books.

(2) The exam result is satisfying to the students.
= The students are _____ with the exam result.

(3) I'm disappointed with the result of the game.
= The result of the game is _____.

(4) The sound shocked William.
= William was _____ by the sound.

교과서 **clown** 광대 **running** 흐르는 **surround** 둘러싸다 **failure** 실패 **run after** ~을 뒤쫓다 **sheep** 양 **meadow** 풀밭 **moss** 이끼
어휘 **fix** 고치다 **take off** 이륙하다 **wounded** 부상 당한 **shock** 충격을 주다

2 분사구문 Grammar

D 분사구문 만들기

1 분사구문: 분사를 이용하여 부사절(접속사＋주어＋동사 ～)을 부사구로 바꿔 쓴 것으로 아래의 방법으로 만든다.

① 접속사 생략	When he saw the dog, he got scared.
② 부사절의 주어가 주절과 같으면 주어 생략	he saw the dog, he got scared.
③ 부사절과 주절의 시제가 같으면 부사절의 동사를 〈동사원형＋ing〉로 바꿈	Seeing the dog, he got scared.

2 분사구문 만들 때 주의할 점

- 부사절의 시제가 주절의 시제보다 앞서면 분사를 〈having＋과거분사〉로 쓴다.

  As I learned this before, I can teach it to you now.

  → **Having learned** this before, I can teach it to you now.

- 분사구문의 부정문은 분사 앞에 not이나 never를 써서 만든다.

  As I didn't know what to say, I kept silent.

  → **Not** knowing what to say, I kept silent.

◆ Plus Grammar

〈Being / Having been 생략〉
분사구문의 Being 또는 Having been은 생략할 수 있다.
Because she was running in the sunglasses, she couldn't see me.
→ **(Being)** Running in the sunglasses, she couldn't see me. (선글라스를 쓰고 뛰고 있었기 때문에, 그녀는 나를 볼 수 없었다.)

E 분사구문의 의미

시간	～할 때, ～하는 동안, ～하기 전에(후에)	양보		～하지만
이유	～하기 때문에, ～하므로	부대 상황	동시 동작	～하면서
조건	～한다면, ～하지 않는다면		연속 상황	～하고 나서

Buying this ice cream, you'll get another one free. 〈조건〉

→ **If** you buy this ice cream, you'll get another one free.

Being young, he is very wise. → **Though** he is young, he is very wise. 〈양보〉

cf. '～가 …한 채로'의 의미로 동시 동작을 나타내는 분사구문 〈with＋명사(구)＋분사〉에서 (대)명사와 분사의 관계가 능동이면 현재분사, 수동이면 과거분사를 쓴다.

Bruce was waving his hands **with his tears running**.

The actress sat **with her legs crossed**.

F 주의해야 할 분사구문

1 독립분사구문: 분사구문의 주어가 주절의 주어와 다른 경우, 분사 앞의 주어를 생략하지 않으며 이를 독립분사구문이라고 한다.

It being fine, they decided to go on a picnic. (→ As it was fine, ～)

2 비인칭 독립분사구문: 분사구문의 주어가 일반인인 경우에는 주절의 주어와 다르더라도 생략한다. 관용적 표현으로 암기해 두어야 한다.

Frankly speaking, Bryan seemed to forget my name.

◆ Plus Grammar

[비인칭 독립분사구문]
generally speaking (일반적으로 말해서)
frankly speaking (솔직히 말해서)
briefly speaking (간단히 말해서)
speaking of (～에 관해 말하자면)
judging from (～로 판단하건대)
considering (～을 고려해 보면)

Grammar Practice >>

Answer p. 4

D1 다음을 분사구문을 이용하여 바꿔 쓸 때 빈칸에 알맞은 말을 쓰시오.

(1) As I got up late, I had to hurry.

= _____ up late, I had to hurry.

(2) Because Scott walked all day long, he is tired.

= _____ _____ all day long, Scott is tired.

(3) As we didn't have lunch, we were very hungry.

= _____ _____ lunch, we were very hungry.

D2 밑줄 친 부분을 분사구문으로 바꿔 쓰시오.

(1) As Sam was absent, I called him.

→ _____

(2) Because I had lost the key, I couldn't unlock the door.

→ _____

(3) As I hadn't learned to swim, I was very worried.

→ _____

E1 밑줄 친 부분의 의미를 〈보기〉에서 고르시오.

┌ 보기 ─────────────────┐
ⓐ 시간   ⓑ 이유   ⓒ 조건
ⓓ 양보   ⓔ 동시 동작
└──────────────────────┘

(1) Living near the school, Vincent always comes late.

(2) He was standing with his arms folded.

(3) Getting a high score, you'll be happy.

(4) Being tired, I went to bed early.

(5) Arriving here, we found Nicole had been sick.

E2 두 문장의 의미가 일치하도록 빈칸에 알맞은 말을 쓰시오.

(1) Dining out without a coat, you'll catch a cold.

= _____ you dine out without a coat, you'll catch a cold.

(2) Not wanting to disappoint my mom, I worked harder.

= _____ I didn't want to disappoint my mom, I worked harder.

(3) Not having a driver's license, Nathan drove his father's car.

= _____ Nathan didn't have a driver's license, he drove his father's car.

(4) Karen fell asleep and the TV was still turned on.

= Karen fell asleep _____ the TV turned on.

F1 괄호 안에서 알맞은 것을 고르시오.

(1) (Raining, It raining) hard, I didn't go.

(2) (Judging, Judged) from Max's gesture, he didn't know the answer.

(3) (We frankly, Frankly) speaking, Helen's boyfriend is not handsome.

F2 주어진 단어들을 바르게 배열하여 문장을 완성하시오.

(1) _____, I couldn't buy it. (not, enough money, having)

(2) _____ in the fridge, we had to buy some. (food, being, no, there)

(3) _____, I'm interested in making movies. (speaking, frankly)

교과서 scared 두려워하는 free 무료로 frankly 솔직하게 all day long 하루 종일 unlock 열다 fold 접다 dine out 외식하다
어휘 disappoint 실망시키다 fall asleep 잠들다 fridge 냉장고

Grammar Test

01 괄호 안에서 알맞은 것을 고르시오.

(1) The girl (played, playing) the piano is my friend.

(2) Archer fixed the (broken, breaking) chair.

(3) Look at the girl (standing, stood) over there.

서술형 평가

02 〈보기〉와 같이 문장을 바꿔 쓸 때 빈칸에 알맞은 말을 쓰시오.

> **보기**
> Joining the musical club, I made a lot of friends.
> = After I joined the musical club, I made a lot of friends.

Getting angry at other people sometimes, he is always kind to me.

= _____ _____ _____ angry at other people sometimes, he is always kind to me.

서술형 평가

03 다음을 분사구문을 이용하여 바꿔 쓸 때 빈칸에 알맞은 말을 쓰시오.

(1) When he came into the house, he found a lizard.

= _____ into the house, he found a lizard.

(2) As I didn't have money, I could not buy the purse.

= _____ _____ money, I could not buy the purse.

04 밑줄 친 부분을 바르게 고친 것은?

The novel was very bore.

① boring   ② bored
③ to bore   ④ bores
⑤ be bored.

서술형 평가

05 우리말과 일치하도록 밑줄 친 부분을 바르게 고쳐 쓰시오.

Iris listened to music with her eyes close.
(Iris는 그녀의 눈을 감은 채로 음악을 들었다.)

→ _____

06 밑줄 친 ①~⑤ 중 어법상 어색한 것은?

I am <u>interested</u> in <u>that</u> boy <u>used</u> <u>his</u> cell
　　　　①　　　　　②　　　　③　　④
phone <u>at the gate</u>.
　　　　⑤

서술형 평가

07 우리말과 일치하도록 빈칸에 알맞은 말을 쓰시오.

일반적으로 말해서, 남자아이들이 여자아이들보다 키가 더 크다.

→ _____, boys are taller than girls.

교과서 **join** 합류하다 **get angry at** ~에게 화내다 **lizard** 도마뱀 **purse** 지갑 **novel** 소설 **gate** 문
어휘

08 밑줄 친 부분 중 어법상 어색한 것은?

① Sam had his bike <u>stolen</u>.

② I got my watch <u>repairing</u>.

③ Her performance was <u>moving</u>.

④ I'm <u>interested</u> in modern art.

⑤ I saw Sally <u>waiting</u> for the subway.

[09~10] 두 문장의 의미가 일치하도록 할 때 빈칸에 알맞은 것을 고르시오.

09

Because Austin is overweight, he has to work out.

= _____ overweight, Austin has to work out.

① Is   ② Be

③ Being   ④ To be

⑤ Having been

10

Having been bored with his job, he is searching for another one.

= _____ bored with his job, he is searching for another one.

① As he is   ② As he was

③ Though he is   ④ Though was

⑤ As has been

서술형 평가

11 다음을 분사구문을 이용하여 바꿔 쓰시오.

(1) When she saw a police officer, she ran away.

→ _____

(2) If it is rainy tomorrow, I think the picnic will be canceled.

→ _____

12 빈칸에 공통으로 들어갈 말로 알맞은 것은?
(대소문자 무시)

• _____ finished my homework, I went to bed.

• Not _____ seen Lucy for a long time, I couldn't recognize her.

① Being   ② Be   ③ To be

④ Having   ⑤ Had

서술형 평가

13 주어진 단어를 이용하여 우리말을 영어로 옮기시오.

(1) 그녀의 나이를 고려해 보면, 그녀는 매우 나이 들어 보인다. (considering)

→ _____

(2) 솔직히 말해서, 나는 그에게 관심이 없다. (speaking)

→ _____

교과서 **performance** 공연, 활동 **modern** 현대의 **overweight** 과체중인 **work out** 운동하다 **search for** ~을 검색하다
어휘 **run away** 도망치다 **cancel** 취소하다 **recognize** 알아보다

Reading

[1~2] 다음을 끊어 읽고 ☑, 해석을 쓰시오. ✍

The Secret of My Father (I)

In the 1920's, (A) when people saw me in the village, they would say, "There goes the *parakho's*

daughter." My father, Kim Yonghwan, was a son from a very ⓐrich family, but he was always at the gambling

house. That is why he was called a *parakho*, which means someone who ⓑruins his family's fortune.

When I was sixteen, my family had already made an arrangement for me to

ⓒmarry Mr. Seo. As part of the wedding tradition, Mr. Seo's family sent my

family some money to buy a new chest for clothes.

Right before the wedding day, my mother came into my room and said,

"Your father has taken the money for the chest. We have no choice. You'll

have to take your aunt's ⓓold chest."

"How ⓔdelightful for the family," people would whisper behind my back. Since

the first day of marriage, life at my husband's house had been difficult for me.

1 밑줄 친 (A)를 분사구문을 이용하여 바꿔 쓸 때 빈칸에 알맞은 말을 쓰시오.

→ _____, people would say, "There goes the *parakho's* daughter."

2 밑줄 친 ⓐ-ⓔ 중 글의 흐름상 어색한 것은?

① ⓐ   ② ⓑ   ③ ⓒ   ④ ⓓ   ⑤ ⓔ

> 교과서 **gambling** 도박 **ruin** 망치다 **fortune** 재산 **make an arrangement** 합의하다 **marry** ~와 결혼하다 **wedding** 결혼 **chest** 옷장
> 어휘 🎧 **delightful** 기분 좋은 **whisper** 속삭이다 **marriage** 결혼

3 글쓴이의 아버지의 말을 한 문장으로 요약할 때, 빈칸에 들어갈 말로 가장 적절한 것은?　일화

My dad and I were driving home and suddenly a truck jumped right in front of us. **Stepping** on his brakes, dad missed the truck by just inches! The driver started yelling at us. But dad just smiled **waving** at the guy. "Dad, it wasn't your fault. Why did you just do that?" My dad replied, "Some people are like garbage trucks full of anger and disappointment. When their garbage piles up, they may dump it on you. When it happens, don't take it personally, just smile, wave, and wish them well. Don't take their garbage and return them. It only hurts them."

→ When others make you feel bad, ＿＿＿＿＿＿＿＿＿＿＿＿.

① go and tell them how you felt　　② admit your fault to be forgiven
③ don't fight back and wish them well　　④ ask them the reason why they did so
⑤ control your anger and talk with them about it

4 글의 흐름으로 보아, 빈칸에 들어갈 말로 가장 적절한 것은?　심리

There is an interesting experiment to show the backward motion effect. Three groups of people were shown a video of a staged crime. First group imagined walking forward or backward **watching** the video. Second group actually walked forward or backward during the experiment. The last group sat still. The result showed that backward motion – whether real or imagined – helped people recall the information better than sitting still or forward motion. Maybe the backward motion mentally helps us move back in time to the point when we get the information. Next time when you try to remember something, ＿＿＿＿＿＿＿＿＿.

① walk backward　　② stand or sit still
③ run as fast as possible　　④ imagine walking forward
⑤ watch a video of a staged crime

3　**by inches** 가까스로　**yell** 소리 지르다　**pile up** 쌓이다　**dump** 버리다　**take personally** 기분 나쁘게 생각하다
4　**motion** 행동, 동작　**staged** 연출된, 일부러 꾸민　**forward** 앞으로　**still** 가만히　**recall** 기억해내다　**mentally** 정신적으로

Expression

1 만족 여부에 대해 묻고 답하기

● 만족 여부에 대해 묻기

- Are you satisfied(happy) with ...?
- How do(did) you like(find) ...?

● 만족 여부 말하기

- I'm (not) satisfied(happy) with ....
- I (don't) like it.

2 감사하기

● 감사하기

- I don't know how to thank you.
- That's very nice of you.
- I (really) (do) appreciate your help.
- I can't thank you enough.
- I am thankful(grateful) for your effort.

● 감사 표현에 답하기

- No problem. / Anytime.
- (It was) My pleasure.
- Don't mention it.
- You would do the same.
- I'm pleased to be able to help you.
- You're welcome.

Expression Test

Answer p. 6

1 의도하는 바가 나머지와 다른 것은?

① I can't thank you enough.

② I am grateful for your help.

③ I'm thankful for your help.

④ I don't know how to thank you.

⑤ I am pleased to be able to help you.

2 빈칸에 알맞은 것은?

A How was your weekend, Dennis?

B It was great. I went to a winter camp.

A _____

B Yes. I learned how to ski and built an igloo.

① Which program did you like most?

② Have you been to a winter camp?

③ How did you like the winter camp?

④ Were you upset about the program?

⑤ Were you satisfied with the program?

3 밑줄 친 부분과 바꿔 쓸 수 없는 것은?

A I can't thank you enough. You've helped me a lot.

B No problem. You would do the same thing.

A Anyway, I really appreciate your help.

① it's my pleasure

② that's very nice of you

③ I am grateful for your help

④ I am thankful for your help

⑤ I don't know how to thank you

4 짝지어진 대화가 어색한 것은?

① A How do you like the contest?

   B I'm happy with the result.

② A I can't thank you enough.

   B Don't mention it.

③ A I'm not happy with the test result.

   B Good job. It's my pleasure.

④ A How did you like the school festival?

   B Well, I was very satisfied with it.

⑤ A How did you like the movie?

   B I loved its story.

5 자연스러운 대화가 되도록 ⓐ-ⓓ를 바르게 배열한 것은?

ⓐ I'm very satisfied with the color.

ⓑ Right. Here it is. Doesn't it look cool?

ⓒ I heard you bought a cell phone, Joyce.

ⓓ Yes, it looks nice.

① ⓑ – ⓒ – ⓐ – ⓓ   ② ⓑ – ⓓ – ⓒ – ⓐ

③ ⓒ – ⓑ – ⓓ – ⓐ   ④ ⓒ – ⓓ – ⓐ – ⓑ

⑤ ⓓ – ⓒ – ⓑ – ⓐ

서술형 평가

6 빈칸에 알맞은 말을 쓰시오.

A Did you win first prize in English writing contest?

B Yeah, I did.

A I'm glad that you won.

B Thanks to you, I could get this prize.

_____

A Don't mention it. It was my pleasure.

서술형 평가

Answer p. 6

1 주어진 단어들을 이용하여 밑줄 친 우리말을 영어로 옮기시오.

> A Hi, can I help you with anything?
> B Yes, can I try on the cap over there?
> A Okay. Here it is. [pause] 모자가 어떠세요?
>   (the cap, like, how)
> B The design is nice, but I don't think the color suits me. Do you have it in black?
> A Yes. I'll get one soon. [pause] Here it is.
> B Great. I'll take it.

→ _____

2 두 문장의 의미가 일치하도록 빈칸에 들어갈 말을 〈보기〉에서 고르시오.

┌─ 보기 ─────────────────────────┐
│ when   though   because   while │
└──────────────────────────────┘

(1) Being old, she wasn't afraid of new challenge.
    = _____ she was old, she wasn't afraid of new challenge.
(2) Going on a vacation, he should pack his bag.
    = _____ he goes on a vacation, he should pack his bag.
(3) Walking along the river, I met Jane.
    = _____ I walked along the river, I met Jane.

3 우리말과 일치하도록 주어진 단어들을 이용하여 빈칸에 알맞은 말을 쓰시오.

(1) 나는 지난주에 놀라운 소식을 들었다. (surprise, news)
    → I heard _____ _____ last week.
(2) 솔직히 말해서, 나는 요리에 서툴다. (frank, speak)
    → _____ _____, I am poor at cooking.
(3) 나는 삶은 계란을 먹고 싶어요. (boil, egg)
    → I would like to eat an _____ _____.

4 다음을 분사구문을 이용하여 바꿔 쓰시오.

(1) When I opened the box, I found an old letter in it.
    → _____
(2) Because I had no money, my friend bought a train ticket for me.
    → _____
(3) Dad went out of the house as he said "Good-bye."
    → _____
(4) When Tom arrived, we started for home.
    → _____

5 그림을 보고, 주어진 단어들을 이용하여 빈칸에 알맞은 말을 쓰시오.

> A Who is the girl (1) _____?
>   (wave, her hands)
> B She is my cousin, Lucy. We went to the beach together.
> A Which kid is your brother, Danny?
> B Danny is the boy (2) _____.
>   (wear, cap)
>   He's holding a (3) _____.
>   (break, shovel)
> A What happened to his shovel?
> B The dog (4) _____ broke it.
>   (follow, a cat)
> A Oh, that's too bad.

Final Test

Answer p. 6

난이도: 상 ★★★ 중 ★★ 하 ★

★
01 두 단어의 관계가 나머지와 <u>다른</u> 것은?

① fix – repair   ② ruin – spoil

③ reply – answer   ④ success – failure

⑤ wedding – marriage

★★
02 빈칸에 들어갈 말로 바르게 짝지어진 것은?

· The police officer ran _____ a thief.

· The flight was delayed and took _____ at 11 p.m.

① to – off   ② to – out   ③ by – out

④ after – on   ⑤ after – off

★ 서술형 평가
03 주어진 단어를 이용하여 밑줄 친 우리말을 영어로 옮기시오.

A Here is the red laptop. <u>너는 그 색깔에 만족하니?</u> (satisfied)

B No, I don't think so. It's not what I wanted.

→ _____

★★ 시험에 잘 나오는 문제
04 대화를 순서대로 바르게 배열하시오.

ⓐ No problem.

ⓑ Put the paper here and dial the number. And lastly press this green button.

ⓒ I don't know how to use this fax machine.

ⓓ Oh, it really works! I appreciate your help.

→ _____

★★
05 빈칸에 알맞은 것은?

A Are you satisfied with your new shoes?

B Yes, _____.

① they're too big

② I don't like them

③ I am happy with them

④ they're too expensive

⑤ they're not satisfactory to me

★★
06 빈칸에 알맞지 <u>않은</u> 것은?

A You helped me to handle the situation.

_____

B My pleasure. It was just nothing.

① I can't thank you enough.

② I really appreciate your help.

③ I am thankful for your effort.

④ Happy to be able to help you.

⑤ I don't know how to thank you.

★★
07 밑줄 친 부분과 바꿔 쓸 수 있는 것은?

A Your new bike looks really cool. <u>Are you happy with it?</u>

B No, I'm not. It's too heavy.

① Are you sure of it?

② Are you interested in it?

③ Are you going to sell it?

④ Are you satisfied with it?

⑤ Are you planning to buy it?

교과서
어휘 🎧   **spoil** 망치다   **delayed** 지연된   **laptop** 노트북 컴퓨터   **lastly** 마지막으로   **work** 작동하다   **satisfactory** 만족스러운   **handle** 다루다   **cool** 멋있는

★★★
08 밑줄 친 부분과 의미가 같은 것은?

If you turn to the left, you'll find the bank.

① Turned to the left
② Turning to the left
③ To turning to the left
④ Having turned to the left
⑤ Though you turn to the left

서술형 평가
[09~10] 어법상 어색한 부분을 찾아 바르게 고쳐 쓰시오.
★★
09

Write your answers on the paper with your book closing.

_____ → _____

★★
10

Lived in the country, Emma has few visitors.

_____ → _____

★★★
11 빈칸에 알맞은 것은?

_____ my cell phone yesterday,
I have to buy a new one now.

① Lost
② Losing
③ Having lost
④ Being lost
⑤ Being losing

★★
12 밑줄 친 부분을 과거분사로 써야 하는 문장의 개수는?

ⓐ Look at the sing shepherd.
ⓑ Can you open this lock door?
ⓒ I'll catch that jump grasshopper.
ⓓ The boy wear glasses is my friend.
ⓔ There are many fall leaves on the street.

① 1개   ② 2개   ③ 3개   ④ 4개   ⑤ 5개

★★ 시험에 잘 나오는 문제
13 밑줄 친 부분의 형태로 알맞은 것끼리 짝지어진 것은?

• The woman stand outside in the rain is looking at us.
• I heard my name call.

① stood – call   ② standing – calling
③ stood – calling   ④ standing – called
⑤ stood – called

★★ 서술형 평가
14 두 문장을 한 문장으로 바꿔 쓸 때 빈칸에 알맞은 말을 쓰시오.

Jack visited Ms. White in the hospital. And then he gave her a bouquet with words of comfort.

→Jack visited Ms. White in the hospital, _____ her a bouquet with words of comfort.

교과서   shepherd 양치는 사람 grasshopper 메뚜기 glasses 안경 leaf 나뭇잎 bouquet 꽃다발 comfort 위로, 위안
어휘

★★
15 우리말과 일치하도록 할 때 빈칸에 알맞은 것은?

그의 억양으로 판단하건대, 그는 남부 출신임에 틀림없다.
→ _____ from his accent, he must be from the south.

① Judged
② Judging
③ To be judged
④ Having judged
⑤ Being judging

★★ 시험에 잘 나오는 문제
16 밑줄 친 부분의 쓰임이 같은 것끼리 짝지어진 것은?

ⓐ Look at the sleeping cats.
ⓑ I have to fix a washing machine.
ⓒ My hobby is collecting wrapping paper.
ⓓ His daughter was playing soccer with her friends.
ⓔ My kids were making sand castles on the beach.

① ⓐ, ⓑ
② ⓐ, ⓓ
③ ⓐ, ⓓ, ⓔ
④ ⓑ, ⓒ, ⓓ
⑤ ⓑ, ⓒ, ⓔ

[17~18] 밑줄 친 부분이 어법상 올바른 것을 고르시오.
★★★
17
① The baby slept in the cradle is cute.
② The kids raised in countryside are healthy.
③ There are two people waited for the bus.
④ I tried to fix the breaking TV, but I couldn't.
⑤ Only the inviting people are allowed to enter the hall.

★★
18
① Jenny was sitting watched TV.
② I found the document torn in the drawer.
③ I saw a stranger walked around my house.
④ The door remained locking during the day.
⑤ Around 10 o'clock, I heard someone approached my room.

★★ 서술형 평가
19 두 문장의 의미가 일치하도록 빈칸에 알맞은 말을 쓰시오.

(1) Having seen that movie last week, I don't want to see it again.
= Because _____ _____ that movie last week, I don't want to see it again.

(2) Having seen that movie before, I didn't want to see it again.
= Because _____ _____ _____ that movie before, I didn't want to see it again.

★★
20 어법상 올바른 것끼리 짝지어진 것은?

ⓐ Having finished the work, I went to bed.
ⓑ Who is that woman running there?
ⓒ Having used the cup, it was thrown away.
ⓓ Looking around, Tyler took a few steps forward.
ⓔ Some of the people inviting to the party were my coworkers.

① ⓐ, ⓔ
② ⓑ, ⓒ
③ ⓑ, ⓔ
④ ⓐ, ⓑ, ⓓ
⑤ ⓐ, ⓒ, ⓓ

교과서 **accent** 억양 **washing machine** 세탁기 **wrapping paper** 포장지 **sand castle** 모래성 **cradle** 요람 **countryside** 시골
어휘 **document** 문서 **torn** 찢어진 **drawer** 서랍 **approach** 다가가다 **throw away** 버리다 **coworker** 동료

★★ 서술형 평가
21 두 문장의 의미가 일치하도록 빈칸에 알맞은 말을 쓰시오.

To be brief, you'd better accept his offer.
= _____, you'd better accept his offer.

★★ 시험에 잘 나오는 문제
22 밑줄 친 부분의 의미로 알맞은 것은?

When Molly got in her house, she saw a mouse in the living room. Frightened by the mouse, she ran into her room.

① If she was frightened
② While she was frightened
③ Unless she was frightened
④ Though she was frightened
⑤ Because she was frightened

★★ 서술형 평가
23 어법상 어색한 부분을 찾아 바르게 고쳐 쓰시오.

Recycling is one of the best things that you can do for the environment. While reduce piles of garbage, you're also protecting natural resources.

_____ → _____

★★
24 밑줄 친 부분과 바꿔 쓸 수 없는 것은?

With a credit card, we tend to purchase something we don't need, so it can make people spend more money. Using a credit card, you have to handle your expenses more carefully.

① If you use
② As you use
① When you use
③ While you use
⑤ Unless you use

★★
25 다음 글의 주제로 알맞은 것은?

Brain activity during dreaming increases as when we are awake. In fact, dreaming may help you solve problems dealing with stress. A Harvard Medical School study showed that people who dreamed while sleeping were better able to detect positive emotions in other people. However, those who did not dream were more sensitive to negative emotions. Generally speaking, dreams help the brain let go of negative emotions safely.

① 꿈의 긍정적인 효과
② 밤에 잠을 자야 하는 이유
③ 스트레스를 다루는 방법
④ 뇌 활동을 촉진시키는 행동
⑤ 부정적인 감정이 생기는 원인

교과서 **to be brief** 요컨대 **frightened** 겁에 질린 **pile** 더미 **natural resource** 천연자원 **purchase** 구입하다 **expense** 소비
어휘 **medical school** 의과 대학 **detect** 감지하다 **sensitive** 예민한, 민감한 **let go of** ~을 놓다

★★
26 밑줄 친 부분에 함축된 의미로 가장 적절한 것은?

One evening over dinner, a son asked his father, "Dad, are bugs good to eat?" Not understanding why he's asking the question, the father answered, "That's disgusting. We don't talk about things like that while we're eating." "Okay, I'm sorry." said the son. After dinner, the father asked, "Now, son. Why did you ask the bug question suddenly?" "Oh, never mind." the boy said. "There was a bug in your soup, now it's gone."

① The father's soup went bad.
② The father ate a bug in his soup.
③ A bug was in the soup, but it flew away.
④ The son ate a bug in the father's soup.
⑤ A bug in the father's soup disappeared.

[27~28] 다음을 읽고, 물음에 답하시오.

There is a unique exhibition ⓐcall The Museum of Failure. Dr. Samuel West, innovation researcher, first started the exhibition with his collection of failures. ⓑFind that 80-90 percent of industries' projects fail, he felt that people need to be told stories of failure and the lessons within them. Among the artifacts are a plastic bicycle and the Amazon Fire phone. The bicycle cost twice the price of a regular one but was easily breakable. The Amazon Fire phone had a 'buy' button, but people hated it.

★★ 서술형 평가
27 위 글에서 밑줄 친 ⓐ와 ⓑ의 알맞은 형태를 쓰시오.
ⓐ _____   ⓑ _____

★★
28 위 글의 내용으로 답할 수 <u>없는</u> 것은?
① What is the name of the unique exhibition?
② Who started the exhibition for the first time?
③ How were the artifacts collected?
④ Why did the plastic bicycle fail?
⑤ What did people hate about the Amazon Fire phone?

[29~30] 다음을 읽고, 물음에 답하시오.

Do you want to sound smarter? Just summarize other people's smart points! The person who simply restate good points ⓐ made by others will often be better remembered. In a similar way, ⓑ have a hard time in getting a word in at a meeting, you'd better ⓒ take notes on the best comments that other people deliver. Near the end of the meeting, summarize these ideas in a simple and clear way. Even when ⓓ praising other people, you'll sound smarter. Remember! ⓔTo sound smart, you don't always have to present a great idea.

*get a word in 대화에 끼다

★★
29 밑줄 친 ⓐ-ⓔ 중 어법상 <u>어색한</u> 것은?
① ⓐ   ② ⓑ   ③ ⓒ   ④ ⓓ   ⑤ ⓔ

★★★
30 위 글에서 제시한 똑똑해 보이기 위한 방법으로 알맞은 것은?
① Present a smart idea.
② Speak in a simple and clear way.
③ Restate other people's great points.
④ Take notes of what you're going to say.
⑤ Summarize again what you've just said.

교과서 어휘 **bug** 벌레 **disgusting** 더러운 **mind** 신경 쓰다 **go bad** 썩다 **innovation** 혁신 **artifact** 작품 **breakable** 깨지기 쉬운 **summarize** 요약하다 **restate** 재진술하다 **deliver** (의견을) 말하다, 전하다 **praise** 칭찬하다

.... >> Grammar

A 분사의 형태와 의미

현재분사	과거분사
동사원형+ing (능동, 진행)	동사원형+(e)d / 불규칙 과거분사 (수동, 완료)

Look at that clown **smiling** at us! 〈능동 · 진행〉   This doll was **made** by me. 〈수동〉

My sister has just **finished** her homework. 〈완료〉

B 분사의 역할

• 분사는 명사를 수식하거나 보어 역할을 하는 등, 형용사처럼 쓰인다.

　Wash vegetables with **running** water. 〈명사 수식〉　　Sally sat **watching** TV. 〈주격보어〉

• 현재분사와 같은 형태의 동명사는 명사의 역할을 한다.

현재분사	~하고 있는 (진행)	형용사 역할
동명사	~하는 것, ~하기 (용도)	명사 역할

Look at that **waiting** boy. (= a boy who is waiting) 〈현재분사〉

Betty is entering the **waiting** room. (= a room for waiting) 〈동명사〉

C 분사 형태의 감정 형용사

현재분사	~한 감정을 유발하는	surprising, exciting, interesting, satisfying, tiring 등
과거분사	~한 감정을 느끼는	surprised, excited, interested, satisfied, tired 등

D 분사구문 만들기

• 분사구문 만드는 방법

① 접속사 생략	When he saw the dog, he got scared.
② 부사절의 주어가 주절과 같으면 주어 생략	he saw the dog, he got scared.
③ 부사절과 주절의 시제가 같으면 부사절의 동사를 〈동사원형+ing〉로 바꿈	Seeing the dog, he got scared.

• 부사절의 시제가 주절의 시제보다 앞서면 분사를 〈having+과거분사〉로 쓰고,
  부정문은 분사 앞에 not이나 never를 써서 만든다.

As I learned this before, I can teach it to you now. → **Having learned** this before, ….

As I didn't know what to say, I kept silent. → **Not** knowing what to say, ….

E 분사구문의 의미

시간	~할 때, ~하는 동안, ~하기 전에(후에)	양보		~하지만
이유	~하기 때문에, ~하므로	부대 상황	동시 동작	~하면서
조건	~한다면, ~하지 않는다면		연속 상황	~하고 나서

Buying this ice cream, you'll get another one free. 〈조건〉
Being young, he is very wise. 〈양보〉

cf. '~가 …한 채로'의 의미로 동시 동작을 나타내는 분사구문 〈with + (대)명사 + 분사〉
에서 (대)명사와 분사의 관계가 능동이면 현재분사, 수동이면 과거분사를 쓴다.
Bruce was waving his hands **with his tears running**.
The actress sat **with her legs crossed**.

F 주의해야 할 분사구문

독립분사구문	분사구문의 주어가 주절의 주어와 달라서 분사 앞에 주어를 남긴 분사구문
비인칭 독립분사구문	분사구문의 주어가 주절의 주어와 다르지만 일반인이어서 주어를 생략한 분사구문

It being fine, they decided to go on a picnic. (= As it was fine, ~)
Frankly speaking, Bryan seemed to forget my name.

>> Expression

1 만족 여부에 대해 묻고 답하기

❤만족 여부에 대해 묻기
• Are you satisfied(happy) with ...?
• How do(did) you like(find) ...?

❤만족 여부 말하기
• I'm (not) satisfied(happy) with ....
• I (don't) like it.

2 감사하기

❤감사하기
• I don't know how to thank you.
• That's very nice of you.
• I (really) (do) appreciate your help.
• I can't thank you enough.
• I am thankful(grateful) for your effort.

❤감사 표현에 답하기
• No problem. / Anytime.
• (It was) My pleasure.
• Don't mention it.
• You would do the same.
• I'm pleased to be able to help you.
• You're welcome.

Lesson 03

접속사

Grammar Preview

1 접속사

- that은 '~하는 것'의 의미로 주어, 목적어, 보어로 쓰이는 명사절을 이끈다.

  It is true **that Brenda became a teacher.** 〈주어〉　　I believe **that David is guilty.** 〈목적어〉

  The surprising fact is **that Daisy didn't even read it.** 〈보어〉

  The news **that they won the game** was not true. 〈동격절〉

- if와 whether는 '~인지 아닌지'의 의미로 명사절을 이끈다. if가 이끄는 절은 목적어로만 쓰인다. whether 뒤에는 or not을 함께 쓸 수 있다.

  Whether Victoria may come (or not) doesn't matter. 〈주어〉

  I wonder **if(whether) Terry is honest.** 〈목적어〉

  Pamela's interest is **whether I move to Chicago (or not).** 〈보어〉

- 부사절을 이끄는 접속사 I

when	~할 때	while	~하는 동안	as	~할 때, ~하면서
before / after	~하기 전에 / 후에	until / till	~할 때까지	since	~ 이래로
if	만약 ~하다면	unless	만약 ~하지 않는다면 (= if ~ not)		

2 접속사 / 접속부사

- 부사절을 이끄는 접속사 II

이유	because, as, since	~ 때문에
양보	although(though), even though, even if	비록 ~하지만, 만약 ~할지라도
목적	so that (= in order to)	~하기 위해서, ~하도록
결과	so ~ that ... can / can't	너무 ~해서 …할 수 있다 / 없다

- 접속부사

결과	so, therefore, thus, consequently, as a result	첨가	besides, moreover, furthermore, in addition
역접	however, nevertheless, still, yet, on the other hand	조건	otherwise

- 상관접속사

both A and B	A와 B 둘 다	not A but B	A가 아닌 B	not only A but (also) B	A뿐만 아니라 B도
either A or B	A, B 둘 중 하나	neither A nor B	A, B 둘 다 아닌	= B as well as A	

Ⓐ 명사절을 이끄는 접속사 that

that은 '~하는 것'의 의미로 주어, 목적어, 보어로 쓰이는 명사절을 이끈다.
That Brenda became a teacher is true. 〈주어〉
= It is true **that Brenda became a teacher**.
I believe **that David is guilty**. 〈목적어〉
The surprising fact is **that Daisy didn't even read it**. 〈보어〉
cf. that은 특정 명사(fact, news, idea, information 등) 뒤에서 동격절을 이끈다.
　　The news **that they won the game** was not true.

> **Plus Grammar**
> ・that이 이끄는 명사절이 주어이면 가주어 it을 쓰고 that절은 문장 뒤쪽에 쓴다.
> **That** he became a teacher is true.
> = It is true **that** he became a teacher.
> ・타동사의 목적절을 이끄는 that은 생략할 수 있다.
> I believe **(that)** he is guilty.

Ⓑ 명사절을 이끄는 접속사 if, whether

if와 whether는 '~인지 아닌지'의 의미로 명사절을 이끈다. 단, if가 이끄는 절은
목적어로만 쓰인다. whether 뒤에는 or not을 함께 쓸 수 있다.
Whether Victoria may come (or not) doesn't matter. 〈주어〉
I wonder **if(whether) Terry is honest**. 〈목적어〉
Pamela's interest is **whether I move to Chicago (or not)**. 〈보어〉

Ⓒ 부사절을 이끄는 접속사 I

1 시간을 나타내는 접속사

when	~할 때	while	~하는 동안	as	~할 때, ~하면서
before / after	~하기 전에 / 후에	until / till	~할 때까지	since	~ 이래로

When I arrived at the office, Louis was arguing with Stella.
While you were sleeping, we had dinner.
As my sister studies, she listens to classical music.
I go to work by 10 **after** I drive my child to school.
We were waiting for the supervisor **until** he comes.
It has been two years **since** I graduated from college.

> **Plus Grammar**
> 시간 부사절을 이끄는 접속사구
> ・every time (~할 때마다)
> **Every time** you fall down, I'll be there to catch you.
> (네가 넘어질 때마다, 내가 그곳에서 너를 잡을게.)
> ・as soon as (~하자마자)
> **As soon as** I put food in the bowl, the cat showed up.
> (내가 음식을 그릇에 놓자마자 고양이가 나타났다.)

2 조건을 나타내는 접속사

if	만약 ~하다면	unless	만약 ~하지 않는다면 (= if ~ not)

If you are tired, you'd better take a rest.
Unless you run faster, you'll lose the race.
→ **If** you **don't** run faster, you'll lose the race.

Grammar Practice >>

Answer p. 8

A1 밑줄 친 부분의 역할을 〈보기〉에서 고르시오.

> 보기
> ⓐ 주어　　　ⓑ 목적어　　　ⓒ 보어

(1) It is doubtful that he made dinner.

(2) I thought that you didn't like math.

(3) That you remember me is surprising.

(4) The actor's secret is that he is married.

A2 다음을 한 문장으로 바꿔 쓸 때 빈칸에 알맞은 말을 쓰시오.

(1) We're late for the meeting. That's true.

→ _____ for the meeting.

(2) I should escape from here. I think so.

→ I think _____ from here.

(3) You have long experience in this field. That's important.

→ It's important _____ in this field.

(4) Plants need water to grow. That's certain.

→ It's _____ to grow.

B1 밑줄 친 부분의 쓰임이 〈보기〉와 같으면 ○를 쓰고, 다르면 ×를 쓰시오.

> 보기
> I wonder if I can stay two days longer.

(1) I don't know if I should pay or not.

(2) If Alan comes, I will tell him the truth.

(3) I doubt if many people will come to the party.

B2 우리말과 일치하도록 빈칸에 알맞은 말을 쓰시오.

(1) Jack이 해결책을 가지고 있는지가 이 상황의 요점이다.

→ _____ Jack has the solution is the key to this situation.

(2) 나는 Susan이 그녀의 숙제를 끝냈는지 모르겠다.

→ I don't know _____ Susan finished her homework.

(3) Luke가 돈을 가지고 있는지 아닌지는 중요하지 않다.

→ It's not important _____ or not Luke has money.

(4) 나의 유일한 의문점은 Sophia가 생존해 있는지 여부이다.

→ My only doubt is _____ Sophia is alive.

C1 우리말과 일치하도록 주어진 단어들을 이용하여 문장을 완성하시오.

(1) 네가 먹는 동안에는 말을 많이 하지 마라. (are, you, eating)

→ _____, don't speak much.

(2) 네가 만약 그것에 주의를 기울이지 않으면, 네게 문제가 좀 생길지도 모른다. (careful with, you, it, are)

→ _____, you may have some problem.

(3) 물이 끓은 후에 냄비에 달걀들을 넣어라. (boiled, the, is, water)

→ Put the eggs into the pot _____ _____.

(4) 내가 Joe의 졸업식에서 그를 만났던 이래로 그를 본 적이 없다. (met, at, graduation, him, I, his)

→ I haven't seen Joe _____ _____.

교과서　**guilty** 유죄인　**matter** 중요하다　**argue with** ～와 논쟁하다　**supervisor** 감독(관)　**doubtful** 의심스러운
어휘　**escape from** ～에서 달아나다　**field** 분야　**doubt** 궁금해하다; 의문점　**alive** 살아 있는　**boil** 끓이다, 삶다

Ⓓ 부사절을 이끄는 접속사 II

이유	because, as, since	~ 때문에
양보	although(though), even though	비록 ~하지만
	even if	만약 ~할지라도
목적	so that (= in order to)	~하기 위해서, ~하도록
결과	so ~ that ... can / can't	너무 ~해서 …할 수 있다 / 없다

I can't eat anymore **as** I'm full. 〈이유〉
Because Andrea lost the way, she took a taxi.
cf. I can't see anything **because of** the fog. 〈because of + 명사(구)〉
Although(Though) the ring is expensive, I could buy it for you. 〈양보〉
Even if you don't like ice cream, try this chocolate ice cream. 〈양보〉
Exercise regularly **so that** you can stay in shape. 〈목적〉
→ Exercise regularly **in order to stay** in shape.
Cathy is **so** rich **that** she **can** buy the expensive car. 〈결과〉

● **Plus** Grammar
〈양보를 나타내는 전치사(구)〉
· He enjoys bungee jumping **in spite of** all the danger. (그는 그 모든 위험에도 불구하고 번지점프를 즐긴다.)
· **Despite** his effort, he failed the exam. (그의 노력에도 불구하고 그는 시험에서 떨어졌다.)

Ⓔ 접속부사

접속부사(구)는 두 개의 문장 사이에서 그 둘을 이어 주는 역할을 하는 부사(구)이다.

결과	so, therefore, thus, consequently, as a result	첨가	besides, moreover, furthermore, in addition
역접	however, nevertheless, still, yet, on the other hand	조건	otherwise

We have a growing population. **Therefore** we need more food.
I was late for lunch; **however**, there was still plenty of food.
Cynthia is a great scientist. **Besides**, she is a talented painter.
You'd better leave now. **Otherwise**, you will miss the train.

Ⓕ 상관접속사

	의미	주어일 경우 수의 일치
both A and B	A와 B 둘 다	복수 취급
not A but B	A가 아닌 B	B에 일치
either A or B	A, B 둘 중 하나	
neither A nor B	A, B 둘 다 아닌	
not only A but (also) B = B as well as A	A뿐만 아니라 B도	

The survey will take **both** time **and** money.
I'll enjoy **either** snowboarding **or** horseriding this weekend.
Emma was confident **not only** on the stage **but also** in real life.
→ Emma was confident in real life **as well as** on the stage.

Grammar Practice >

Answer p. 8

D1 우리말과 일치하도록 빈칸에 알맞은 말을 〈보기〉에서 고르시오.

┌─보기─────────────────────┐
so   can   that   can't

though   even   because
└─────────────────────────┘

(1) _____ I had a headache, I skipped the meal. (나는 두통이 있었기 때문에 식사를 걸렀다.)

(2) Jake still looks pale _____ he recovered his health. (비록 Jake가 건강을 회복했지만, 그는 여전히 창백해 보인다.)

(3) Mark studied math hard _____ _____ he could pass the test. (Mark는 시험에 통과하기 위해서 수학 공부를 열심히 했다.)

(4) Emily is _____ tired _____ she can't walk any more. (Emily는 너무 피곤해서 더 이상 걸을 수가 없다.)

(5) Edward is _____ tall _____ he _____ be a model. (Edward는 키가 매우 커서 모델이 될 수 있다.)

(6) _____ _____ it is August, the weather is rather cool. (8월이지만, 날씨가 다소 시원하다.)

E1 괄호 안에서 알맞은 것을 고르시오.

(1) Donald tried his best. (As a result, However), he lost the game.

(2) Watch out! (Moreover, Otherwise), you can get hurt.

(3) The weather was too windy. (Thus, Nevertheless), we put on our coats.

(4) Andy is smart and handsome. (Thus, Besides), he is kind.

(5) Ann didn't like the color of the product. (Nevertheless / Otherwise), she bought it anyway.

F1 밑줄 친 부분을 어법에 맞게 고쳐 쓰시오.

(1) Both my wife <u>nor</u> I are responsible for the accident. → _____

(2) We need not only a new doctor <u>and</u> also a new nurse. → _____

(3) <u>Neither</u> Eric or you should finish this project. → _____

(4) It is not you <u>and</u> me that our mom really worried about. → _____

F2 다음 문장을 우리말로 옮기시오.

(1) Both you and your brother were wrong.
→ _____

(2) I will play either soccer or baseball in the afternoon.
→ _____

(3) Not only men but also women have to learn how to ride a bike.
→ _____

(4) Not Judith but you should drive the truck.
→ _____

(5) Neither Linda nor Kyle participated in the meeting.
→ _____

(6) Police officers as well as firefighters were hurt.
→ _____

교과서 **stay in shape** 건강을 유지하다 **talented** 재능 있는 **horseriding** 승마 **skip** 거르다 **pale** 창백한 **windy** 바람이 부는
어휘 **be responsible for** ~에 책임이 있다 **participate in** ~에 참석하다

Grammar Test

01 빈칸에 알맞은 것은?

> Jinsu is good at singing. _____, he plays the guitar well.

① However ② Therefore ③ As a result
④ Otherwise ⑤ Besides

서술형 평가

02 주어진 문장의 의미와 일치하도록 빈칸에 알맞은 말을 쓰시오.

> Mr. Smith as well as Mr. Baker seems to know the news.

= Not only _____.

---

03 밑줄 친 부분 중 어법상 어색한 것은?

① I can't delay it longer <u>because</u> it's too late.
② The hotel is cheap <u>because of</u> it is old.
③ Madeline said such things <u>because of</u> her jealousy.
④ <u>Because</u> I am a foreigner, I should carry my passport.
⑤ <u>Because</u> Eric won the gold medal, his parents are proud of him.

---

04 밑줄 친 that의 쓰임이 〈보기〉와 같은 것은?

> 보기
> I think <u>that</u> Mr. Potter will be a president.

① Which is worse, this or <u>that</u>?
② I finally realized <u>that</u> I had met Jane before.
③ Where is the girl <u>that</u> sells tickets?
④ Tell me the story <u>that</u> you heard from Joe.
⑤ I'd like to recommend <u>that</u> skirt to you.

---

05 우리말과 일치하도록 할 때 빈칸에 알맞은 것은?

> 만약 당신이 더 좋은 아이디어를 가지고 있지 않다면, 나는 Henry에게 기회를 줄 것이다.
>
> → _____ you have a better idea, I'll give Henry a chance.

① As ② If ③ Unless
④ Though ⑤ Even

[06~07] 빈칸에 들어갈 말이 바르게 짝지어진 것을 고르시오.

06

> • Both Jason _____ his girlfriend are baseball fans.
> • The musical was not only interesting _____ also successful.

① or – but ② or – either
③ and – and ④ and – but
⑤ and – neither

07

> • We sat in front of the stage _____ that we could see the actors closely.
> • The plate is so hot that I _____ touch.

① and – can't ② and – can
③ so – can ④ so – can't
⑤ but – can

교과서 **be good at** ~을 잘하다 **delay** 미루다, 연기하다 **jealousy** 시기심, 질투 **foreigner** 외국인 **passport** 여권
어휘 **president** 대통령, 의장 **realize** 알아채다 **recommend** 추천하다 **closely** 바싹, 접근하여

Answer p. 8

08 밑줄 친 부분의 의미와 일치하도록 빈칸에 알맞은 말을 쓰시오.

A Did you do your homework?
B Not yet. I'll do it after finishing the game.
A <u>If you don't stop it right away</u>, I'll turn off the computer.

= _____ _____ _____ it right away, I'll turn off the computer.

09 밑줄 친 If(if)의 쓰임이 나머지와 다른 것은?
① Please help me <u>if</u> you are free.
② <u>If</u> you don't get up now, you'll be late.
③ You will succeed <u>if</u> you make every effort.
④ I wonder <u>if</u> she has an interest in Korean food.
⑤ <u>If</u> you don't stop lying, we can't trust you.

10 빈칸에 알맞지 <u>않은</u> 것은?

I'll start early _____.

① unless I oversleep
② though I am so tired
③ until I pack up my things
④ so that I can catch the bus
⑤ and I will arrive there earlier than you

11 우리말과 일치하도록 주어진 단어들을 이용하여 문장을 완성하시오.

나는 Albert가 그 선물을 좋아하는지 아닌지를 알고 싶다. (whether, or not, present)

→ I want to know _____.

12 주어진 문장과 의미가 같은 것은?

Unless you can answer my question, you must find someone who can.

① If you can answer my question, you must find someone who can.
② If you answer my question, you must find someone who can.
③ Unless you can answer my question, you must not find someone who can.
④ Unless you can't answer my question, you must not find someone who can.
⑤ If you can't answer my question, you must find someone who can.

13 주어진 문장들의 의미와 일치하도록 빈칸에 알맞은 말을 쓰시오.

Ella doesn't like yogurt. She doesn't like ice cream, either.

= Ella likes _____ yogurt _____ ice cream.

교과서 **turn off** 끄다 **free** 한가한 **make an effort** 노력하다 **have an interest in** ~에 관심이 있다 **lie** 거짓말하다
어휘 **trust** 믿다, 신뢰하다 **oversleep** 늦잠 자다 **pack up** 짐을 싸다

Reading

[1~2] 다음을 끊어 읽고 ☑, 해석을 쓰시오. ✎

The Secret of My Father (II) _____

In 1946, a strange man visited me and asked, "Are you Mr. Kim Yonghwan's daughter?" For me, this was

3 an odd question ___(A)___ I was more used to being called the daughter of a *parakho*. "I'm your father's

friend," the man said. At that moment, I was expecting disappointing news since I did not have good

memories of my father.

6 My father's friend continued his story. "ⓐHe was not a gambler. Your father sent the family money to the

independence fighters in Manchuria. ⓑHe made himself look like a gambler to keep this a secret from the

Japanese officers." At first, I was not sure ___(B)___ ⓒhe was telling the truth. But afterwards, I found out

9 the truth about my father and I realized ___(C)___ I had been wrong about

ⓓhim. Ever since that moment, I have been proud to be the daughter of a

parakho who had devoted ⓔhis life to the independence movement.

1 빈칸 (A)–(C)에 알맞은 말을 〈보기〉에서 골라 쓰시오.

┌─ 보기 ───┐
│   because   if   that   │
└──┘

(A) _____   (B) _____   (C) _____

2 밑줄 친 ⓐ–ⓔ 중 가리키는 대상이 나머지와 다른 것은?

① ⓐ   ② ⓑ   ③ ⓒ   ④ ⓓ   ⑤ ⓔ

교과서 **odd** 이상한 **be used to** ~에 익숙하다 **disappointing** 실망스러운 **gambler** 도박꾼 **independence** 독립 **Manchuria** 만주
어휘 🎧 **officer** 경찰관 **afterwards** 나중에 **wrong** 잘못 생각한, 오해한 **devote A to B** A를 B에 바치다

Answer p. 8

3 밑줄 친 ⓐ–ⓔ 중 글 전체의 흐름상 어색한 것은?

의학

Artificial intelligence(AI) can give medical advice, detect skin cancer or perform surgery with expert-level accuracy. It is said **that** AI will soon replace as much as 80% of what doctors are doing now. ⓐWill patients prefer AI to human doctors? ⓑA recent study shows **that** patients are reluctant to choose AI. ⓒPatients view themselves as unique, but they believe AI will treat them **not** as a special patient **but** as an average one. ⓓPatients are likely to say "my" cold instead of "a" cold and to think "my" cold is a unique illness. ⓔ**Thus**, they want their illness to be treated as an average case.

① ⓐ   ② ⓑ   ③ ⓒ   ④ ⓓ   ⑤ ⓔ

4 다음 글에서 언급되지 <u>않은</u> 것은?

동물

When you see yourself in a mirror, you know **that** the reflection is another you. Can other animals do the same? In the 1970s, Dr. Gordon Gallup created the mirror test to learn how intelligent animals were. He thought more intelligent animals might know **that** their reflections show themselves. Since then, researchers have given the test to many kinds of animals. So far, only eight have passed the test including humans, chimpanzees, dolphins, and elephants. They all have a lot in common. **Not only** do they have large and complicated brain, **but** they **also** live in social groups helping each other.

① 거울 검사의 창시자   ② 거울 검사를 하게 된 이유
③ 거울 검사를 통과한 동물들   ④ 동물들에게 거울 검사하는 방법
⑤ 거울 검사를 통과한 동물들의 공통점

3 artificial intelligence 인공 지능 surgery 수술 accuracy 정확성 be reluctant to ～하는 데 주저하다 average 보통의
4 reflection 상, 모습 in common 공통의 complicated 복잡한 social 사회의

Expression

1 이유 묻고 답하기

Comic books are really useful for adults.

Really? Why do you say so?

They help us think more creatively. We need to think outside the box to find the answers.

🐨 이유 묻기

- Can you tell me (the reason) why ...?
- What's the matter with you?
- What makes you ...?
- Why are(do) you ...?

🐨 이유 답하기

- Because ....
- It's because ....

2 가능성 정도 묻고 답하기

Jake. He lived in space for one year, and he grew 2 inches while in space.

Really? How is that possible?

I'm not sure, but maybe it's because there's no gravity in space.

That's so cool. I wish I could live in space. That way, I could become taller.

🐨 가능성 정도 묻기

- Can you ...?
- Are you able to ...?
- Is he likely to ...?
- How is that(it) possible?
- Is it possible(impossible) to(that) ...?
- Is it probable(likely) to(that) ...?

🐨 가능성 정도 표현하기

- I can(am able to) ....
- They should(ought to) ....
- Maybe(Perhaps, Possibly) they can(will) ....
- It is possible(impossible) to(that) ....
- It is probable(likely) to(that) ....

Expression Test

(Answer p. 9)

1 주어진 질문에 대한 답으로 알맞지 <u>않은</u> 것은?

Why are you bringing your umbrella?

① Maybe it'll rain later.
② It cannot rain today.
③ It may rain in the afternoon.
④ Possibly it'll rain in the afternoon.
⑤ My mom said it'll rain this afternoon.

서술형 평가
2 빈칸에 알맞은 말을 쓰시오.

A Hey, you look upset. _____ _____
_____ with you?
B It's because I lost my wallet.
A That's too bad.

3 자연스러운 대화가 되도록 ⓐ–ⓓ를 바르게 배열한 것은?

ⓐ Because Mike has to leave Korea next week.
ⓑ I feel so sad today.
ⓒ What makes you feel that way?
ⓓ Oh, you must feel so sad.

① ⓐ – ⓒ – ⓓ – ⓑ
② ⓑ – ⓐ – ⓓ – ⓒ
③ ⓑ – ⓒ – ⓐ – ⓓ
④ ⓒ – ⓐ – ⓓ – ⓑ
⑤ ⓒ – ⓑ – ⓐ – ⓓ

서술형 평가
4 밑줄 친 우리말과 일치하도록 괄호 안의 단어를 이용하여 문장을 완성하시오.

A Dr. Smith's seminar was postponed until the following day.
B Really? <u>왜 그가 그렇게 했는지 나에게 말해 줄 수 있습니까?</u> (tell, reason)
A He had an accident, so he is in the hospital now.

→ _____ he did it?

5 빈칸에 알맞은 것은?

A _____ reading the book today?
B I'm afraid I can't. Today I have to meet my friend, Dobin.

① Is it likely finish
② Is it likely finishing
③ Is it possible finishing
④ Is it possible to finish
⑤ Is it probable finishing

6 의도하는 바가 나머지와 <u>다른</u> 것은?
① He may go to England next month.
② Maybe he will go to England next month.
③ He had better go to England next month.
④ Perhaps he will go to England next month.
⑤ Possibly he will go to England next month.

1 밑줄 친 문장의 의미와 일치하도록 괄호 안에 제시된 단어들을 이용하여 문장을 바꿔 쓰시오.

A Irene, what was the best food you ate in the space station?

B Hmm…. I can't really answer to that.

A (1) What makes you think so? (why, say)

B We grew some vegetables and ate them every day. They were all fresh and tasty!

A (2) Are we able to grow vegetables in the space station? (it, is, possible)

B Yes. Since there's no gravity in space, we had to grow them in special bags. The bags helped the roots to grow.

(1) _____

(2) _____

2 두 문장을 접속사 that을 이용하여 한 문장으로 바꿔 쓰시오.

(1) We don't know as much as we think. It is the truth.

→ The truth is _____.

(2) Beckett is actually a Mexican. It is true.

→ _____ is true.

3 빈칸에 알맞은 말을 (A), (B)에서 골라 각 문장을 완성하시오.

(A)	(B)
whether	the rumor is true or not
though	it snowed heavily

(1) We went on a picnic _____.

(2) _____ is not important at all.

4 표를 보고, 괄호 안의 상관접속사를 이용하여 빈칸에 알맞은 말을 쓰시오.

⟨List of Sports I Can Do⟩

	ride a bike	skate	swim
Tom	○	×	○
Jina	○	○	×
Minsu	○	–	×
Jihoon	–	○	○

(1) _____ can ride a bike.
　　　(both … and ~)

(2) Jina cannot _____.
　　　　　　　(not … but ~)

(3) _____ can swim.
　　　(neither … nor ~)

(4) _____ can swim.
　　(not only … but also ~)

5 대화창을 보고, 밑줄 친 부분과 접속사 that, if, because를 한 번씩 써서 요약문을 완성하시오.

Lucy

I visited my grandmother in New York during the vacation. Have you been there before?

Minsu

Sure. I enjoyed watching musicals in Broadway. Did you go to watch musicals? There are so many famous musicals there.

Lucy

No. My grandmother wanted me to spend time with her, so I just stayed at her house cooking with her.

Lucy said (1) _____ in New York during her vacation. Knowing that there are many famous musicals there, Minsu asked her (2) _____. Lucy said that she stayed at her grandmother's house (3) _____ _____.

★
01 짝지어진 단어의 관계가 나머지와 <u>다른</u> 것은?

① careful – careless　　② honest – dishonest

③ lower – raise　　④ envy – jealousy

⑤ innocent – guilty

★★ 서술형 평가
02 다음 영영풀이가 설명하는 단어를 〈보기〉에서 골라 쓰시오.

┌─보기─
│　　fiction　　　delay　　　doubt
└

(1) books and stories about imaginary people and events: _____

(2) to make something or someone take longer than planned: _____

★★
03 빈칸에 공통으로 들어갈 말로 알맞은 것은?

• His main _____ is studying space science.

• Banks lend money and charge _____.

① fan　　　② battle　　　③ interest

④ chance　　⑤ gravity

★★ 서술형 평가
04 우리말과 일치하도록 주어진 단어들을 이용하여 문장을 완성하시오.

A <u>스마트폰 없이 사는 게 가능할까?</u>

(it, live, possible, is, to)

B Yeah, I think it's possible.

→ _____ without smartphones?

★★
05 빈칸에 알맞지 <u>않은</u> 것은?

A My best friend doesn't want to talk to me.

B _____

A Actually, I told others her big secret.

B You should apologize to her first.

① Can you tell me why?

② Why didn't you tell her?

③ What makes her act that way?

④ Why do you think she doesn't talk to you?

⑤ What happened between you and your friend?

★
06 의도하는 바가 나머지와 <u>다른</u> 것은?

① Can an animal live over 100 years?

② Is it possible to drink water in space?

③ Is Mary likely to finish the work in time?

④ Is it likely that you win first place?

⑤ Is it necessary to wear a helmet when riding a bike?

★★★
07 주어진 말에 이어질 ⓐ–ⓓ의 순서를 바르게 배열한 것은?

How do you like your dish?

ⓐ I'm really satisfied with the food here. How about you?

ⓑ Because the food is too greasy. I don't like greasy food.

ⓒ Why don't you like it?

ⓓ Actually, I'm not satisfied with mine at all.

① ⓐ – ⓒ – ⓓ – ⓑ　　② ⓐ – ⓓ – ⓒ – ⓑ

③ ⓑ – ⓓ – ⓐ – ⓒ　　④ ⓒ – ⓓ – ⓐ – ⓑ

⑤ ⓓ – ⓐ – ⓒ – ⓑ

교과서 **careless** 부주의한　**dishonest** 정직하지 않은　**envy** 부러움　**innocent** 무죄의　**imaginary** 상상의　**battle** 싸움　**gravity** 중력
어휘 **secret** 비밀　**apologize to** ～에게 사과하다　**dish** 요리　**greasy** 기름진

Final Test

08 밑줄 친 ①-⑤ 중 어법상 어색한 것은?

I don't know ① if or not Sumin ② will meet the director ③ after she ④ finishes ⑤ writing the scenario.

①   ②   ③   ④   ⑤

★★
09 빈칸에 공통으로 들어갈 말로 알맞은 것은?

I don't know _____ it will rain tomorrow, but _____ it rains, I'd rather stay home than go out.

① unless   ② if   ③ whether
④ that   ⑤ as

서술형 평가 · 시험에 잘 나오는 문제
10 두 문장의 의미가 일치하도록 빈칸에 알맞은 말을 〈보기〉에서 고르시오.

┌ 보기 ┐
since   if   although

They took a taxi in order to get there on time.
= They took a taxi _____ they wanted to get there on time.

★★ 서술형 평가
11 두 문장의 의미가 일치하도록 빈칸에 알맞은 말을 쓰시오.

English as well as math is a required subject.
= _____ only math _____ also English is a required subject.

★★ 시험에 잘 나오는 문제
12 밑줄 친 부분의 쓰임이 〈보기〉와 같은 것은?

┌ 보기 ┐
I believe that there were more witnesses to the accident.

① That is why all the people helped him.
② I found the ring that Jim had given to Alice.
③ After that, he began to talk about the fact.
④ The girl that visited us yesterday is a pianist.
⑤ Nara recommended that you should try the new dish at the restaurant.

★★
13 밑줄 친 ①-⑤ 중 어법상 어색한 것은?

A Hi, Robin. ① Let's go hiking this Saturday.
B ② I'd love to. But did you hear the weather forecast?
A No, I didn't. I don't know ③ either it will rain or not, but let's go anyway.
B ④ If there's a chance of rain, maybe ⑤ we'd better go another time.

①   ②   ③   ④   ⑤

★★
14 밑줄 친 부분의 쓰임이 나머지와 다른 것은?
① When does Fred leave for Canada?
② When I am alone, I usually paint.
③ Sam was out when the bell rang.
④ When you watch TV with kids, watch out for violent scenes.
⑤ Please give my regards to your mom when you go to your hometown.

교과서   **scenario** 각본, 시나리오   **on time** 제시간에   **require** 요구하다   **witness** 목격자   **leave for** ~을 향해 떠나다   **paint** 그리다
어휘   **ring** (벨이) 울리다   **violent** 폭력적인   **scene** 장면   **give one's regards to** ~에게 …의 안부를 전하다

15 밑줄 친 부분 중 어법상 어색한 것은?

① We didn't stay outside long <u>as</u> it was too cold.

② Light up the candles <u>before</u> you turn off the lights.

③ <u>While</u> Ms. Green was waiting for her son, she read a newspaper.

④ Elena was not allowed to go out <u>because</u> she had done her homework.

⑤ <u>After</u> Dan bought some food at the market, he prepared a delicious meal.

16 밑줄 친 부분의 의미가 나머지와 다른 것은?

① Kate has kept a diary <u>since</u> she was ten.

② <u>Since</u> he wasn't there, I couldn't meet him.

③ I couldn't ride a bike <u>since</u> my bike broke down.

④ <u>Since</u> I took the wrong bus, I must get off now.

⑤ We can't afford the car <u>since</u> we don't have enough money.

17 괄호 안에서 알맞은 표현을 선택한 것은?

① It's late. (<u>Moreover</u>, Therefore), please hurry up.

② Emilia is not rich. (However, <u>As a result</u>), she has donated a lot of money.

③ I went to the store. (<u>Otherwise</u>, However), I did not buy anything.

④ I love dance music. (For instance, <u>On the other hand</u>), my sister loves jazz.

⑤ Patrick is young. (Moreover, <u>Therefore</u>) he is wise.

18 어법상 옳은 것은?

① Grace will dance as well as sing on the stage.

② The novel was not only exciting also moving.

③ Both walking and run are needed for good health.

④ Jacob gets either what he likes and what he hates.

⑤ In the jail, Howard can see neither the sun or the moon.

서술형 평가

[19~21] 빈칸에 알맞은 것을 〈보기〉에서 골라 쓰시오.

보기

besides	therefore	though	since

19

How about covering the walls of your room with sticky notes? There are so many pretty colors to choose from and it is easy to change the color later. _____, they are very cheap! Try them out right now!

20

There are many tourists who can't speak French; _____, the government needs to hire more employees who speak English and other languages.

21

Many achievements of the Roman Empire still exist _____ it ended more than a thousand years ago.

교과서
어휘 **candle** 초 **be allowed to** ~하는 것이 허용되다 **get off** (탈것에서) 내리다 **afford** ~을 감당하다 **jail** 감옥 **government** 정부
hire 고용하다 **employee** 직원 **achievement** 성취 **empire** 제국

Lesson 03 접속사 65

★★★
22 어법상 올바른 것끼리 짝지어진 것은?

ⓐ It's getting dark and cloudy, so it's going to rain soon.

ⓑ Even though I was tired, I went to the party.

ⓒ Daniel is not American also German.

ⓓ I wonder if or not that is true.

ⓔ Both my brother and I like pasta with cream sauce.

① ⓐ, ⓑ, ⓒ   ② ⓐ, ⓑ, ⓔ   ③ ⓑ, ⓓ, ⓔ
④ ⓑ, ⓒ, ⓔ   ⑤ ⓒ, ⓓ, ⓔ

★★
23 빈칸에 들어갈 말이 바르게 짝지어진 것은?

- Ethan speaks to his mom _____ loudly that she can hear his saying.
- When it _____ raining, we will go to the market.

① very – stopped   ② very – will stop
③ so – stopped   ④ so – will stop
⑤ so – stops

★★
24 밑줄 친 ⓐ~ⓔ 중 어법상 어색한 것은?

Many insects have bright colors ⓐ to protect themselves. For example, ladybugs advertise ⓑ the fact what they taste bad ⓒ by being colorful. Birds and other predators soon learn ⓓ that creatures with bright colors and bold patterns ⓔ might be poisonous.

① ⓐ   ② ⓑ   ③ ⓒ   ④ ⓓ   ⑤ ⓔ

★★
25 글의 흐름으로 보아, 빈칸에 알맞은 것은?

If you're trying to decide between going on a trip and buying the latest cell phone, choose the trip. According to some studies, you'll get more happiness not from spending money on physical objects, but from _____. Why? The studies shows the pleasure disappears as we get used to new goods. However, an experience keeps bringing you a little burst of joy whenever you remember it.

① experiences   ② money   ③ time
④ appearance   ⑤ relationships

★★★
26 주어진 글 다음에 이어질 (A)-(C)의 순서로 알맞은 것은?

How are you sitting now? When you sit with your shoulder and head bent, you may not think clearly nor remember things.

(A) Thus, when you have trouble in solving a difficult math problem, just sit up straight.

(B) What's more, this defeated position actually brings feelings of anxiety and depression.

(C) On the other hand, when you sit upright, it improves blood and oxygen flow to the brain by up to 40 percent!

① (A) – (C) – (B)   ② (B) – (A) – (C)
③ (B) – (C) – (A)   ④ (C) – (A) – (B)
⑤ (C) – (B) – (A)

교과서 **insect** 곤충 **ladybug** 무당벌레 **advertise** 광고하다 **predator** 포식자 **poisonous** 독성의 **latest** 최신의 **according to** ~에 따르면
어휘 **get used to** ~에 익숙해지다 **defeated** 패배한, 패배의 **anxiety** 불안감 **depression** 좌절감 **upright** 꼿꼿하게 **flow** 흐름

[27~28] 다음을 읽고, 물음에 답하시오.

During World War I, some animals helped soldiers. Horses not only carried soldiers _____ⓐ_____ they also pulled some of the gigantic guns and ambulances. Gas from their droppings were used to power lamps. Both pet dogs _____ⓑ_____ pet pigeons carried messages since they were too fast to shoot at. Goldfish did their jobs, too. How? After gas attack, soldiers washed the gas masks in water and put a goldfish in the water. If the goldfish died, it meant that the masks still had poison on them.

*dropping (짐승의) 배설물

★★
27 빈칸 ⓐ와 ⓑ에 각각 들어갈 말로 알맞은 것은?
① and – but
② but – and
③ if – with
④ and – with
⑤ but – or

★★
28 위 글의 내용으로 알맞지 <u>않은</u> 것은?
① 말은 큰 총과 구급차를 끌었다.
② 말의 배설물에서 나온 가스는 전등을 켜는 데 이용되었다.
③ 비둘기는 너무 빨라서 총에 잘 맞지 않았기 때문에 메시지를 전달했다.
④ 가스 공격 후에 군인들은 방독면을 물에 씻었다.
⑤ 물에 있는 금붕어들이 방독면에 있는 독을 없애 주었다.

[29~30] 다음을 읽고, 물음에 답하시오.

Every year, many new hurricanes are seen on TV. Have you wondered how they got their names? The World Meteorological Organization (WMO) gives names to hurricanes ⓐ<u>each one, that, distinguish, so, we, can.</u> The WMO develops a list of names and a storm is given a name in an alphabetical order. Thus, the first storm of the year is given a name starting with A, the second with B and so on. That name stays with the storm until it develops into a hurricane.

★★ 서술형 평가
29 밑줄 친 ⓐ의 단어들을 바르게 배열하여 문장을 완성하시오.

→ _____

★★
30 위 글의 제목으로 가장 알맞은 것은?
① The Funniest Hurricane Names
② The Worst Hurricane in History
③ How to Give a Hurricane Its Name
④ The Effect of Hurricanes on Sea Life
⑤ Storms Developing into Hurricanes

교과서
어휘 ⌒ **gigantic** 거대한 **pigeon** 비둘기 **goldfish** 금붕어 **poison** 독 **meteorological** 기후의, 기상학의 **distinguish** 구별하다
alphabetical 알파벳순의 **order** 순서 **effect** 영향; 효과

A 명사절을 이끄는 접속사 that

that은 '~하는 것'의 의미로 주어, 목적어, 보어로 쓰이는 명사절을 이끈다.

That Brenda became a teacher is true. = It is true **that Brenda became a teacher**. 〈주어〉

I believe **that David is guilty**. 〈목적어〉

The surprising fact is **that Daisy didn't even read it**. 〈보어〉

The news **that they won the game** was not true. 〈동격절〉

B 명사절을 이끄는 접속사 if, whether

if와 whether는 '~인지 아닌지'의 의미로 명사절을 이끈다. if가 이끄는 절은 목적어로만 쓰인다.

Whether Victoria may come (or not) doesn't matter. 〈주어〉

I wonder **if(whether) Terry is honest**. 〈목적어〉

Pamela's interest is **whether I move to Chicago (or not)**. 〈보어〉

C 부사절을 이끄는 접속사 I

when	~할 때	while	~하는 동안	as	~할 때, ~하면서
before / after	~하기 전에 / 후에	until / till	~할 때까지	since	~ 이래로
if	만약 ~하다면	unless	만약 ~하지 않는다면 (= if ~ not)		

When I arrived at the office, Louis was arguing with Stella.

We were waiting for the supervisor **until** he comes.

It has been two years **since** I graduated from college.

If you are tired, you'd better take a rest.

Unless you run faster, you'll lose the race. (= **If** you **don't** run faster, ~)

D 부사절을 이끄는 접속사 II

이유	because, as, since	~ 때문에
양보	although(though), even though / even if	비록 ~하지만 / 만약 ~할지라도
목적	so that (= in order to)	~하기 위해서, ~하도록
결과	so ~ that ... can / can't	너무 ~해서 …할 수 있다 / 없다

I can't eat anymore **as** I'm full. 〈이유〉

Although(Though) the ring is expensive, I could buy it for you. 〈양보〉

Exercise regularly **so that** you can stay in shape. 〈목적〉

Cathy is **so** rich **that** she **can** buy the expensive car. 〈결과〉

E 접속부사

두 개의 문장 사이에서 그 둘을 이어 주는 역할을 하는 부사(구)

결과	so, therefore, thus, consequently, as a result	첨가	besides, moreover, furthermore, in addition
역접	however, nevertheless, still, yet, on the other hand	조건	otherwise

We have a growing population. **Therefore** we need more food.
I was late for lunch; **however**, there was still plenty of food.
Cynthia is a great scientist. **Besides**, she is a talented painter.
You'd better leave now. **Otherwise**, you will miss the train.

F 상관접속사

both A and B	A와 B 둘 다	not A but B	A가 아닌 B	not only A but (also) B = B as well as A	A뿐만 아니라 B도
either A or B	A, B 둘 중 하나	neither A nor B	A, B 둘 다 아닌		

The survey will take **both** time **and** money.
I'll enjoy **either** snowboarding **or** horseriding this weekend.
Emma was confident **not only** on the stage **but also** in real life.
→ Emma was confident in real life **as well as** on the stage.

▶▶ Expression

1 이유 묻고 답하기

❤ 이유 묻기
- Can you tell me (the reason) why ...?
- What's the matter with you?
- What makes you ...?
- Why are(do) ...?

❤ 이유 답하기
- Because .....
- It's because ....

2 가능성 정도 묻고 답하기

❤ 가능성 정도 묻기
- Can you ...?
- Are you able to ...?
- Is he likely to ...?
- How is that(it) possible?
- Is it possible(impossible) to(that) ...?
- Is it probable(likely) to(that) ...?

❤ 가능성 정도 표현하기
- I can(am able to) ....
- They should(ought to) ....
- Maybe(Perhaps, Possibly) they can(will) ....
- It is possible(impossible) to(that) ....
- It is probable(likely) to(that) ....

Lesson 04

가정법

Grammar Preview

1 가정법 I

• 가정법 과거는 현재 사실에 반대되는 일이나 실현 가능성이 희박한 일을 가정한다.

형태	조건절	If+주어+동사의 과거형 …, (cf. be동사는 were 사용)
	주절	주어+과거형 조동사(would/could/might/should)+동사원형 ….
의미		(사실은 그렇지 않지만) 만약 ～하다면, …할 텐데

If I **were** a millionaire, I **could buy** a great mansion.

• 가정법 과거완료는 과거 사실에 반대되는 일을 가정한다.

형태	조건절	If+주어+had+p.p. …,
	주절	주어+과거형 조동사(would/could/might/should)+have+p.p. ….
의미		(사실은 그렇지 않았지만) 만약 ～했다면, …했을 텐데

If Albert **had been** honest, the company **would have employed** him.

• if가 생략된 가정법

조건절의 동사가 were나 〈had+p.p.〉이면 if를 생략할 수 있는데, 이때 조건절의 주어와 동사는 도치된다.

If I were my brother, I wouldn't read comic books. → **Were** I my brother, ….

If the captain had been more careful, the ship would not have sunk.

→ **Had the captain been** more careful, ….

2 가정법 II

• I wish+가정법

형태	의미
I wish+가정법 과거(주어+동사의 과거형[were])	～하다면 좋을 텐데(현재의 실현 불가능한 소망)
I wish+가정법 과거완료(주어+had+p.p.)	～했다면 좋을 텐데(과거의 일에 대한 유감)

• as if+가정법

형태	의미
as if+가정법 과거(주어+동사의 과거형[were])	마치 ～한 것처럼(주절과 같은 시제의 일)
as if+가정법 과거완료(주어+had+p.p.)	마치 ～했던 것처럼(주절보다 이전 과거의 일)

• Without[But for]+가정법

형태	의미
Without[But for] ~, +가정법 과거	～이 없다면, (지금) …할 텐데
Without[But for] ~, +가정법 과거완료	～이 없었다면, (이전에) …했을 텐데

A 가정법 과거

가정법 과거는 현재 사실에 반대되는 일이나 실현 가능성이 희박한 일을 가정한다. 동사의 형태는 과거이지만 해석은 현재로 한다. 가정법 과거는 현재 시제의 직설법으로 바꿔 쓸 수 있으며 이때 긍정문은 부정문으로, 부정문은 긍정문으로 쓴다.

형태	조건절	If+주어+동사의 과거형 …, (cf. be동사는 were 사용)
	주절	주어+과거형 조동사(would/could/might/should)+동사원형 ….
의미		(사실은 그렇지 않지만) 만약 ～하다면, …할 텐데

If I **were** a millionaire, I **could buy** a great mansion.

→ As I am not a millionaire, I can't buy a great mansion. 〈직설법〉

If Arthur **felt** hungry, he **would taste** my dish.

→ As Arthur doesn't feel hungry, he doesn't taste my dish. 〈직설법〉

◆ Plus Grammar

조건문과 가정법 문장
• 조건문: 실현 가능한 일을 가정
 If I see her, I will be happy.
 (그녀를 본다면 나는 행복할 것이다.
 → 그녀를 볼 가능성이 있음)
• 가정법 조건절: 실현 가능성이 희박한 일을 가정
 If I saw her, I would be happy.
 (만약 내가 그녀를 보게 된다면 나는 행복할 텐데. → 그녀를 볼 가능성이 희박함)

B 가정법 과거완료

가정법 과거완료는 과거 사실에 반대되는 일을 가정한다. 동사의 형태는 과거완료이지만 해석은 과거로 한다. 가정법 과거완료는 과거 시제의 직설법으로 바꿔 쓸 수 있으며 이때 긍정문은 부정문으로, 부정문은 긍정문으로 쓴다.

형태	조건절	If+주어+had+p.p. …,
	주절	주어+과거형 조동사(would/could/might/should)+have+p.p. ….
의미		(사실은 그렇지 않았지만) 만약 ～했다면, …했을 텐데

If Albert **had been** honest, the company **would have employed** him.

→ As Albert was not honest, the company didn't employ him.

If I **had got** up earlier, I **wouldn't have been** late for school.

→ As I didn't get up earlier, I was late for school.

C if가 생략된 가정법

조건절의 동사가 were나 〈had+p.p.〉인 경우 if를 생략할 수 있는데, 이때 조건절의 주어와 동사는 도치된다.

If I were my brother, I wouldn't read comic books.

→ **Were** I my brother, I wouldn't read comic books.

If the captain had been more careful, the ship would not have sunk.

→ **Had the captain been** more careful, the ship would not have sunk.

Grammar Practice >

Answer p. 11

A1 두 문장의 의미가 일치하도록 빈칸에 알맞은 말을 쓰시오.

(1) If Mark were not old, he could apply for the job.
→ As Mark is old, he _____ apply for the job.

(2) If my parents didn't encourage me, I couldn't succeed.
→ As my parents _____ me, I _____ succeed.

(3) If Nora accepted his proposal, we would be pleased.
→ _____ Nora _____ _____ his proposal, we aren't pleased.

A2 우리말과 일치하도록 밑줄 친 부분을 알맞은 형태로 고쳐 쓰시오.

(1) If Japanese was not difficult, I would learn it. (만약 일본어가 어렵지 않다면, 나는 그것을 배울 텐데.) → _____

(2) If I have enough money, I could buy you a computer. (만약 내게 돈이 충분히 있다면, 너에게 컴퓨터를 사 줄 텐데.) → _____

(3) If you went there, you can meet Laura. (네가 거기에 간다면, 너는 Laura를 만날 수 있을 텐데.) → _____

B1 밑줄 친 부분을 어법에 맞게 고쳐 쓰시오.

(1) If Judy studied French, she could have read the book in French. → _____

(2) If Linda agreed with you, everything should have been fine. → _____

(3) If I drank less coffee, I could have slept well. → _____

(4) If it had been fine, we would go on a picnic. → _____

B2 우리말과 일치하도록 주어진 단어들을 이용하여 빈칸에 알맞은 말을 쓰시오.

(1) 만약 어제 눈이 내렸다면, 나는 스키 타러 갔을 텐데. (will go)
→ If it had snowed yesterday, I _____ _____ _____ skiing.

(2) 만약 수민이가 더 일찍 왔다면, 그녀는 너를 만날 수 있었을 텐데. (have)
→ If Sumin _____ come earlier, she could _____ met you.

(3) Lauren이 아프지 않았으면, 그녀는 그녀의 작품을 마무리할 수 있었을 텐데. (be)
→ If Lauren _____ _____ sick, she could have finished her work.

C1 괄호 안에서 알맞은 것을 고르시오.

(1) (Were you, You were) well, you could hang out with me.

(2) (Owen had helped, Had Owen helped) me, I could have done it.

(3) (I had known, Had I known) the truth, I wouldn't have punished Milo.

C2 접속사 If를 생략할 때 빈칸에 알맞은 말을 쓰시오.

(1) If today were Saturday, I would not have to work.
→ _____ _____ Saturday, I would not have to work.

(2) If Joseph were trustworthy, the teacher would give him a chance.
→ _____ _____ trustworthy, the teacher would give him a chance.

(3) If I had been you, I would have looked after the patients.
→ _____ _____ _____ you, I would have looked after the patients.

교과서 **millionaire** 백만장자 **mansion** 대저택 **comic book** 만화책 **captain** 선장, 주장 **sink** 가라앉다 **apply for** ~에 지원하다
어휘 **accept** 받아들이다 **proposal** 제안 **agree with** ~에 동의하다 **hang out with** ~와 놀다 **punish** 처벌하다 **trustworthy** 믿을 만한

D | I wish + 가정법

〈I wish + 가정법〉은 현재나 과거 사실의 반대에 대한 소망과 유감을 나타낼 때 쓰며, 〈I am(was) sorry (that) + 주어 + 동사〉로 바꿔 쓸 수 있다.

형태	의미
I wish + 가정법 과거(주어 + 동사의 과거형(were))	~하다면 좋을 텐데(현재의 실현 불가능한 소망)
I wish + 가정법 과거완료(주어 + had + p.p.)	~했다면 좋을 텐데(과거의 일에 대한 유감)

I wish I had a cute puppy.
→ I am sorry (that) I don't have a cute puppy.
I wish you had seen the car parade.
→ I am sorry (that) you didn't see the car parade.

Plus Grammar

hope는 실현 가능한 소망에, wish는 실현 가능성이 적은 소망에 쓰인다.
I **hope** you can come.
(나는 네가 올 수 있기를 희망해.)
→ I expect you can come.
I **wish** you could come.
(네가 올 수 있다면 좋을 텐데.)
→ I'm sorry you can't come.

E | as if + 가정법

〈as if + 가정법〉은 현재나 과거 사실에 반대되는 가정을 나타낼 때 쓰며, 〈In fact, 주어 + 동사〉로 바꿔 쓸 수 있다.

형태	의미
as if + 가정법 과거(주어 + 동사의 과거형(were))	마치 ~한 것처럼(주절과 같은 시제의 일)
as if + 가정법 과거완료(주어 + had + p.p.)	마치 ~했던 것처럼(주절보다 이전 과거의 일)

Somin walks **as if** she **were** a super model.
→ In fact, Somin is not a super model.
Mr. Song talks **as if** he **had found** the solution.
→ In fact, Mr. Song didn't find the solution.

Plus Grammar

• I wish(ed) / as if + 가정법 과거: 주절 동사의 시제와 동일한 때에 관한 표현
• I wish(ed) / as if + 가정법 과거완료: 주절 동사의 시제보다 이전 시기에 관한 표현

F | Without(But for) + 가정법

Without(But for)가 이끄는 어구는 '~이 없(었)다면'의 의미로 현재 또는 과거 사실과 반대되는 가정을 나타내며, if를 이용한 가정법으로 바꿔 쓸 수 있다.

Without(But for) ~, + 가정법 과거	~이 없다면, (지금) …할 텐데	→ If it were not for ~ → Were it not for ~
Without(But for) ~, + 가정법 과거완료	~이 없었다면, (이전에) …했을 텐데	→ If it had not been for ~ → Had it not been for ~

Without(But for) air, nothing **could live**.
→ **If it were not for** air, nothing **could live**.
→ **Were it not for** air, nothing **could live**.
But for(Without) the policeman, Glenn **would have got** lost.
→ **If it had not been for** the policeman, Glenn **would have got** lost.
→ **Had it not been for** the policeman, Glenn **would have got** lost.

Plus Grammar

otherwise 구문
• 〈직설법 현재, otherwise, 가정법 과거〉: 그렇지 않다면
He works hard, otherwise, he would fail. (그는 열심히 일한다, 그렇지 않다면 그는 실패할 것이다.)
→ If he didn't work hard, he would fail.
• 〈직설법 과거, otherwise, 가정법 과거완료〉: 그렇지 않았다면
I was ill, otherwise, I would have gone there. (나는 아팠다, 그렇지 않았다면 거기 갔을 것이다.)
→ If I had not been ill, I would have gone there.

Grammar Practice >>

(Answer p. 11)

D1 우리말과 일치하도록 괄호 안에서 알맞은 것을 고르시오.

(1) I wish I (am, were) a famous movie star. (내가 유명한 영화배우라면 좋을 텐데.)

(2) I wish I (were, had been) a translator. (내가 번역가였다면 좋을 텐데.)

(3) I wish I (can, could) turn back time. (내가 시간을 되돌릴 수 있으면 좋을 텐데.)

(4) I wish you (have told, had told) me the story before. (네가 전에 그 이야기를 내게 했다면 좋을 텐데.)

D2 다음을 우리말로 옮기시오.

(1) I wish I didn't have to work all day long.

→ _____

(2) I wish he had come to the party last night.

→ _____

(3) I wish I had studied hard in the past.

→ _____

E1 괄호 안에서 알맞은 것을 고르시오.

(1) Alan talks as if he (have been, were) a director.

(2) Abigail talks as if she (is, had been) rich when young.

(3) Mary looks as if she (took, take) a lot of exercise.

(4) Henry talked as if he (are, had been) a champion last year.

E2 우리말과 일치하도록 괄호 안에서 알맞은 것을 고르시오.

(1) Jeffrey talks as if he (had known, knew) the password. (Jeffrey는 마치 암호를 아는 것처럼 말한다.)

(2) The girl looks as if she (had been, were) ill before. (그 소녀는 마치 전에 아팠던 것처럼 보인다.)

(3) James treats me as if I (be, were) a child. (James는 마치 내가 어린아이인 것처럼 나를 대한다.)

(4) Julie talked as if she (had visited, visits) Canada before. (Julie는 그녀가 전에 캐나다에 가 봤던 것처럼 말했다.)

F1 두 문장의 의미가 일치하도록 빈칸에 알맞은 말을 쓰시오.

(1) If it were not for his help, I couldn't finish it.

→ _____ his help, I couldn't finish it.

(2) Without your courage, you might fail.

→ If it _____ _____ for your courage, you might fail.

(3) Without your caring, I wouldn't get well so soon.

→ _____ for your caring, I wouldn't get well so soon.

F2 어법상 어색한 부분을 찾아 바르게 고쳐 쓰시오.

(1) With water, we could not live anymore.

_____ → _____

(2) But him, we would have lost the game.

_____ → _____

(3) If it were for the sun, nothing could live on the earth.

_____ → _____

교과서 **puppy** 강아지 **get lost** 길을 잃다 **translator** 번역가 **turn back** 되돌아가게 하다 **director** 감독 **take exercise** 운동을 하다
어휘 **password** 암호 **get well** 건강을 회복하다

Grammar Test

[01~03] 빈칸에 알맞은 것을 고르시오.

01

> I wish you _____ us last night.

① join   ② joined

③ would join   ④ had joined

⑤ would have joined

02

> If I were rich, I _____ lots of money to charity.

① donate   ② donated

③ will donate   ④ would donate

⑤ would have donated

03

> I don't have time now. I wish _____.

① I will play tennis with them

② I can play tennis with them

③ I could play tennis with them

④ I am playing tennis with them

⑤ I could have played tennis with them

04 밑줄 친 ①–⑤ 중 어법상 어색한 것은?

> ①If I ②hadn't talked so long ③on the phone with Eric, I ④wouldn't ⑤miss Helen's call yesterday.

05 우리말을 영어로 바르게 옮긴 것은?

> 만약 네가 아프지 않았다면, 나와 함께 여행을 갔을 텐데.

① If you had not been sick, you would have traveled with me.

② If you had been sick, you would have traveled with me.

③ If you were not sick, you would travel with me.

④ If you had not been sick, you would travel with me.

⑤ If you were not sick, you would have traveled with me.

06 밑줄 친 부분과 의미가 같은 것은?

> Without your support, I couldn't pass the exam.

① As if you support me

② I wish you support me

③ Is it not for your support

④ Had it not been for your support

⑤ If it were not for your support

서술형 평가

07 두 문장의 의미가 일치하도록 빈칸에 알맞은 말을 쓰시오.

(1) If Sam had a key, he could unlock the door.

→ As Sam _____, he _____ the door.

(2) If you had not seen the fire on the gas stove, the house would have burned down.

→ As _____ on the gas stove, _____.

교과서 **charity** 자선 단체   **donate** 기부하다   **support** 지원   **unlock** 열다   **burn down** 다 타 버리다
어휘

Answer p. 11

08 어법상 어색한 것은?

① Lena acts as if she were ill.

② I wish I were such a good cook.

③ If I knew Janet, I could speak to her.

④ Were I rich, I could buy that house.

⑤ If I had a digital camera, I would have taken pictures.

09 다음 중 문장의 전환이 어색한 것은?

① I wish I were free.

  → I'm sorry I'm not free.

② Aaron walks as if he were an old man.

  → In fact, Aron is not an old man.

③ If James had not been busy, he would have been present at the meeting.

  → As James was busy, he wasn't present at the meeting.

④ Without computers, our lives would be completely different.

  → But for computers, our lives would be completely different.

⑤ If Chloe had started writing a report earlier, she could have finished it in time.

  → As Chloe didn't start writing a report earlier, she couldn't have finished it in time.

10 다음 문장과 의미가 같은 것은?

Julie acts as if she were a captain.

① In fact, Julie is a captain.

② In fact, Julie was a captain.

③ In fact, Julie was not a captain.

④ In fact, Julie is not a captain.

⑤ In fact, Julie had not been a captain.

서술형 평가

11 〈보기〉와 같이 문장을 바꿔 쓰시오.

보기

I'm sorry that I don't have a lot of money.

→ I wish I had a lot of money.

I'm sorry that you didn't join the club meeting.

→ I wish _____.

12 두 문장의 의미가 일치하도록 할 때 빈칸에 들어갈 말이 바르게 짝지어진 것은?

· Stella talks as if she were a champion.

  → In fact, Stella _____ a champion.

· I wish I had mastered English.

  → I am sorry I _____ master English.

① was – do   ② is – do

③ isn't – didn't   ④ wasn't – don't

⑤ isn't – don't

서술형 평가

13 밑줄 친 부분을 바르게 고쳐 쓰시오.

A I saw you talking with a foreigner.

B Yeah, he was French, but I couldn't speak French at all.

A What did he say?

B I think he asked me for directions. If I am able to speak French, I can show him the way.

→ _____

_____

교과서   **ill** 아픈   **cook** 요리사   **free** 자유로운   **present** 출석한   **completely** 완전히   **report** 보고서   **in time** 제시간에   **master** 통달하다
어휘   **ask for directions** 길을 묻다

Reading

[1~2] 다음을 끊어 읽고 ☑, 해석을 쓰시오. ✎

Wormholes: Fact or Theory?

Hi, science fans. I'm Dr. Sci. Today, I'm going to talk about space travel. If we travel at the speed of light,

3 we should be able to get to another planet very quickly. Einstein figured out that space and time are

ⓐconnected. He called it space-time. He thought that space-time could actually be bent. When it is bent,

parts that are far away from each other get ⓑcloser. Let me explain this with a sheet of paper. Make small

dot each at the top and bottom of the paper. Then fold it with the dots ⓒmatched up. Punch a hole on the

6 dots in the paper and they will be connected. 웜홀이라고 불리는 그런 지름길이 우주에 존재한다면, 우리는 수백

만 광년 떨어진 곳에 빠르게 도착할 수 있을 것입니다!

But it's too early to celebrate. Wormholes exist in

9 theory only. Even if we find one, the wormhole would be very ⓓstable. If a spaceship flew into one, it might

be crushed or broken into pieces. I hope we'll eventually find one and learn how to ⓔtravel through it.

---

1 밑줄 친 우리말을 영어로 옮길 때 주어진 단어들을 빈칸에 알맞은 형태로 쓰시오.

→ If such a shortcut, called wormhole, _____ in space, we _____ _____ to places billions of light-years away quickly! (can, exist, get)

2 밑줄 친 ⓐ-ⓔ 중 글의 흐름상 어색한 것은?

① ⓐ   ② ⓑ   ③ ⓒ   ④ ⓓ   ⑤ ⓔ

교과서 wormhole 웜홀 **theory** 이론 **figure out** 알아내다, 이해하다 **space-time** 시공간 **bend** 휘다 **dot** 점 **punch** 구멍을 내다
어휘 ∩ celebrate 기념하다, 축하하다 **spaceship** 우주선 **into pieces** 조각으로 **eventually** 결국 **shortcut** 지름길 **light-year** 광년

Answer p. 12

3 다음 글의 내용을 한 문장으로 요약할 때, 빈칸에 들어갈 말을 본문에서 찾아 쓰시오.

동물

Why do birds fly in a V-shape? It turns out that the V formation has a lot to do with efficiency. Birds can use the least amount of effort when they fly in a V. Scientists found that the lead bird at the front of the V works the hardest while the others behind it have an easier time. That's because flapping wings make little swirls of air flowing upward so birds flying into them get a helpful boost. **If it were not for the leader, the rest would have to make more effort to fly.** Birds take turns as leader since the lead bird gets tired. *swirl 소용돌이

→ Birds fly in a V-shape so that they can use as little _____ as possible.

4 다음 글의 내용과 일치하지 <u>않는</u> 것은?

예술

Allegri's Miserere is one of the most beautiful pieces of choir music, but **you might not be able to hear it without Mozart**. It used to be performed only in the Vatican once a year, and the composition was carefully guarded. It was not allowed be copied, so it was kept secret for almost 150 years. However, when a 14-year-old Mozart heard it once in the Vatican, he wrote it down by ear. When the Vatican found it out, they were surprised by how exact the copy was. That is how we know and love the music to this day.

*composition (음악, 미술) 작품

① Allegri's Miserere는 바티칸에서만 일 년에 한 번 연주되었다.
② Allegri's Miserere의 악보는 철저하게 지켜졌으며, 복제가 금지되었다.
③ Allegri's Miserere의 악보는 거의 150년 동안 비밀로 유지되었다.
④ 모차르트는 Allegri's Miserere를 반복해서 들은 끝에 마침내 그 악보를 적었다.
⑤ 14살의 모차르트가 적은 Allegri's Miserere의 악보는 매우 정확했다.

3 **turn out** ~이 밝혀지다 **have to do with** ~와 관련이 있다 **lead** 선두의 **flap** 퍼덕거리다 **boost** 추진력 **take turns** 교대로 하다
4 **choir** 성가 **guard** 지키다, 보호하다 **copy** 복사하다; 복제물 **by ear** 악보를 보지 않고 **exact** 정확한

Expression

1 상상한 내용 묻고 답하기

🌑 상상하여 묻기

- What would you do if you ...?
- If you ..., what would you do?

🌑 상상하여 묻는 말에 답하기

- I would(could) ....
- I guess I would(could) ....

2 바람, 소원 말하기

🌑 바람, 소원 말하기

- I wish I could ....
- I want (to) ....
- I'd like (to) ....

- I look forward to ....
- I'm looking forward to ....

Expression Test

서술형 평가

1 주어진 단어들을 이용하여 빈칸에 알맞은 말을 쓰시오.

> wish, can

A New Zealand is famous for its beautiful mountains.

B _____ travel to New Zealand.

2 질문에 대한 답으로 알맞은 것은?

> What would you do if you were free today?

① Let's go snowboarding.
② I would watch TV all day long.
③ How about going dining out tonight?
④ I'm thinking of walking my puppies.
⑤ I'm going to stay in my bed all day long.

3 밑줄 친 부분이 의미하는 바로 알맞은 것은?

A I wish I could go to the history museum with you.
B Oh, come on! Are you busy?
A Yes, I have to study for an exam.

① I can't go
② I shouldn't go
③ I'm going to go
④ I don't want to go
⑤ I'm supposed to go

4 밑줄 친 부분과 바꿔 쓸 수 없는 것은?

A What do you want to do this summer?
B I'd like to take a swimming class.

① I want to take
② I'd like to take
③ I wish I could take
④ I used to take
⑤ I'm looking forward to taking

5 빈칸에 공통으로 알맞은 것은?

A What _____ you do if you were very tall?
B I _____ become a basketball player.

① will   ② can   ③ would
④ were   ⑤ can't

6 자연스러운 대화가 되도록 ⓐ-ⓓ를 바르게 배열한 것은?

ⓐ I would play catch with him.
ⓑ No, I'm an only son, so I really want a brother.
ⓒ What would you do if you had a brother?
ⓓ Do you have a brother?

① ⓐ – ⓑ – ⓒ – ⓓ   ② ⓑ – ⓐ – ⓓ – ⓒ
③ ⓑ – ⓒ – ⓓ – ⓐ   ④ ⓓ – ⓐ – ⓑ – ⓒ
⑤ ⓓ – ⓑ – ⓒ – ⓐ

서술형 평가

1 주어진 단어들을 이용하여 밑줄 친 우리말을 영어로 옮기시오.

> A Look at these colorful pictures of the universe.
> B Oh, they're beautiful. (1) 나는 우주에서 지구를 볼 수 있으면 좋겠어. (wish, from space, see the earth)
> A What else would you do if you were in space?
> B (2) 나는 우주인처럼 떠다닐 거야. (an astronaut, like, around, float)
> A Actually, you can do that at the National Youth Space Center.
> B Really?
> A Yeah, you can use the VR glasses. I heard that you feel like you are actually in space!

(1) _____

(2) _____

2 우리말과 일치하도록 주어진 단어들을 바르게 배열하시오.

(1) 그 집이 너무 멀리에 있지 않다면, 우리가 그것을 샀을 텐데. (we, buy, it, not, so far away, were, would)

→ If the house _____.

(2) 내가 키가 더 크다면, 나는 농구 선수가 될 수 있을 텐데. (could, a, I, taller, were, be, basketball player)

→ If I _____.

(3) 내가 당신이었다면, 나는 그 코트를 사지 않았을 텐데. (have, If, I, been, I would, that coat, not, bought, had, you)

→ _____.

3 두 문장의 의미가 일치하도록 빈칸에 알맞은 말을 쓰시오.

(1) In fact, Kane is not a bus driver.

= Kane talks as if _____.

(2) I'm sorry my daughter lost her wallet on the street.

= I wish _____ her wallet on the street.

(3) In fact, they don't have much time.

= They act _____.

4 주어진 단어들을 이용하여 빈칸에 알맞은 말을 쓰시오.

(1) If I were an adult, I _____. (buy, that car)

(2) If it had rained a lot, _____. (go, camping)

(3) If I had had my own skates, I _____. (enjoy, skating)

5 그림을 보고, 주어진 단어들을 이용하여 남자아이의 말을 완성하시오.

> I am so sick that I can't participate in the science contest.
> (1) If I weren't sick, I _____. (win)
> (2) If I won the contest, I _____ for prize. (get, an electric car)

Answer p. 13

난이도: 상 ★★★ 중 ★★ 하 ★

★
01 짝지어진 단어의 관계가 나머지와 <u>다른</u> 것은?

① gain – lose
② succeed – fail
③ present – absent
④ proposal – suggestion
⑤ encourage – discourage

★★
02 빈칸에 알맞은 것은?

A _____ is a vehicle for carrying people through space.

① courage   ② garbage   ③ spaceship
④ proposal   ⑤ wisdom

★★
03 다음 영영풀이가 설명하는 단어로 알맞은 것은?

to go down below the surface of water, mud, etc.

① employ   ② accept   ③ donate
④ sink   ⑤ celebrate

★★
04 밑줄 친 부분의 의도로 알맞은 것은?

A Did you see the movie *Mamma Mia*?
B Not yet.
A Why don't we see that movie together? <u>I'd like to see that movie.</u>
B Sure. I've heard it's very interesting.

① 소망 말하기   ② 충고 말하기   ③ 동의하기
④ 확신하기   ⑤ 제안하기

★★
05 빈칸에 알맞은 것은?

A Sarah, _____?
B I'm not sure. Maybe I'd travel all around the world.
A What country would you like to visit?
B Well, I'm interested in Peru these days.

① what should I do to become rich
② what about taking a trip with me
③ what are you going to do after school
④ what would you like to be in the future
⑤ what would you do if you were rich

★★
06 짝지어진 대화가 <u>어색한</u> 것은?
① A What would you do if you were free?
   B I would volunteer at the daycare center.
② A Can you come to the party tonight?
   B I'd like to but I can't.
③ A I wish I could study abroad.
   B I'm sorry to hear that.
④ A I wish I could be a great musician.
   B I believe you can do it.
⑤ A If you had wings, where would you fly to?
   B I would fly up to Mount Everest.

★★ 시험에 잘 나오는 문제
07 자연스러운 대화가 되도록 ⓐ-ⓓ를 바르게 배열하시오.

ⓐ I wonder the way he thought.
ⓑ Why would you meet him?
ⓒ If you could meet anyone in history, who would you meet?
ⓓ I'd meet Newton.

교과서   **suggestion** 제안   **vehicle** 탈것   **garbage** 쓰레기   **surface** 표면   **mud** 진흙   **volunteer** 자원봉사를 하다   **wonder**: 궁금해하다
어휘

Final Test

[08~09] 빈칸에 알맞은 말을 고르시오.

★★
08

If he were with me, I _____ it.

① can do   ② can't do

③ could do   ④ would be

⑤ could have done

★★
09

If you _____ my advice, you would not have caught a cold.

① take   ② took

③ had taken   ④ would take

⑤ would have taken

★★
10 두 문장의 의미가 일치하도록 할 때 빈칸에 알맞은 것은?

In fact, Jude doesn't do everything for me.
= Jude talks _____ he would do everything for me.

① if   ② like   ③ as if

④ unless   ⑤ because

★★
11 밑줄 친 부분을 어법에 맞게 고쳐 쓰시오.

During my high school days, I didn't study very hard. I failed the exam and I couldn't gain admission to the college that I wanted. If I don't neglect my studies, I would have passed the exam.

→ _____

★★
12 밑줄 친 부분이 어법상 어색한 것은?

① I wish I were a genius.

② I wish my son had succeeded in skiing.

③ Mr. smith talks as if he saw the ghost yesterday.

④ If my wife were with me, I would be happy.

⑤ If Rick had been honest, I could have forgiven him.

[13~14] 우리말을 영어로 바르게 옮긴 것을 고르시오.

★★
13

만약 그가 그의 친구들에게 친절하지 않다면, 그들은 그를 좋아하지 않을 텐데.

① Were he kind to his friends, they would like him.

② If he isn't kind to his friends, they would have liked him.

③ If he hadn't been kind to his friends, they would like him.

④ If he were not kind to his friends, they wouldn't like him.

⑤ Had he not been kind to his friends, they wouldn't have liked him.

★★
14

내가 그들과 함께 놀이 공원에 갈 수 있으면 좋을 텐데.

① I wish I go to the theme park with them.

② I wish I can go to the theme park with them.

③ I wish I could go to the theme park with them.

④ I wished I could go to the theme park with them.

⑤ I wished I could have gone to the theme park with them.

★★ 〔서술형 평가〕
15 우리말과 일치하도록 빈칸에 알맞은 말을 쓰시오.

내가 어젯밤에 그런 어리석은 일을 하지 않았다면 좋을 텐데.

→I wish I _____ _____ _____ such a silly thing last night.

★★★
16 다음 문장의 밑줄 친 ①–⑤를 고쳐 쓴 것 중 어법상 <u>어색한</u> 것은?

If the clerk ①has ②being ③as kindly as you, we ④will ⑤had gone to the shop again.

① has → had
② being → been
③ as kindly as → as kind as
④ will → would
⑤ had gone → go

〔시험에 잘 나오는 문제〕
★★
17 밑줄 친 부분과 바꿔 쓸 수 있는 것을 <u>모두</u> 고르면?

Without your help, I would have failed to win.

① But for your help
② Were it for your help
③ If it were not for your help
④ If it had been for your help
⑤ If it had not been for your help

〔서술형 평가〕
[18~19] 우리말과 일치하도록 주어진 단어들을 바르게 배열하시오.
★★
18

운동화가 없다면, 나는 울퉁불퉁한 길에서 뛰지 못할 것이다. (if, sneakers, for, it, not, were)

→ _____, I couldn't run on bumpy roads

★★
19

만약 수진이가 좀 더 부지런했다면 그녀는 숙제를 끝냈을 텐데. (been, Sujin, had, diligent, more)

→ _____, she would have finished her homework.

[20~21] 어법상 <u>어색한</u> 것을 고르시오.
★★★
20
① I wish I had met you.
② Teresa acts as if she were a queen.
③ Were I my sister, I wouldn't play the game.
④ If Amy met you, she would have been surprised.
⑤ If it had not been for your help, I could not have made it.

★★★
21
① I wish it weren't raining.
② Walter felt as if something were touching his shoulders.
③ They wish they had chosen a different leader.
④ John screamed as if he were really angry.
⑤ Nick wishes he lives in Paris.

교과서 **silly** 어리석은 **clerk** 점원 **sneakers** 운동화 **bumpy** 울퉁불퉁한 **diligent** 부지런한 **queen** 여왕 **make it** 해내다
어휘 **scream** 소리 지르다 **angry** 화난

★★★
22 빈칸에 had가 들어갈 수 <u>없는</u> 것의 개수는?

ⓐ If I _____ been there, I would have told her the truth.

ⓑ If I _____ left earlier, I would not have missed the bus.

ⓒ If my daughter _____ had a key, she could open the door.

ⓓ If he _____ had lunch, he would not have eaten too much at dinner.

ⓔ If we _____ finished the work, we could go home.

① 1개 ② 2개 ③ 3개 ④ 4개 ⑤ 5개

서술형 평가

[23~24] 두 문장의 의미가 일치하도록 빈칸에 알맞은 말을 쓰시오.

★★
23

I'm sorry I didn't have better relationships with my classmates.

= _____ better relationships with my classmates.

★★
24

As I'm not taller, I am not good at playing volleyball.

= If _____ good at playing volleyball.

★★
25 글의 흐름으로 보아, 빈칸에 알맞은 것은?

Steve Jobs was thinking of what to name his computer company. As it happened, Steve had just cut the branches of apple trees in a farm. When his coworker started throwing many names like Matrix, Steve suggested the name Apple Computer. He said "I really enjoyed working at the apple farm. Apple sounds fun and not scary." If he had not worked with _____, then we would not have had the chance to see the logo of the world's most famous computer company.

① apple trees   ② his coworker
③ Matrix   ④ farmers
⑤ famous companies

★★
26 밑줄 친 부분으로 유추할 수 있는 것은?

Before a man enters a barber's shop, he saw this sign on the door: DANGER. BEWARE OF DOG! He carefully opens the door, but all he can see is a fat old dog asleep on the floor. "Is this the dog that people are supposed to beware of?" He asks the barber. "Yes, that's him." "But he doesn't look dangerous to me." The barber replies, "<u>If I didn't post that sign, you too would fall over him.</u>"

① 손님들이 개를 무서워해서 경고 표지판을 붙여 놓았다.
② 주인은 개를 보호하기 위해 경고 표지판을 붙여 놓았다.
③ 많은 손님들이 개를 보지 못하고 개에 걸려 넘어졌다.
④ 개가 가게로 들어오는 손님들을 물어 넘어뜨렸다.
⑤ 경고 표지판을 붙여 놓은 이후로 개가 얌전해졌다.

교과서   **truth** 진실   **relationship** 관계   **volleyball** 배구   **branch** 나뭇가지   **coworker** 동료   **barber** 이발사   **beware of** ~을 조심하다
어휘   **post** 붙이다, 게재하다   **fall over** ~에 걸려 넘어지다

[27~28] 다음을 읽고, 물음에 답하시오.

Everyone has fears, but too many fears can be harmful because it may stop us from ⓐ trying new things. What we're afraid of is learned, and there is one way ⓑ to beat our own fears. Instead of ⓒ listening to our imagination, we can learn the facts about what makes us scared. Knowledge can help a person ⓓ feel less afraid. Are you afraid of dogs? Study about them. If you know for sure how to protect yourself from dogs, you would not ⓔ felt afraid.

★★
27 밑줄 친 ⓐ~ⓔ 중 어법상 어색한 것은?

 ①ⓐ   ②ⓑ   ③ⓒ   ④ⓓ   ⑤ⓔ

★★ 시험에 잘 나오는 문제
28 글쓴이가 주장하는 바로 알맞은 것은?
① 두려움을 유발하는 것을 최대한 피하라.
② 두려움을 극복하고 새로운 것에 도전하라.
③ 특정 사물에 대한 지나친 두려움을 경계하라.
④ 긍정적으로 상상하는 훈련을 통해 두려움을 극복하라.
⑤ 두려움에서 극복하기 위해 두려움의 대상에 관해 연구하라.

[29~30] 다음을 읽고, 물음에 답하시오.

"Follow your passion." When I read this advice, I thought it was great. I felt that I could succeed in life if I found my passion that I was born with. So, I decided to look for it. I travelled to many places and experienced new things. However, I spent years only to waste valuable time and money. Now I realize that passion isn't something you're born with; it's something you develop. I wish I <u>be</u> given the advice to "_____" from the beginning.

★★ 서술형 평가
29 밑줄 친 be를 알맞은 형태로 고쳐 쓰시오.

_____

★★
30 글의 흐름으로 보아, 빈칸에 들어갈 말로 알맞은 것은?
① Follow your passion.
② Take a trip to many places.
③ Experience something new.
④ Develop your passion.
⑤ Save your time and money.

교과서   **harmful** 해로운   **beat** 이기다, 극복하다   **imagination** 상상력   **protect** 지키다, 보호하다   **passion** 열정   **waste** 낭비하다
어휘   **valuable** 소중한   **develop** 개발하다

··· >> Grammar

A 가정법 과거

가정법 과거는 현재 사실에 반대되는 일이나 실현 가능성이 희박한 일을 가정한다.

형태	조건절	If+주어+동사의 과거형 ..., (cf. be동사는 were 사용)
	주절	주어+과거형 조동사(would/could/might/should)+동사원형 ….
의미		(사실은 그렇지 않지만) 만약 ~하다면, …할 텐데

If I **were** a millionaire, I **could buy** a great mansion.
→ As I am not a millionaire, I can't buy a great mansion. 〈직설법〉

B 가정법 과거완료

가정법 과거완료는 과거 사실에 반대되는 일을 가정한다.

형태	조건절	If+주어+had+p.p. ...,
	주절	주어+과거형 조동사(would/could/might/should)+have+p.p. ....
의미		(사실은 그렇지 않았지만) 만약 ~했다면, …했을 텐데

If Albert **had been** honest, the company **would have employed** him.
→ As Albert was not honest, the company didn't employ him.

C if가 생략된 가정법

조건절의 동사가 were나 〈had+p.p.〉인 경우 if를 생략할 수 있는데,
이때 조건절의 주어와 동사는 도치된다.
If I were my brother, I wouldn't read comic books. → **Were I** my brother, ~.
If the captain had been more careful, the ship would not have sunk.
→ **Had the captain been** more careful, ~.

D I wish + 가정법

〈I wish+가정법〉은 현재나 과거 사실의 반대에 대한 소망과 유감을 나타낼 때 쓰며,
〈I am〔was〕 sorry (that)+주어+동사〉로 바꿔 쓸 수 있다.

형태	의미
I wish+가정법 과거(주어+동사의 과거형(were))	~하다면 좋을 텐데(현재의 실현 불가능한 소망)
I wish+가정법 과거완료(주어+had+p.p.)	~했다면 좋을 텐데(과거의 일에 대한 유감)

I wish I had a cute puppy. → I am sorry (that) I don't have a cute puppy.
I wish you had seen the car parade. → I am sorry (that) you didn't see the car parade.

E as if + 가정법

〈as if + 가정법〉은 현재나 과거 사실에 반대되는 가정을 나타낼 때 쓰며,
〈In fact, 주어+동사〉로 바꿔 쓸 수 있다.

형태	의미
as if + 가정법 과거(주어+동사의 과거형(were))	마치 ~한 것처럼(주절과 같은 시제의 일)
as if + 가정법 과거완료(주어+had+p.p.)	마치 ~했던 것처럼(주절보다 이전 과거의 일)

Somin walks **as if** she **were** a super model.

→ In fact, Somin is not a super model.

Mr. Song talks **as if** he **had found** the solution.

→ In fact, Mr. Song didn't find the solution.

F Without[But for] + 가정법

Without(But for)가 이끄는 어구는 '~이 없(었)다면'의 의미로 현재 또는 과거 사실과
반대되는 가정을 나타내며, if를 이용한 가정법으로 바꿔 쓸 수 있다.

Without(But for) ~, + 가정법 과거	~이 없다면, (지금) …할 텐데	→ If it were not for ~ → Were it not for ~
Without(But for) ~, + 가정법 과거완료	~이 없었다면, (이전에) …했을 텐데	→ If it had not been for ~ → Had it not been for ~

Without(But for) air, nothing **could live.**

→ **If it were not for** air, nothing **could live.**

→ **Were it not for** air, nothing **could live.**

But for(Without) the policeman, Glenn **would have got** lost.

→ **If it had not been for** the policeman, Glenn **would have got** lost.

→ **Had it not been for** the policeman, Glenn **would have got** lost.

·· ≫ **Expression**

1 상상한 내용 묻고 답하기

❤상상하여 묻기
- What would you do if you ...?
- If you ..., what would you do?

❤상상하여 묻는 말에 답하기
- I would(could) ....
- I guess I would(could) ....

2 바람, 소원 말하기

❤바람, 소원 말하기
- I wish I could ....
- I want (to) ....
- I'd like (to) ....

- I look forward to ....
- I'm looking forward to ....

Lesson 05

일치, 화법, 특수 구문

Grammar Preview

❶ 일치, 화법

- 주어의 수에 따라 동사의 수를 일치시키는 것을 수의 일치라고 하며, 주절과 종속절의 동사의 시제를 일치시키는 것을 시제의 일치라고 한다.

  Mathematics is an interesting subject.　　**Not only she but also I am** interested in jazz.

  I **know** that she **is** happy.　　I **knew** that she **was** happy.

- 다른 이의 말을 전달하는 화법에는, 인용부호를 써서 그대로 전하는 직접화법과, 전하는 이의 말로 바꿔서 전하는 간접화법이 있다.

  Joe said to me, "I will return your books tomorrow." 〈직접화법〉

  → Joe **told** me **that she would** return **my** books **the next day**. 〈간접화법〉

❷ 특수 구문

- 동사, 명사 강조

	형태	예문
동사 강조	do(does/did)+동사원형	They **did eat** all of my chocolate cookies. (정말로 먹었다)
명사 강조	the very+명사	This is **the very watch** I've been looking for. (바로 그 시계)

- 〈It is(was) ~ that ...〉 강조: 강조할 대상을 It is(was)와 that 사이에 두어 '…하는 것은 바로 ~이(었)다'라는 의미를 나타낸다. 강조 대상에 따라 that 대신 who, which, where, when을 쓸 수도 있다.

  Henry found the key under the table.

  → It was **Henry** that(who) found the key under the table. 〈주어 강조〉

- 문장성분의 위치를 바꾸는 것을 도치라고 하며, 주로 강조하기 위해 도치한다.

	형태	비고
장소 부사(구) 도치	부사(구)+동사+주어	주어가 인칭대명사이면 〈주어+동사〉
부정어 도치	부정어+ ┌ 동사+주어 ├ 조동사+주어+동사원형 └ have(had)+주어+p.p.	not, never, little, hardly, seldom 등의 부정어 강조
so, neither 도치	so(neither)+(조)동사+주어	동의를 나타내는 관용 표현

- 앞에서 언급된 후에 반복되는 어구와, 부사절에서 〈주절의 주어와 같은 주어+be동사〉는 생략할 수 있다.

  My shoes are wet. So I'll wear my sister's (**shoes**).

  Though (**she is**) young, she is very thoughtful.

1 일치, 화법

A 수의 일치

주어의 수에 동사의 수를 일치시키되, 주어의 형태에 따라 다음과 같이 한다.

단수 취급하는 주어의 형태	복수 취급하는 주어의 형태
• 수(거리, 시간, 길이 등), 국가, 학문, 질병, 책, 영화, 음식, 신문 • some(most, none, half, the rest, 분수)+of+단수 명사 • to부정사(구), 동명사(구), 명사절 • the number of+복수 명사 • every(each, no)+단수 명사 • 두 단어로 된 동일 개체	• some(most, none, half, the rest, 분수)+of+복수 명사 • a number of+복수 명사 • no+복수 명사 • both A and B

Mathematics is an interesting subject.
Most of the people don't agree with the idea.

> **Plus Grammar**
> • 집합명사의 수 일치
> My family **is** large. (나의 가족은 대가족이다.) 〈전체 묘사 → 단수〉
> My family **are** early birds. (나의 가족은 일찍 일어난다.) 〈각 구성원 묘사 → 복수〉
> • 다음 어구가 주어이면 B에 수 일치
> not only A but also B (= B as well as A) / neither A nor B / either A or B / not A but B

B 시제의 일치

주절 동사의 시제에 종속절 동사의 시제를 일치시키되, 주절의 시제에 따라 다음과 같이 한다.

주절이 현재 → 종속절에 모든 시제 가능	I **know** that she **is(was, will be, has been)** happy.
주절이 과거 → 종속절은 과거, 과거완료	I **knew** that she **was(had been)** happy.

cf. 진리, 속담, 현재의 습관 등은 항상 현재 시제로, 역사적 사실은 항상 과거 시제로 쓴다.

My teacher explained that the Earth **is** round. 〈진리〉
Mandy says that the Korean War **broke** out in 1950. 〈역사〉

> **Plus Grammar**
> 비교구문의 시제 일치
> 과거와 현재 사실을 비교할 때, 시제 일치를 따르지 않고 의미에 따라 시제를 결정한다.
> I **have** more books than he **had.** (나는 그가 가졌던 것보다 더 많은 책을 가지고 있다.)

C 화법

다른 이의 말을 전달하는 화법에는, 인용부호를 써서 그대로 전하는 직접화법과, 전하는 이의 말로 바꿔서 전하는 간접화법이 있다.

직접화법	간접화법		
	인용문이 평서문	인용문이 의문문	인용문이 명령문
say (to)+ (대)명사	• say → say • tell+(대)명사	ask+(대)명사	tell(ask, advise, order)+(대)명사
인용문	접속사 that+인용문	• 의문사+주어+동사 • if(whether)+주어+동사	• 긍정: to부정사 • 부정: not(never) to부정사
인용문의 인칭	1인칭 → 주절의 주어의 인칭 / 2인칭 → 인용문 청자의 인칭 / 3인칭 → 그대로 유지		
인용문의 시제	시제 일치의 원칙에 따라 주절의 동사의 시제에 일치		
기타	인용문의 지시대명사나 부사(구)를 전하는 이의 말로 전환		

Joe said to me, "I will return your books tomorrow." 〈직접화법〉
→ Joe **told** me **that she would** return **my** books **the next day.** 〈간접화법〉
Larry **said to** me, "Are you busy?"   My mom **said to** me, "Enter your room."
→ Larry **asked** me **if** I was busy.   → My mom **ordered** me **to enter** my room.

> **Plus Grammar**
> 지시대명사, 부사구의 전환
> (직접화법 → 간접화법)
> this / these → that / those
> ago → before
> now → then
> here → there
> today → that day
> tonight → that night
> tomorrow
> → the next day,
> the following day
> yesterday
> → the day before,
> the previous day
> last night
> → the night before,
> the previous night

Grammar Practice >>

Answer p. 15

A1 괄호 안에서 알맞은 것을 고르시오.

(1) *Hansel and Gretel* (is / are) the title of a German fairy tale.

(2) To take a rest (is / are) what Audrey really wants now.

(3) Fifty kilometers (is / are) too far to run in one day.

(4) Half of the birds (is / are) already gone.

(5) Not apples but a piece of cake (is / are) served.

A2 밑줄 친 부분이 맞으면 ○를, 틀리면 바르게 고쳐 쓰시오.

(1) To stay with Felix <u>makes</u> me pleasant.

(2) The rest of the food <u>is</u> thrown away.

(3) Thirty years <u>are</u> such a long time.

(4) *The Dreamers* <u>are</u> my favorite book.

(5) Both Alex and I <u>know</u> her name.

(6) Every <u>vets</u> loves animals so much.

(7) The number of the dishes <u>were</u> hard to count.

B1 괄호 안에서 알맞은 것을 고르시오.

(1) Eric thought that it (is / was) 10 a.m.

(2) I wondered if you (do / had done) the work.

(3) Do you know Shakespeare (writes / wrote) many plays?

(4) Judy said that the first class always (starts / started) at 9 o'clock.

(5) Brian told me that he (is / was) supposed to write a letter to Mr. Smith.

B2 우리말과 일치하도록 주어진 단어를 빈칸에 알맞은 형태로 쓰시오.

(1) 우리는 세종대왕이 한글을 발명했다고 배웠다.
→ We learned that the King Sejong _____ hangeul. (invent)

(2) Ann은 물이 섭씨 100도에서 끓는 것을 몰랐다.
→ Ann didn't know that water _____ at 100°C. (boil)

(3) 그녀가 어제 나를 공원에서 봤다고 그녀가 말했다.
→ She says that she _____ me in the park yesterday. (see)

C1 화법을 바꿔 쓸 때 괄호 안에서 알맞은 것을 고르시오.

(1) Naomi said, "I need your help."
→ Naomi (said / told) that (I / she) needed my help.

(2) I said to Mila, "I can't speak French."
→ I (said to / told) Mila that (you / I) couldn't speak French.

(3) Jim said to me, "I came here to see you."
→ Jim told me that he (comes / had come) (here / there) to see me.

C2 화법을 바꿔 쓸 때 빈칸에 알맞은 말을 쓰시오.

(1) Mike said that he had solved that problem the day before.
→ Mike said, "I _____ _____ problem yesterday."

(2) I said to him, "Don't be afraid of skiing."
→ I told him _____ _____ _____ afraid of skiing.

(3) She asked me what my problem was.
→ She said to me, "_____ _____ _____ problem?"

교과서 **round** 둥근 **break out** 일어나다 **return** 돌려주다 **fairy tale** 동화 **pleasant** 유쾌한 **vet** 수의사 **play** 희곡
어휘 **be supposed to** ~하기로 하다

D 강조

1 동사, 명사 강조

강조	형태(의미)	예문
동사	do(does/did)+동사원형 (정말로(꼭) ~하다)	They **did eat** all of my chocolate cookies. (그들은 내 초콜릿 쿠키 전부를 정말로 먹었다.)
명사	the very+명사 (바로(그) ~)	This is **the very watch** I've been looking for. (이것이 내가 찾고 있었던 바로 그 시계이다.)

2 〈It is(was) ~ that ...〉 강조: 강조할 대상을 It is(was)와 that 사이에 두어 '…하는 것은 바로 ~이(었)다'라는 의미를 나타낸다. 강조 대상에 따라 that 대신 who, which, where, when을 쓸 수도 있다.

Henry found the key under the table.

→ It was **Henry** that(who) found the key under the table. 〈주어 강조〉

→ It was **the key** that(which) Henry found under the table. 〈목적어 강조〉

→ It was **under the table** that(where) Henry found the key. 〈부사구 강조〉

● **Plus** Grammar

• 의문사 강조
〈의문사+on earth〉로 '도대체 ~'의 의미를 나타낸다.
What on earth were you thinking at that time?
(도대체 너는 그때 무슨 생각을 하고 있었니?)

• 부정어 강조
not ~ at all은 '전혀 ~ 않는'의 의미를 나타낸다.
I **didn't** understand what he said **at all**. (나는 그가 말했던 것을 전혀 이해하지 못했다.)

E 도치

문장성분의 위치를 바꾸는 것을 도치라고 하며, 주로 강조하기 위해 도치한다.

형태		비고
장소 부사(구) 도치	부사(구)+동사+주어	주어가 인칭대명사이면 〈주어+동사〉
부정어 도치	부정어+ ┌ 동사+주어 ├ 조동사+주어+동사원형 └ have(had)+주어+p.p.	not, never, little, hardly, seldom 등의 부정어 강조
so, neither 도치	so(neither)+(조)동사+주어	동의를 나타내는 관용 표현

Over my head passed the ball.

Here she is to buy a car.

Never does the author come here on time.

I don't like tomatoes and **neither does Jimin**.

F 생략

1 앞에서 언급된 후에 반복되는 어구는 생략할 수 있다.

My shoes are wet. So I'll wear my sister's (**shoes**).

I think my car can't go further, but Alice says it can (**go further**).

Diane looked tired, but actually she wasn't (**tired**).

You don't have to eat if you don't want to (**eat**).

Jeremy was 30 years old, and his wife (**was**) 27 (**years old**).

2 부사절에서 〈주절의 주어와 같은 주어+be동사〉는 생략할 수 있다.

Though (**she is**) young, she is very thoughtful.

When (**I was**) a boy, I used to catch insects with a butterfly net.

Grammar Practice >

Answer p. 15

D1 우리말과 일치하도록 빈칸에 알맞은 말을 쓰시오.

(1) Athens is _____ _____ city I visited last year. (아테네는 내가 작년에 방문했던 바로 그 도시이다.)

(2) Amy _____ _____ dancing every day. (Amy는 매일 반드시 춤을 연습한다.)

(3) It was 65 million years ago _____ dinosaurs died out. (공룡들이 멸종했던 것은 바로 6천5백만 년 전이었다.)

(4) It was the _____ _____ Cheryl discovered last month. (Cheryl이 지난달에 발견했던 것이 바로 그 행성이었다.)

D2 강조된 대상을 〈보기〉에서 고르시오.

┌─보기─────────────────────┐
│ ⓐ 주어 ⓑ 동사 ⓒ 목적어 ⓓ 부사구 │
└──────────────────────────┘

(1) It was Sam that I met on the street.

(2) It was my sister who threw an egg at the man.

(3) She did meet her best friends last night.

(4) It was at the dance party that Jack wore his best suit last night.

(5) It was the book that I bought yesterday.

E1 괄호 안에서 알맞은 것을 고르시오.

(1) (Never did I expect, Never I expected) to see him again.

(2) On the platform (a strange man stood, stood a strange man) last night.

(3) Brian can't ride a bicycle, and neither (I can, can I).

(4) Jisu read the book, and so (I did, did I).

E2 두 문장의 의미가 일치하도록 빈칸에 알맞은 말을 쓰시오.

(1) The bus leaves there now.
→ There _____ _____ _____ now.

(2) Jack stood under the tree.
→ Under the tree _____ _____.

(3) The sun shone over the rainbow.
→ Over the rainbow _____ _____ _____.

(4) Adam didn't do his homework at all and Karen didn't either.
→ Adam didn't do his homework at all and _____ _____ Karen.

F1 생략할 수 있는 부분에 밑줄을 그으시오.

(1) If you can't go, someone else should go.

(2) When I was in L.A. I met Mr. Johnson.

(3) Though he is poor, he is very generous.

(4) You can wear this if you want to wear.

(5) I was happy, and my mother was happy, too.

F2 다음 문장에서 빈칸에 생략된 말을 대화에서 찾아 쓰시오.

(1) A Let's take a walk.
B I don't like to _____.

(2) A What did your parents do last night?
B My dad went to bed and my mom _____ to the market.

(3) A When did you watch *Romeo and Juliet*?
B When _____ a boy, I watched the movie.

교과서 **on time** 제시간에 **actually** 실제로 **thoughtful** 사려 깊은 **butterfly** 나비 **die out** 멸종하다 **platform** 승강장
어휘 **generous** 너그러운, 관대한

Grammar Test

01 밑줄 친 ①-⑤ 중 어법상 어색한 것은?

We ① know ② that ③ South Korea ④ hosts ⑤ the 2002 World Cup.

02 빈칸에 들어갈 말이 바르게 짝지어진 것은?

- The rest of the food _____ given to the homeless yesterday.
- Half of the boys _____ still laughing now.

① was – is   ② was – are

③ were – is   ④ were – are

⑤ was – were

03 밑줄 친 부분 중 어법상 어색한 것은?

① They think that Bill <u>wasn't</u> polite.
② We learned that water <u>freezes</u> at 0°C.
③ Jim said that slow and steady <u>wins</u> the race.
④ Austin found out that Elena <u>prints</u> the valuable data.
⑤ I heard that the house <u>had burned</u> before.

04 어법상 어색한 부분을 찾아 바르게 고쳐 쓰시오.

(1) What you say to me are not true.

   _____ → _____

(2) Not Mr. Brown but Ms. Brown were the thief.

   _____ → _____

05 빈칸에 is를 쓸 수 없는 것은?

① Economics _____ hard to study.
② Not the author but the professor _____ arriving tonight.
③ One third of the nations _____ developed countries.
④ Ten minutes _____ too short for me to fall asleep.
⑤ Whether you believe in God _____ your choice.

06 생략할 수 있는 부분에 밑줄을 그으시오.

A Why don't we go camping this weekend?
B I'd love to go camping, but I have lots of homework to do this weekend.

07 우리말과 일치하도록 빈칸에 알맞은 말을 〈보기〉에서 고르시오.

보기

do	does	did	doing

(1) 나는 그의 치아가 정말로 걱정이 된다.

  → I _____ worry about his teeth.

(2) Willy는 작년 이 마을에 공장을 정말로 건설했다.

  → Willy _____ construct a factory in this town last year.

(3) 나는 테니스화를 가지고 있고 내 아내도 그렇다.

  → I have tennis shoes and so _____ my wife.

교과서 **host** 주최하다 **homeless** 집이 없는 **polite** 공손한 **freeze** 얼다 **steady** 꾸준한 **economics** 경제학 **author** 저자
어휘🎧 **developed country** 선진국 **construct** 건설하다

[08~09] 어법상 <u>어색한</u> 것을 고르시오.

08

① Charlotte said she didn't hurt my leg.
② David asked me what I do yesterday.
③ John told me to carry that chair back to its place.
④ Prof. Hughes asked me if I understood the meaning of the idiom.
⑤ The scientist said that the goal of the research was to clone humans.

09

① I washed the dishes and so did my husband.
② On the table was my watch.
③ Not both of us failed the entrance exam.
④ It was at 8 o'clock when Lydia arrived here.
⑤ I the very know the reason why Jade missed the class.

10 우리말을 영어로 바르게 옮긴 것은?

나의 옆집에 Andy가 살고 있다.

① Next to Andy's house I live.
② My house lives next to Andy.
③ My house next to Andy lives.
④ Next to my house lives Andy.
⑤ Lives Andy next to my house.

11 밑줄 친 부분을 강조하는 문장으로 바꿀 때 빈칸에 알맞은 말을 쓰시오.

Mr. Cuban was promoted to the position of manager in <u>September</u>.

→_____ Mr. Cuban was promoted to the position of manager.

12 두 문장의 의미가 일치하도록 할 때 빈칸에 들어갈 말이 바르게 짝지어진 것은?

Ron said to me "I'll leave for Rome tomorrow."
→Ron told me that he _____ leave for Rome _____.

① will – the day
② will – that day
③ would – the day
④ would – the next day
⑤ would – the previous day

13 〈보기〉와 같이 밑줄 친 부분을 강조하는 문장으로 바꿔 쓰시오.

┌─보기─
Jenny saw <u>a very famous singer</u> in the park.
→ It was a very famous singer that Jenny saw in the park.
└─

<u>My English teacher</u> will visit Canada next week.

→_____

_____

교과서   **hurt** 다치게 하다   **idiom** 관용구   **goal** 목표   **clone** 복제하다   **promote** 승진시키다   **manager** 관리자   **leave for** ~을 향해 떠나다
어휘

Reading

[1~2] 다음을 끊어 읽고 ☑, 해석을 쓰시오. ✎

A Father's Wisdom

A rich and wise father had two sons, Puru and Puneet. Before he passed away, he called his

sons, and gave them last words of advice. "My dear sons. (A) Build a house in every city. Sleep

comfortably. Enjoy your food. Lastly, spend money like a rich man." After his death, his sons

took their share of the father's wealth, settled in different cities and followed their father's words. Five years

passed and Puru had no money left. But Puneet was richer than ever. Puru visited Puneet

to find out where he had gone wrong. "Puneet, did you not follow our father's wisdom?"

Puneet said, "I did. When (B) our father said to us, "build a house in every city," I took it as

having a place to stay. So I made friends in every city. Also, I slept comfortably each night because I would

be tired after a hard day's work. I ate only when I was hungry, so even a simple meal tasted

great. Spend money like a rich man? I tried to spend money on something that would bring

me back more money. For me, it was this wisdom that our father tried to explain."

1 밑줄 친 (A)에 관해 Puneet이 생각한 바를 우리말로 쓰시오.

_____

2 밑줄 친 (B)를 간접화법으로 바꿔 쓸 때 빈칸에 알맞은 말을 쓰시오.
→ our father _____ in every city

교과서 **pass away** 세상을 떠나다 **dear** 친애하는 **comfortably** 편안하게 **share** 몫 **wealth** 재산 **settle in** ~에 정착하다
어휘 🎧 **go wrong** 잘못되다 **meal** 끼니

3 아버지의 마지막 말의 의미로 가장 알맞은 것은? **교훈**

There was a little boy with a bad temper. His father had him hammer a nail into the fence every time he lost his temper. Finally the day came when the boy didn't lose his temper. Next, the father had him pull out one nail every time he could hold his temper. He finally **told his father that** all the nails were gone. Then, the father led him to the fence and said, "My son, look at the holes in the fence. The fence will never be the same. No matter how many times you say I'm sorry, the wound is still there."

① When you make others feel bad, say sorry right away.
② Instead of saying sorry, do good things to others.
③ Don't ever lose your temper to avoid hurting others.
④ When you say sorry, say it from the heart.
⑤ After losing your temper, don't say sorry.

4 글의 흐름으로 보아, 주어진 문장이 들어가기에 알맞은 곳은? **미디어**

For example, videos can create people who never existed, and make people say things they never said.

There are thousands of videos online and you may think what you see in the video is true. (①) However, using advanced technology, people can edit clips in many new ways. (②) Those clips are called deepfakes. (③) **It is** because of deepfakes **that** China is planning to apply new laws to fight it. (④) Under the new laws, any video or audio using AI(artificial intelligence) or VR(virtual reality) must be labeled. (⑤) Officials in Beijing **said that** the law would help stop the spread of fake news.

3 **bad temper** 고약한 성미   **hammer** 망치로 두드리다; 망치   **nail** 못   **fence** 울타리   **lose one's temper** 화를 내다   **wound** 상처
4 **exist** 존재하다   **edit** 편집하다   **clip** 영상   **apply** 적용하다   **label** 표식을 붙이다   **spread** 확산   **fake news** 거짓 뉴스

Expression

1 안타까움, 후회 표현하기

❤ 안타까움 표현하기

- You should (not) have done ....
- I'm sorry (that) you (didn't) ....

❤ 후회하기

- I(We) should (not) have done ....

2 제안, 권유하기

❤ 제안, 권유하기

- I suggest (that) ....
- You'd better ....
- I think you should ....

- Why don't you ....?
- How(What) about -ing ....?

Expression Test

Answer p. 16

1 의도하는 바가 나머지와 <u>다른</u> 것은?

① You'd better take a break.

② Why do you take a break?

③ How about taking a break?

④ Why don't you take a break?

⑤ I suggest that you take a break.

서술형 평가

2 우리말과 일치하도록 put을 이용하여 빈칸에 알맞은 말을 쓰시오.

A I feel very cold.

B So do I. We _____ _____ _____
on warm coats. (우리는 따뜻한 코트를 입었어
야 했는데.)

A I wish I had listened to my mom.

3 빈칸에 알맞지 <u>않은</u> 것은?

A Can you tell me what I need for go up a
mountain?

B Hmm... First of all, _____
wear comfortable clothes and shoes.
They will keep you from getting hurt.

A Okay. Thanks.

① I'd like to

② I suggest you

③ You'd better

④ I think you should

⑤ I think you had better

4 밑줄 친 부분과 바꿔 쓸 수 <u>없는</u> 것은?

A Are we late?

B Yes, we are. The movie starts at 7 and it's
6:40 now.

A See? <u>We should have taken the bus.</u>

① We must have taken the bus.

② I regret we didn't take the bus.

③ We ought to have taken the bus.

④ We had to take the bus, but we didn't.

⑤ It would be better if we had taken the bus.

서술형 평가

5 주어진 단어들을 배열하여 빈칸에 알맞은 말을 쓰시오.

A What makes you hurry?

B I have so many things to do.
_____ in advance.
(them, done, have, I, should)

A Hmm ... Let me give you a hand.

6 자연스러운 대화가 되도록 ⓐ–ⓓ를 바르게 배열한
것은?

ⓐ It looks exciting. I'd like to try it. Do you
think I can?

ⓑ Yes. It's really fun. I felt like a bird in the
sky.

ⓒ Sure. I suggest that you learn from an
expert.

ⓓ Sandy, this picture is cool. Is that you?

① ⓐ – ⓒ – ⓓ – ⓑ   ② ⓐ – ⓓ – ⓑ – ⓒ

③ ⓑ – ⓓ – ⓐ – ⓒ   ④ ⓒ – ⓑ – ⓓ – ⓐ

⑤ ⓓ – ⓑ – ⓐ – ⓒ

1 주어진 조건에 맞게 대화를 완성하시오.

조건

(1) 주어진 단어를 활용하여 후회하는 말을 쓸 것
(2) 주어진 단어를 활용하여 제안하는 말을 쓸 것

A Oh, this coat is too uncomfortable.
B Why? What's wrong with it?
A It's too tight.
B Didn't you try it on before buying it?
A No. It was my size, so I just bought it.
  (1) _____ (should, try it on)
B (2) _____ Or, you'll able to exchange it for free. (why, get a refund)

2 밑줄 친 부분을 어법에 맞게 고쳐 쓰시오.

(1) Most of the people in this country is very poor. → _____
(2) A number of cities was destroyed due to the hurricane. → _____
(3) Our history teacher said that Jang Yeongsil had invented Jagyeongnu. → _____
(4) Luna said that she is going to go shopping after school. → _____

3 주어진 문장의 밑줄 친 부분을 강조해서 쓰시오.

I saw (1) Alice (2) in the bakery (3) this morning.

(1) _____
(2) _____
(3) _____

4 두 문장의 의미가 일치하도록 빈칸에 알맞은 말을 쓰시오.

(1) Jack didn't eat a single piece of cake.
  = Not a single piece of cake _____.
(2) Larry has never been to aborad.
  = Never _____ to abroad.
(3) An old building stood on the hill.
  = On the hill _____.

5 다음 글의 밑줄 친 문장을 간접화법 문장으로 바꿔 쓰시오.

I suddenly felt hungry. (1) I said to Mom "Is there anything to eat?" (2) She said to me "I can make some omelet for you." (3) She took out a frying pan and said to me "Bring some eggs from the refrigerator." Soon, Mom made me a delicious cheese omelet.

⇩

I suddenly felt hungry.
(1) _____
  _____
(2) _____
  _____
(3) _____
  _____
Soon, Mom made me a delicious cheese omelet.

01 영영풀이가 설명하는 단어로 알맞은 것은?

person who treats sick animals

① clerk ② author ③ vet
④ patient ⑤ lawyer

02 밑줄 친 부분과 의미가 같은 것은?

He was injured in a car accident.

① counted ② served ③ cloned
④ hurt ⑤ hugged

03 다음 중 나머지 넷을 포함하는 것은?
① ant ② bee ③ butterfly
④ insect ⑤ cricket

시험에 잘 나오는 문제
04 자연스러운 대화가 되도록 ⓐ-ⓒ를 바르게 배열하시오.

ⓐ Oh, no! I forgot to bring an umbrella.
ⓑ Me, too. We should have remembered the weather forecast.
ⓒ Look. It's raining.

_____ → _____ → _____

시험에 잘 나오는 문제
05 밑줄 친 부분과 바꿔 쓸 수 있는 것은?

A I want to be strong. What should I do?
B How about doing weight lifting?

① I hope I can do weight lifting.
② I'm going to do weight lifting.
③ Why do you do weight lifting?
④ You're very good at weight lifting.
⑤ I suggest that you do weight lifting.

06 빈칸에 알맞은 것은?

A: You're late for the class.
B: I know. _____

① I'm sorry to hear that.
② The school is not far from here.
③ I should have got up earlier.
④ I think you should go to school now.
⑤ Why don't we go to school together?

서술형 평가
07 밑줄 친 우리말과 일치하도록 빈칸에 알맞은 말을 쓰시오.

A Swimming was really fun. I felt like a fish in the sea.
B It sounds fun, but I can't swim. Can you teach me how to swim?
A Sure, I can, but 전문 수영 강사에게 배우는 게 어때?

→ _____ _____ learning from a professional swimming instructor?

교과서 **treat** 치료하다 **injured** 다친 **cricket** 귀뚜라미 **weather forecast** 일기 예보 **weight lifting** 역도 **professional** 전문적인
어휘 🎧 **instructor** 강사

★★
08 밑줄 친 부분의 쓰임이 나머지와 <u>다른</u> 것은?

① I <u>do</u> miss all of you.
② Allison <u>does</u> want a new assistant.
③ I <u>did</u> tell you that it was not yours.
④ They <u>did</u> not establish the corporation.
⑤ Molly <u>did</u> make an effort to finish the work.

★★ 서술형 평가
09 우리말과 일치하도록 빈칸에 알맞은 be동사를 쓰시오.

내가 그 상자를 열었을 때, 그 상자 속의 사과들 중 몇 개는 썩어 있었다.

→ When I opened the box, some of the apples _____ in the box were rotten.

★★
10 빈칸에 공통으로 들어갈 말로 알맞은 것은?

• I _____ want to join you.
• Lara doesn't go there and neither _____ we.

① am   ② do   ③ don't
④ does   ⑤ did

★★ 시험에 잘 나오는 문제
11 빈칸에 들어갈 말이 바르게 짝지어진 것은?

• I knew that the Earth _____ around the sun.
• Ms. Hicks says Lincoln _____ slavery.

① revolves – ends   ② revolves – ended
③ revolved – ends   ④ revolved – ended
⑤ revolves – had ended

★★
12 다음 중 강조를 나타내는 문장이 <u>아닌</u> 것은?

① Tony does expand the business.
② It was at the park where I rode a bike.
③ They did the dishes for their mother.
④ It was Julie that I met on my way home.
⑤ This is the very concert that I was looking forward to.

★★★
13 다음을 간접화법으로 바꿀 때 빈칸에 들어갈 말이 순서대로 바르게 짝지어진 것은?

Ted said to me, "I'll hold this box up for you."
→ Ted _____ me that he _____ hold _____ box up for _____.

① said – will – this – me
② told – will – this – him
③ told – would – that – me
④ asked – would – this – me
⑤ asked – will – that – him

★★
14 다음 밑줄 친 부분 중 생략할 수 <u>없는</u> 것은?

① Lena is better at drawing than Martin <u>is</u>.
② Let's go skiing if you'd like to <u>go</u>.
③ I lost my watch. So I'll borrow Jin's <u>watch</u>.
④ Anthony looked bored, but he said he was not <u>bored</u>.
⑤ I waited for Clara when <u>she was</u> driving to me.

교과서 **miss** 그리워하다 **assistant** 보조원 **establish** 설립하다 **corporation** 회사 **rotten** 썩은 **slavery** 노예제도 **revolve** 공전하다
어휘 **expand** 확장하다

★★ 서술형 평가
15 두 문장의 의미가 일치하도록 빈칸에 알맞은 말을 쓰시오.

Not only Nathan but also I am going through a very difficult time.

= I as well as Nathan _____ going through a very difficult time.

★★
16 빈칸에 알맞은 것은?

A Jimin speaks Chinese well.

B _____ He had lived in China for two years.

① So is Minho.
② So has Minho.
③ So does Minho.
④ Neither does Minho.
⑤ Neither has Minho.

★★
17 밑줄 친 부분 중 어법상 어색한 것은?
① Sean said, "I want to see that movie."
② Mom told us to not touch that vase.
③ Diana asked me if I could go with her.
④ Jessie asked Dean when he had met Joe.
⑤ Nick told me that he had passed the exam.

★★ 서술형 평가
18 빈칸에 공통으로 들어갈 알맞은 be동사를 쓰시오.

• A number of boys _____ running now.
• Both Dan and Sue _____ worried.

★★★
19 빈칸에 알맞은 것의 개수는?

Paxton told me that _____.

ⓐ he wanted to see his mom
ⓑ he will be waiting for me
ⓒ he would see his dentist on Friday
ⓓ he is taking a picture
ⓔ a whale is a mammal

① 1개　② 2개　③ 3개　④ 4개　⑤ 5개

🎯 시험에 잘 나오는 문제
[20~21] 두 문장의 의미가 일치하도록 할 때 빈칸에 알맞은 말을 고르시오

★★
20

Brad said to me, "Do you want some more coffee?"
= Brad asked me _____ I wanted some more coffee.

① that　②if　③ what
④ do　⑤ did

★★
21

Eva said to Gabriel, "What are we going to do after dinner?"
= Eva asked Gabriel _____ going to do after dinner.

① what we are　② what we were
③ what she was　④ what was she
⑤ what they were

교과서 **go through** ~을 겪다　**dentist** 치과의사　**whale** 고래　**mammal** 포유류
어휘 🎧

★★★ 서술형 평가

22 다음 문장을 바꿔 쓸 때 빈칸에 알맞은 말을 쓰시오.

Max has never thought about immigrating to America.

→ Never _____.

★★★

23 밑줄 친 부분 중 생략이 가능한 것끼리 짝지어진 것은?

ⓐ Matt is poor but he is honest.
ⓑ While I was waiting for you, I ate some cookies.
ⓒ Because my cat is old, I care about him very much.
ⓓ You may come if you want to come.
ⓔ Glenn visited my house when I was out.

① ⓐ, ⓑ, ⓓ
② ⓐ, ⓓ, ⓔ
③ ⓑ, ⓒ, ⓓ
④ ⓑ, ⓓ, ⓔ
⑤ ⓒ, ⓓ, ⓔ

★★

24 괄호 안에서 알맞은 것끼리 바르게 짝지어진 것은?

(a) It was Mike (which / who) won first prize.
(b) It was at the park (who / where) I found the ring.
(c) It was last Sunday (when / where) we watched a movie.

① which – who – where
② which – where – when
③ who – where – when
④ who – who – when
⑤ who – where – where

★★

25 다음 글의 내용과 일치하지 않는 것은?

Have you ever seen spots after a camera flashes and wondered why? This is because of your photoreceptors. They are special cells in the back of your eye that let you see light. They change light into electrical signals that are sent to the brain. It is the brain that produces the images you see. When a camera flash goes off, however, it is so bright that the photoreceptors can't operate well. While the photoreceptors are recovering, your brain "sees" nothing and fills in the blanks with spots.

*photoreceptor 광수용체

① 사람의 눈 뒤에는 광수용체가 있다.
② 광수용체는 전기 신호를 빛으로 바꾸고, 이 빛은 뇌로 보내진다.
③ 뇌는 우리가 보는 이미지를 생성한다.
④ 카메라 플래시는 너무 밝아서 광수용체가 잘 작동하지 못한다.
⑤ 광수용체가 회복하는 동안 뇌는 전혀 보지 못한다.

★★

26 밑줄 친 ⓐ~ⓔ 중 나머지 넷과 다른 것은?

Have you heard of a white rainbow? ⓐIt appears during fog. When a fog has very small drops inside ⓑit a surprising white rainbow appears. You can find ⓒit easily standing with your back to the sun and looking toward the fog. ⓓIt can even appear at night when the moon in the sky is very bright. In that case, ⓔit's not called a white rainbow, but a moonbow.

① ⓐ
② ⓑ
③ ⓒ
④ ⓓ
⑤ ⓔ

교과서 어휘 ∩ **immigrate** 이민 가다 **spot** 점 **go off** 터지다 **operate** 작동하다 **blank** 여백 **fog** 안개 **drop** 물방울 **appear** 나타나다
stand with one's back to ~을 등지고 서다 **moonbow** 달무지개

[27~28] 다음을 읽고, 물음에 답하시오.

Mexico City is a warm place and never freezes throughout the year, but citizens can enjoy ice skating. How? There is a huge outdoor staking rink with a surface that isn't covered in ice. It's plastic that covers it. Skaters say that they feel like they're on a frozen rink. ⓐ Not only the rink saves tons of water to make ice, but it also saves energy to keep that ice frozen. The mayor of the city says, "Our eco-rink offers the joy of ice skating without harming the environment."

★★★ 서술형 평가
27 밑줄 친 ⓐ에서 어법상 어색한 부분을 찾아 다시 고쳐 쓰시오.

→ _____

★★ 시험에 잘 나오는 문제
28 위 글의 내용을 보고 답할 수 없는 것은?

① How is the climate in Mexico City?
② What covers the surface of the skating rink in Mexico City?
③ How do skaters feel when they use the skating rink?
④ How many people use the skating rink a day?
⑤ What positive effects does the skating rink have on the environment?

[29~30] 다음을 읽고, 물음에 답하시오.

Sherlock Holmes and Dr. Watson go on a camping. After they have a tasty dinner and a bottle of wine, they go into their tent to sleep. Some hours later, Holmes wakes up Watson.

(A) "What do you deduce from that?" Watson says that there are millions of galaxies and billions of planets.

(B) ⓐ He says to Watson, "Look up at the sky and tell me what you see." "I see millions and millions of stars, Holmes" replies Watson.

(C) "Watson, you idiot!" Holmes says. "Someone has stolen our tent!"

*deduce 추론하다

★★ 서술형 평가
29 밑줄 친 ⓐ와 같은 의미가 되도록 빈칸에 알맞은 말을 쓰시오.

→ He tells Watson _____ look up at the sky and tell _____ what _____ _____.

★★
30 주어진 문장에 이어질 (A)-(C)의 순서로 알맞은 것은?

① (A) – (C) – (B)   ② (B) – (A) – (C)
③ (B) – (C) – (A)   ④ (C) – (A) – (B)
⑤ (C) – (B) – (A)

교과서 **freeze** 추워지다 **citizen** 시민 **outdoor** 실외의 **frozen** 언, 냉동된 **mayor** 시장 **eco-rink** 친환경 스케이트장 **harm** 해치다
어휘 **climate** 기후 **galaxy** 은하계 **idiot** 바보

A 수의 일치

주어의 수에 동사의 수를 일치시키되, 주어의 형태에 따라 다음과 같이 한다.

단수 취급하는 주어의 형태	복수 취급하는 주어의 형태
• 수(거리, 시간, 길이 등), 국가, 학문, 질병, 책, 영화, 음식, 신문 • some(most, none, half, the rest, 분수)+of+단수 명사 • to부정사(구), 동명사(구), 명사절 • the number of+복수 명사 • every(each, no)+단수 명사 • 두 단어로 된 동일 개체	• some(most, none, half, the rest, 분수)+of+복수 명사 • a number of+복수 명사 • no+복수 명사 • both A and B

B 시제의 일치

주절 동사의 시제에 종속절 동사의 시제를 일치시키되, 주절의 시제에 따라 다음과 같이 한다.

주절이 현재 → 종속절은 모든 시제 가능	I **know** that she **is(was, will be, has been)** happy.
주절이 과거 → 종속절은 과거, 과거완료	I **knew** that she **was(had been)** happy.

cf. 진리, 속담, 현재의 습관 등은 항상 현재 시제로, 역사적 사실은 항상 과거 시제로 쓴다.
My teacher explained that the Earth **is** round. 〈진리〉
Mandy says that the Korean War **broke** out in 1950. 〈역사〉

C 화법

다른 이의 말을 전달하는 화법에는, 인용부호를 써서 그대로 전하는 직접화법과,
전하는 이의 말로 바꿔서 전하는 간접화법이 있다.

직접화법	간접화법		
	인용문이 평서문	인용문이 의문문	인용문이 명령문
say (to)+(대)명사	• say → say • tell+(대)명사	ask+(대)명사	tell(ask, advise, order)+(대)명사
인용문	접속사 that+인용문	• 의문사+주어+동사 • if(whether)+주어+동사	• 긍정: to부정사 • 부정: not(never) to부정사
인용문의 인칭	1인칭 → 주절의 주어의 인칭 / 2인칭 → 인용문 청자의 인칭 / 3인칭 → 그대로 유지		
인용문의 시제	시제 일치의 원칙에 따라 주절의 동사의 시제에 일치		
기타	인용문의 지시대명사나 부사(구)를 전하는 이의 말로 전환		

D 강조

강조	형태 / 의미	예문
동사	do(does/did)+동사원형 (정말로(꼭) ~하다)	They **did eat** all of my chocolate cookies. (그들은 내 초콜릿 쿠키 전부를 정말로 먹었다.)
명사	the very+명사 (바로(그) ~)	This is **the very watch** I've been looking for. (이것이 내가 찾고 있었던 바로 그 시계이다.)
기타 문장성분	It is/was ~ that ... (…하는 것은 바로 ~이(었)다)	It was **under the table** that Henry found the key last night. (Henry가 지난밤에 열쇠를 찾아냈 던 것은 바로 탁자 아래였다.)

E 도치

	형태	비고
장소 부사(구) 도치	부사(구)+동사+주어	주어가 인칭대명사이면 〈주어+동사〉
부정어 도치	부정어+┌ 동사+주어 ├ 조동사+주어+동사원형 └ have(had)+주어+p.p.	not, never, little, hardly, seldom 등의 부정어 강조
so, neither 도치	so(neither)+(조)동사+주어	동의를 나타내는 관용 표현

F 생략

앞에서 언급된 후에 반복되는 어구와, 부사절에서 〈주절의 주어와 같은 주어+be동사〉
는 생략할 수 있다.

My shoes are wet. So I'll wear my sister's (**shoes**).

I think my car can't go further, but Alice says it can (**go further**).

Though (**she is**) young, she is very thoughtful.

When (**I was**) a boy, I used to catch insects with a butterfly net.

·· >> Expression

1 안타까움, 후회 표현하기

🍎 안타까움 표현하기
- You should (not) have done ....
- I'm sorry (that) you (didn't) ....

🍎 후회하기
- I(We) should (not) have done ....

2 제안, 권유하기

🍎 제안, 권유하기
- I suggest (that) ....
- You'd better ....
- I think you should ....

- Why don't you ....?
- How(What) about -ing ....?

**It does not matter how slowly you go
as long as you do not stop.**

Confucius

II

듣기 실전
모의고사

01 대화를 듣고, 여자가 찾고 있는 우산을 고르시오.

02 대화를 듣고, 남자가 추천하는 책에 관해 언급되지 <u>않은</u> 것을 고르시오.

① 제목　　　　② 작가
③ 주인공의 나이　④ 주된 내용
⑤ 좋아하는 이유

03 대화를 듣고, 남자가 여자에게 전화한 목적으로 가장 적절한 것을 고르시오.

① 예약을 확인하려고
② 예약을 취소하려고
③ 예약일을 다른 날로 바꾸려고
④ 방을 하나 더 예약하려고
⑤ 4인용 방을 예약하려고

04 대화를 듣고, 두 사람이 새로 생긴 피자 가게에 방문할 시각을 고르시오.

① 12:00　　② 12:30　　③ 1:00
④ 1:30　　⑤ 2:00

05 대화를 듣고, 두 사람이 대화하는 장소로 가장 적절한 곳을 고르시오.

① 바닷가　② 수족관　③ 등산로
④ 중식당　⑤ 잠수함

06 다음 그림의 상황에 가장 적절한 대화를 고르시오.

① 　　② 　　③ 　　④ 　　⑤

07 대화를 듣고, 남자가 여자에게 부탁한 일로 가장 적절한 것을 고르시오.

① 함께 저녁 먹기　② 우체국 방문하기
③ 책 포장하기　　④ 소포 전해 주기
⑤ 아이스크림 사다 주기

08 다음을 듣고, 일정에 관해 언급되지 <u>않은</u> 것을 고르시오.

① 오늘 방문한 곳
② 내일 방문할 곳
③ 내일 아침 식사 시작 시각
④ 내일 아침 식사 장소
⑤ 내일 아침 버스 대기 장소

09 다음을 듣고, 무엇에 관한 설명인지 고르시오.

① 학생증 발급 방법　② 사서 선생님 소개
③ 도서 대출 안내　　④ 종류별 도서 위치
⑤ 도서관 출입 방법

10 다음을 듣고, 두 사람의 대화가 <u>어색한</u> 것을 고르시오.

① 　　② 　　③ 　　④ 　　⑤

11 대화를 듣고, 남자가 할 일로 가장 적절한 것을 고르시오.

① 표지판에 글씨 쓰기　② 콘택트렌즈 구입하기
③ 눈 검사 받기　④ 휴대전화 사용하기
⑤ 안경 착용하기

12 다음 표를 보면서 대화를 듣고, 남자가 만들 물건을 고르시오.

Rainbow Art Club		
Things to make	Price(₩)	Time
① Candle	9,000	60 min
② Bag Charm	5,000	30 min
③ Pencil Case	6,000	20 min
④ Coin Bank	7,000	40 min
⑤ Clock	10,000	50 min

13 대화를 듣고, 여자가 예금을 찾을 날짜를 고르시오.

① January 20th　② January 21st
③ January 22nd　④ February 20th
⑤ February 22nd

14 대화를 듣고, 남자가 어제 한 일로 가장 적절한 것을 고르시오.

① TV 드라마 보기　② 커피 마시러 가기
③ 컴퓨터 게임 하기　④ 축구 하기
⑤ 스키 타기

15 다음을 듣고, 방송의 목적으로 가장 적절한 것을 고르시오.

① 세제 광고　② 가전제품 광고
③ 의류 할인 안내　④ 세탁비 할인 안내
⑤ 특별 할인 기간 안내

16 대화를 듣고, 여자가 세탁비로 지불한 금액을 고르시오.

① ₩2,000　② ₩3,000　③ ₩7,000
④ ₩7,600　⑤ ₩10,000

17 대화를 듣고, 여자의 마지막 말에 대한 남자의 응답으로 가장 적절한 것을 고르시오.

Man: _____

① I take the bus at 7:30.
② I ride my bike to school.
③ I usually take No. 2001 bus.
④ It takes at least an hour by bus.
⑤ The bus stop is too far away from my house.

18 대화를 듣고, 남자의 마지막 말에 대한 여자의 응답으로 가장 적절한 것을 고르시오.

Woman: _____

① Never mind.
② Let me help you.
③ That's a good idea.
④ That makes two of us.
⑤ I'm really appreciate that.

19 대화를 듣고, 여자의 마지막 말에 대한 남자의 응답으로 가장 적절한 것을 고르시오.

Man: _____

① About 3 centimeters each.
② They are too long for me.
③ That will cost you extra $5.
④ I'll be back in an hour then.
⑤ They look really good on you.

20 다음 상황 설명을 듣고, Michael이 Sandra에게 할 말로 가장 적절한 것을 고르시오.

Michael: _____

① What would you like to drink?
② Mom likes iced milk tea better.
③ Please call Mom and ask what she wants.
④ Why don't you go with me to the tea shop?
⑤ Do you remember what Mom wanted to drink?

01 대화를 듣고, 여자가 찾고 있는 우산을 고르시오.

① ② ③
④ ⑤

W Excuse me, have you seen an _____ around here?
M What does it look like?
W It's just a _____ _____ umbrella.
M Is it a _____ umbrella?
W Yes. It's inside a black _____. I remember _____ it on this _____ about 10 minutes ago.
M Then this might be yours. I found it on this counter.
W Yes, this is mine. Thank you very much.

02 대화를 듣고, 남자가 추천하는 책에 관해 언급되지 <u>않은</u> 것을 고르시오.

① 제목　　　② 작가
③ 주인공의 나이　④ 주된 내용
⑤ 좋아하는 이유

W Can you recommend me a good book?
M I've read _____ _____ _____ *Wonder* recently. I enjoyed it very much.
W Who is the main character?
M The main character is a _____ boy with a rare disease.
W I see. So, what's the story about?
M It's about how the _____ _____ _____ his situation and achieves success in his school life.
W That sounds interesting. Why did you like the book?
M _____ _____ it was very thought provoking. In addition, it was easy to relate to because it dealt with teenagers.
W That's good to hear. Maybe I should try reading it too.

03 대화를 듣고, 남자가 여자에게 전화한 목적으로 가장 적절한 것을 고르시오.

① 예약을 확인하려고
② 예약을 취소하려고
③ 예약일을 다른 날로 바꾸려고
④ 방을 하나 더 예약하려고
⑤ 4인용 방을 예약하려고

[Telephone rings.]
W Good morning, BS Hotel. How can I help you?
M Hello. I _____ _____ _____ for this Friday.
W May I have your name, sir?
M My name is Mark Smith.
W Hold on, please. Yes, we have a reservation under that name. It's _____ _____ _____ for one night.
M Right. Can four people stay in the room?
W A twin room is for two people. A family room would _____ _____ four people.
M Then can I _____ the twin room and _____ _____ _____ _____ instead?
W Of course. I'll change the reservation right now.

» WORDS　umbrella 우산　counter 계산대　recommend 추천하다　character 배역　rare 희귀한　disease 병
thought provoking 생각을 하게 하는　reservation 예약　twin room 침대가 2개인 방

04 대화를 듣고, 두 사람이 새로 생긴 피자 가게에 방문할 시각을 고르시오.

① 12:00 ② 12:30 ③ 1:00
④ 1:30 ⑤ 2:00

W Tom, did you see the new pizza place in front of the school?
M Yes. Why don't we visit there sometime?
W School _____ _____ 12:30 today. We should go there today.
M Great. Let's meet there at 1.
W Sorry, but can you _____ _____ 1:30? I have to help _____ _____ _____ after school.
M No problem. But we should hurry. I saw that they _____ the lunch special set until 2.
W I _____ _____ _____. See you there at 1:30.
M Okay.

05 대화를 듣고, 두 사람이 대화하는 장소로 가장 적절한 곳을 고르시오.

① 바닷가 ② 수족관 ③ 등산로
④ 중식당 ⑤ 잠수함

M Look at that! Those _____ are very pretty.
W I know. I wish I had some at home.
M It feels great walking _____ _____ _____.
W Right. The weather is really nice, too.
M We should take breaks like this more often.
W Why don't we _____ _____ on a mountain next time?
M Good idea. Let's _____ _____ _____ for it. Oh and by the way, what do you want for lunch?
W Let's try the famous Chinese restaurant near here.

06 다음 그림의 상황에 가장 적절한 대화를 고르시오.

① ② ③ ④ ⑤

① M Have you seen my bag? I think _____ _____ it.
W I think I saw your bag on the bench.
② M This bag is too heavy to _____ _____.
W Let me help you.
③ M What is this table _____ _____?
W It is made of wood.
④ M Are you feeling _____?
W No, I think I have a fever.
⑤ M _____ _____ _____ _____. How have you been?
W I've been doing very well.

>> WORDS **sometime** 언젠가 **hurry** 서두르다 **break** 휴식 **by the way** 그런데 **be made of** ~로 만들어지다 **wood** 목재
have a fever 열이 나다

07 대화를 듣고, 남자가 여자에게 부탁한 일로 가장 적절한 것을 고르시오.

① 함께 저녁 먹기
② 우체국 방문하기
③ 책 포장하기
④ 소포 전해 주기
⑤ 아이스크림 사다 주기

W Dad, you're having dinner with mom tonight, right?

M Yes, we're about to go out. Then can I ask a favor?

W Sure. Is there anything I can do for you?

M Yes. Actually, _____ _____ is coming to get my book any time soon.

W Oh, I see that you decided to _____ it. Do you want me to put it in a package for you?

M No, you don't have to. I already _____ _____ and put it on the table. Please _____ _____ to the deliveryman.

W Okay. No problem. Oh, and Then can you buy me strawberry ice cream _____ _____ _____ _____?

M No problem.

08 다음을 듣고, 일정에 관해 언급되지 않은 것을 고르시오.

① 오늘 방문한 곳
② 내일 방문할 곳
③ 내일 아침 식사 시작 시각
④ 내일 아침 식사 장소
⑤ 내일 아침 버스 대기 장소

M Attention, everyone. I guess you're very tired _____ _____ the tight schedule today. Let me briefly tell you _____ _____ for tomorrow. We are going to visit the National Palace Museum. Breakfast will _____ _____ from 6:30 at the restaurant on the first floor. We're planning to leave at 8:20, so please finish your meals by 8:00 and get on the tour bus by 8:10. The bus will be waiting at _____ _____ _____. Any questions?

09 다음을 듣고, 무엇에 관한 설명인지 고르시오.

① 학생증 발급 방법
② 사서 선생님 소개
③ 도서 대출 안내
④ 종류별 도서 위치
⑤ 도서관 출입 방법

W So, have _____ _____ _____ found the books you want to read? To _____ _____ the books, take them to Ms. Kim, the school librarian. She will help you check them out. Don't _____ _____ _____ your student ID, too. You can borrow _____ _____ three books but you have to return them in two weeks.

10 다음을 듣고, 두 사람의 대화가 어색한 것을 고르시오.

① ② ③ ④ ⑤

① M What's the weather like today?
   W No, I don't like rainy days. I should stay at home today.
② M What kind of movies do you like?
   W I like _____ _____. What about you?
③ M Does the T-shirt _____ _____ _____?
   W I think it's too tight.
④ M Where shall we hang this picture?
   W We should put it on the wall _____ _____ _____.
⑤ M _____ _____ _____ this man in the picture?
   W Yes. This is the man I saw at the hospital.

>> **WORDS** **actually** 사실(은) **deliveryman** 배달원 **tight** 빡빡한 **briefly** 간단하게 **librarian** 사서 **check out** 대출하다 **student ID** 학생증 **return** 반납하다 **hang** 걸다

11 대화를 듣고, 남자가 할 일로 가장 적절한 것을 고르시오.

① 표지판에 글씨 쓰기
② 콘택트렌즈 구입하기
③ 눈 검사 받기
④ 휴대전화 사용하기
⑤ 안경 착용하기

M　Anne, can you read what it says on the blue sign?

W　Yes, it says 'Olympic Expressway.'

M　Oh, my. I can't see it. It seems that _____ _____ _____ _____ _____.

W　I think you are using your cellphone too much nowadays.

M　Maybe I am. I guess I should start _____ _____ now.

W　Why don't you go see the doctor _____ _____ your eyesight?

M　You're right. I'll _____ _____ _____ _____ at the hospital.

---

12 다음 표를 보면서 대화를 듣고, 남자가 만들 물건을 고르시오.

Rainbow Art Club			
	Things to make	Price(₩)	Time
①	Candle	9,000	60 min
②	Bag Charm	5,000	30 min
③	Pencil Case	6,000	20 min
④	Coin Bank	7,000	40 min
⑤	Clock	10,000	50 min

M　Amy, what are you going to make?

W　I'm going to make _____ _____ _____ and buy some snacks with the money left over. How about you?

M　I want to make a candle or a clock, but _____ _____ _____ take too long.

W　Well, maybe I'll also make _____ _____ _____ instead of buying snacks.

M　Can I make _____ _____ _____? I need something to decorate my bag.

W　Sure. It only takes 30 minutes, so let's go eat something after that.

M　That'll be great.

---

13 대화를 듣고, 여자가 예금을 찾을 날짜를 고르시오.

① January 20th
② January 21st
③ January 22nd
④ February 20th
⑤ February 22nd

W　Good morning. How can I help you?

M　I'd like to _____ _____ _____ _____ and make a deposit of 50,000 won a month for one year.

W　Okay. Let me help you. Please _____ _____ these forms.

M　Today is January 20th, so I have to _____ 50,000 won every 20th.

W　You are right. Visit us back on January 20th _____ _____ to get your money back.

M　But I checked the calendar and that day is Saturday. Then when should I come?

W　Then you should come on Monday, _____ _____.

M　Oh, I see. Thank you.

>> WORDS　**expressway** 고속도로　**nowadays** 요즘　**decorate** 장식하다　**bag charm** 가방 장식품　**make a deposit of** ~을 입금하다
form 양식

14 대화를 듣고, 남자가 어제 한 일로 가장 적절한 것을 고르시오.

① TV 드라마 보기
② 커피 마시러 가기
③ 컴퓨터 게임 하기
④ 축구 하기
⑤ 스키 타기

W Mark, you look very tired today.
M I do feel very tired. Maybe I spent too much energy yesterday.
W Let me guess. Did you watch _____ _____ all night?
M No, not yesterday. I couldn't even _____ _____ _____ yesterday.
W Did you _____ _____ with your friends outside?
M Well, actually, I _____ all day long.
W So that's why you feel tired. I'm going to get some coffee. Will you go with me?
M No, _____ _____ get some sleep before class. Thanks anyway.

15 다음을 듣고, 방송의 목적으로 가장 적절한 것을 고르시오.

① 세제 광고
② 가전제품 광고
③ 의류 할인 안내
④ 세탁비 할인 안내
⑤ 특별 할인 기간 안내

M You come back home from work and your clothes are _____ _____ and dirty. However, you don't have time to wash them. What do you do? Just leave them to the Fashion Styler. _____ you put them in, it'll make your clothes so clean as if they were freshly washed. It not only saves your money and cleans your clothes, but it also improves your style. In addition, it's _____ _____. We're giving a 30% discount until this Sunday. You can find the Fashion Styler in the _____ _____.

16 대화를 듣고, 여자가 세탁비로 지불한 금액을 고르시오.

① ₩2,000   ② ₩3,000
③ ₩7,000   ④ ₩7,600
⑤ ₩10,000

M Next, please.
W Okay. I have three shirts and two pairs of pants. How much do I have to pay?
M These shirts are 1,200 won each, and it's 2,000 won for _____ _____ _____ _____.
W So it will be 7,600 won, right?
M Yes, but we are giving a discount _____ _____ now. So each shirt costs 1,000 won.
W That sounds great. Here's 10,000 won. When does the discount end?
M This Friday. Here's _____ _____.
W Thank you.

>> WORDS   tired 피곤한   guess 짐작하다   all day long 하루 종일   wash 세탁하다   freshly 막 (~한)   give a discount 할인을 제공하다

17 대화를 듣고, 여자의 마지막 말에 대한 남자의 응답으로 가장 적절한 것을 고르시오.

① I take the bus at 7:30.
② I ride my bike to school.
③ I usually take No. 2001 bus.
④ It takes at least an hour by bus.
⑤ The bus stop is too far away from my house.

W Jake, are you going home?
M Yes. I am. Are you going home, too?
W Yes. It seems like we are going _____ _____ _____ _____. Where do you live?
M I live in the Castle apartment. How about you?
W Me, too. Why _____ _____ see you on the bus this morning?
M That's because I don't _____ _____ _____ to school.
W Really? Then how do you go to school?

18 대화를 듣고, 남자의 마지막 말에 대한 여자의 응답으로 가장 적절한 것을 고르시오.

① Never mind.
② Let me help you.
③ That's a good idea.
④ That makes two of us.
⑤ I'm really appreciate that.

M I'm so excited. Sports Day is finally tomorrow.
W Yeah, but I'm worried that it _____ _____ _____.
M Why would it be canceled? Is it going to rain tomorrow?
W No, I'm worried about _____ _____. I read it could be bad tomorrow.
M But we can still have Sports Day in the gym.
W Mr. Kim said if the fine dust is too bad, we would _____ _____ instead of Sports Day.
M No way. I hope we have good weather tomorrow.

19 대화를 듣고, 여자의 마지막 말에 대한 남자의 응답으로 가장 적절한 것을 고르시오.

① About 3 centimeters each.
② They are too long for me.
③ That will cost you extra $5.
④ I'll be back in an hour then.
⑤ They look really good on you.

M Excuse me. I'd like to buy these pants.
W Okay. They are $30 each.
M Well, these are a little short for me. I should _____ _____ the hems.
W If you _____ more than $50, we do that for free.
M That sounds great. How long does it take to _____ _____ _____?
W You can get them back in an hour. How much do you want to _____ them?

20 다음 상황 설명을 듣고, Michael이 Sandra에게 할 말로 가장 적절한 것을 고르시오.

① What would you like to drink?
② Mom likes iced milk tea better.
③ Please call Mom and ask what she wants.
④ Why don't you go with me to the tea shop?
⑤ Do you remember what Mom wanted to drink?

W Michael and Sandra went to a tea shop. They _____ _____ _____ buy tea for themselves, and also for their mother. However, Michael _____ what his mother wanted to drink. It was _____ iced milk tea or iced black tea. Before he asks his mother on the phone, he wants to ask Sandra _____ _____ _____ which one it was. In this situation, what would Michael most likely to say to Sandra?

>> WORDS **at least** 적어도 **fine dust** 미세 먼지 **No way!** 절대 안 돼! **That makes two of us.** 그것에 대해 나도 같은 생각이야.
hem (옷 등의) 단 **black tea** 홍차 **on the phone** 전화로

02회 » 듣기 실전 모의고사

01 대화를 듣고, 두 사람이 구입할 것을 고르시오.

① ② ③

④ ⑤

02 대화를 듣고, 두 사람의 주말 약속에 관해 언급되지 <u>않은</u> 것을 고르시오.

① 만날 시간   ② 만나서 할 일
③ 함께 갈 곳   ④ 입고 올 옷
⑤ 가져올 준비물

03 대화를 듣고, 여자가 전화한 목적으로 가장 적절한 것을 고르시오.

① 극장 가는 길을 물어보려고
② 자신을 데리러 오라고 말하려고
③ 표를 지금 구매하라고 말하려고
④ 약속 장소에 못 간다고 말하려고
⑤ 간식을 먹고 싶은지 물어보려고

04 대화를 듣고, 현재 시각을 고르시오.
① 7:20   ② 7:50   ③ 8:00
④ 8:10   ⑤ 8:30

05 다음 그림의 상황에 가장 적절한 대화를 고르시오.

①   ②   ③   ④   ⑤

06 대화를 듣고, 두 사람이 대화하는 장소로 가장 적절한 곳을 고르시오.

① 침실   ② 부엌   ③ 화장실
④ 거실   ⑤ 정원

07 대화를 듣고, 여자가 남자에게 부탁한 일로 가장 적절한 것을 고르시오.

① 고구마 삶기   ② 가스레인지 끄기
③ 접시 가져오기   ④ 창문 열기
⑤ 고구마 버리기

08 다음을 듣고, 상에 관해 언급되지 <u>않은</u> 것을 고르시오.

① 상 이름   ② 수상자
③ 시상 이유   ④ 시상 기관
⑤ 상품

09 다음을 듣고, 무엇에 관한 설명인지 고르시오.

① 지구   ② 자석   ③ 분필
④ 테이프   ⑤ 고무줄

10 다음을 듣고, 두 사람의 대화가 <u>어색한</u> 것을 고르시오.

①   ②   ③   ④   ⑤

11 대화를 듣고, 남자가 대화 직후에 할 일로 가장 적절한 것을 고르시오.

① 핫초콜릿 만들기
② 친구들과 축구 하기
③ 쿠키 통 꺼내기
④ 손 씻기
⑤ 음료수 마시기

12 대화를 듣고, 남자가 13일에 할 운동으로 알맞은 것을 고르시오.

Mon	Tue	Wed	Thu	Fri	Sat	Sun
1	2	3	4	5	6	7
8	9	10	11	12	⑬	14

① curling　　　　② swimming
③ skiing　　　　④ skating
⑤ snowboarding

13 대화를 듣고, 여자가 지갑을 두고 온 자리로 가장 알맞은 것을 고르시오.

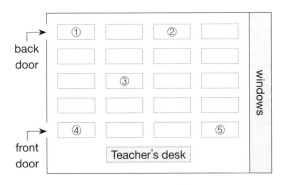

14 대화를 듣고, 상호가 방학 중에 한 일로 가장 적절한 것을 고르시오.
① 우유 많이 마시기　　② 많이 먹기
③ 새 재킷 사기　　　　④ 운동 많이 하기
⑤ 다이어트 하기

15 다음을 듣고, 방송의 목적으로 가장 적절한 것을 고르시오.
① 학교 매점을 홍보하려고
② 보건실 위치를 안내하려고
③ 새 보건 교사를 소개하려고
④ 손 씻는 방법을 설명하려고
⑤ 바이러스 대응법을 안내하려고

16 대화를 듣고, 남자가 지불할 금액을 고르시오.
① $29　　　② $30　　　③ $32
④ $40　　　⑤ $43

17 대화를 듣고, 여자의 마지막 말에 대한 남자의 응답으로 가장 적절한 것을 고르시오.

Man: _____

① I haven't seen it yet.
② I like cats better than dogs.
③ It was hard to get the tickets.
④ Your performance was the best.
⑤ I prefer the musical to the movie.

18 대화를 듣고, 남자의 마지막 말에 대한 여자의 응답으로 가장 적절한 것을 고르시오.

Woman: _____

① I've just turned it off.
② I want it. Give me a lot.
③ Where are the flashlights?
④ It's because people use a lot of electricity.
⑤ I can't help turning on the air conditioner.

19 대화를 듣고, 여자의 마지막 말에 대한 남자의 응답으로 가장 적절한 것을 고르시오.

Man: _____

① I went there already.
② Oh, I shouldn't have.
③ They are looking forward to it.
④ I know nothing about martial arts.
⑤ Can I? That would be really great.

20 다음 상황 설명을 듣고, Anne이 Tom에게 할 말로 가장 적절한 것을 고르시오.

Anne: _____

① How would I look with a perm?
② I'd like to have a hair cut.
③ I'm sorry, I'll visit you later.
④ A short hair won't look good on you.
⑤ Can you recommend a good hairstyle on me?

01 대화를 듣고, 두 사람이 구입할 것을 고르시오.

① ② ③
④ ⑤

W Let's buy some pineapples.

M We have to _____ them if we want to eat them. I have no idea how to do it.

W I don't mean to buy a whole pineapple.

M Okay, then do you want _____ _____?

W They are too little. Why don't we buy that _____ pineapple?

M We don't need to. There're fresh pineapples. Let's buy the sliced pineapple in the _____ _____.

W Okay. That would be best.

02 대화를 듣고, 두 사람의 주말 약속에 관해 언급되지 않은 것을 고르시오.

① 만날 시간 ② 만나서 할 일
③ 함께 갈 곳 ④ 입고 올 옷
⑤ 가져올 준비물

M Why don't you go skating this weekend?

W I don't know how to skate. Can you skate?

M Yes. It's easy. I'll show you how.

W I _____ _____ _____ I'll fall down on the ice too much.

M Don't worry. I'll hold your hands _____ _____.

W Okay, then I'll try skating. Which ice rink are we going to?

M A new ice rink just opened _____ _____ _____. Let's go there.

W Sounds perfect. How about meeting on Saturday at 10 a.m.?

M Fine. Don't forget to _____ _____ _____.

03 대화를 듣고, 여자가 전화한 목적으로 가장 적절한 것을 고르시오.

① 극장 가는 길을 물어보려고
② 자신을 데리러 오라고 말하려고
③ 표를 지금 구매하라고 말하려고
④ 약속 장소에 못 간다고 말하려고
⑤ 간식을 먹고 싶은지 물어보려고

[Cellphone rings.]

M Hello, Hana. Where are you? I'm in front of the ticket booth.

W Brian. I'm sorry, but I'm _____ _____ _____ _____ yet. I have no idea where I am.

M Tell me what you see. I'll _____ _____ you.

W That's okay. I took a taxi. I called you because I'm worried that the tickets might be _____ _____. Why don't you buy tickets now?

M Don't worry, I _____ _____ two.

W Thank you. I think I'll be there in 5 minutes.

M Okay. I'll be waiting for you buying some snacks.

>> **WORDS** **have no idea** 모르다 **whole** 전체의 **slice** 얇게 썰다 **fall down** 넘어지다 **ice rink** 빙상장 **ticket booth** 매표소

04 대화를 듣고, 현재 시각을 고르시오.

① 7:20   ② 7:50   ③ 8:00
④ 8:10   ⑤ 8:30

W   Hurry up. You'll be late for school.

M   Don't worry. It's only 7:20. I'll go out at 8 o'clock. We have _____ _____ _____.

W   What's wrong with the clock? It's 7:50 now.

M   What? Oh, you're right. _____ _____ _____ are not moving at all.

W   I think the battery is dead. I'll _____ you to school today. What time do you have to get to school by?

M   By 8:30.

W   It _____ _____ 15 minutes to get to school, so get in the car by 8:10.

M   Okay. Thank you.

05 다음 그림의 상황에 가장 적절한 대화를 고르시오.

① ② ③ ④ ⑤

① M   I have a headache. I think I have a fever, too.
    W   Let's _____ _____ _____.

② M   Can you bring me the pills? It is time to take them.
    W   Here you are. _____ them with water.

③ M   Are you okay? You look bad.
    W   I think I'm too tired.

④ M   I want to have some apples.
    W   Okay. I'm going to peel one for you.

⑤ M   Do you want to try _____ _____?
    W   Thank you. I was very hungry.

06 대화를 듣고, 두 사람이 대화하는 장소로 가장 적절한 곳을 고르시오.

① 침실   ② 부엌   ③ 화장실
④ 거실   ⑤ 정원

M   Mom, can you please come and help me?

W   What's the matter? I have to go back to the kitchen again.

M   The water's _____ _____ of the pot. Maybe I watered the plant too much.

W   I think we should move the pot to the bathroom.

M   But this is too heavy. I'm wiping the water from the floor, but the bed _____ _____ _____.

W   Well, it seems that the water has stopped. It'll be okay soon.

M   Whew. It is _____ that the pot is not in the living room, where the floor is _____ _____ carpet.

W   I shouldn't have put the pot near the bed. I'll move it to the garden later.

≫ WORDS   **get to** ~에 도착하다   **have a fever** 열이 나다   **pill** 알약   **peel** 껍질을 벗기다   **pot** 화분   **water** 물을 주다   **wipe** 닦다

07 대화를 듣고, 여자가 남자에게 부탁한 일로 가장 적절한 것을 고르시오.

① 고구마 삶기   ② 가스레인지 끄기
③ 접시 가져오기   ④ 창문 열기
⑤ 고구마 버리기

W David, can't you _____ _____ _____?
M Oh my! I forgot I _____ some sweet potatoes.
W That's okay. I turned off the stove.
M Thank you. They must be _____ _____.
W I already checked them, and actually they looked quite delicious.
M That's fortunate. Then let's have them. I'll take out some plates.
W I'll do that. Can you please open the windows to get rid of _____ _____?
M Sure. I will.

08 다음을 듣고, 상에 관해 언급되지 <u>않은</u> 것을 고르시오.

① 상 이름   ② 수상자
③ 시상 이유   ④ 시상 기관
⑤ 상품

M This year, Woodbridge High School gladly _____ the Good Citizenship Award to Mark Thomson. He has been _____ _____ by students and teachers. They said he has a positive attitude, and he studies very hard and actively volunteers. I also know him _____ _____ _____ _____ student. I hope he will be a good role model for everyone. Please give a big hand to Mark, everyone.

09 다음을 듣고, 무엇에 관한 설명인지 고르시오.

① 지구   ② 자석   ③ 분필
④ 테이프   ⑤ 고무줄

W You may have seen this in your science class. This has two poles, the North pole and the South pole. Two North poles _____ each other away, and so do two South poles. However, the North pole and South pole _____ _____ _____. You can put a note, using this, on _____ _____ like blackboards and refrigerator doors, because this _____ _____ to them. However, this doesn't stick to plastic or rubber.

10 다음을 듣고, 두 사람의 대화가 어색한 것을 고르시오.

①   ②   ③   ④   ⑤

① W Do you _____ _____ the door?
  M Of course. I'll do it for you.
② W Let me introduce my younger sister to you. This is Hana.
  M Nice to meet you. I'm Jason.
③ W Where shall we meet tomorrow?
  M See you at _____ _____ _____ of the museum.
④ W How would you like your hair done?
  M Just _____ it a little bit, please.
⑤ W How can a lizard not fall down from the ceiling?
  M People say it has _____ _____.

>> **WORDS** **sweet potato** 고구마 **(gas) stove** 가스레인지 **fortunate** 다행스러운 **gladly** 기쁘게 **award** 상 **positive** 긍정적인 **attitude** 태도 **give a hand to** ~에게 박수를 보내다 **rubber** 고무 **lizard** 도마뱀

11 대화를 듣고, 남자가 대화 직후에 할 일로 가장 적절한 것을 고르시오.

① 핫초콜릿 만들기
② 친구들과 축구 하기
③ 쿠키 통 꺼내기
④ 손 씻기
⑤ 음료수 마시기

M Mom, I'm home. Oh, it's so cold outside.

W Do you want some _____ _____?

M That would be great. Thank you.

W How was school today?

M My _____ _____ seems very nice. I also made some friends already. We _____ _____ together after lunch.

W Sounds great. Can you take out the cookie jar from _____ _____?

M Okay. Here you are. I'll _____ _____ _____ before I eat.

W Good idea.

12 대화를 듣고, 남자가 13일에 할 운동으로 알맞은 것을 고르시오.

Mon	Tue	Wed	Thu	Fri	Sat	Sun
1	2	3	4	5	6	7
8	9	10	11	12	⑬	14

① curling   ② swimming
③ skiing   ④ skating
⑤ snowboarding

W What are you going to do this winter?

M Nothing special, _____ that I will play a lot of sports.

W What sports are you going to play?

M Well, first of all, I'm going to go swimming every morning _____ _____ _____. I'll also take skating lessons in the afternoon during _____ _____ _____.

W Wow. That sounds like quite a lot.

M There's more. During every weekend, my family is going to go skiing.

W Will you go snowboarding, too?

M No, I _____ _____ that yet. I would like to try that and curling someday.

13 대화를 듣고, 여자가 지갑을 두고 온 자리로 가장 알맞은 것을 고르시오.

M Good morning, Jina. What are you doing?

W I'm looking for my wallet. I think I left it in a desk yesterday, but I don't remember _____ _____ _____.

M I remember you sat _____ _____ _____ in your last class.

W I checked the back seats, but I couldn't find it there.

M Wait. Didn't you move to _____ _____ _____ later?

W Oh you're right. Now I remember, I _____ _____ the front door. It's here. Thank you very much.

>> **WORDS** jar 통, 단지 first of all 우선 lesson 강습 wallet 지갑 front door 앞문

14 대화를 듣고, 상호가 방학 중에 한 일로 가장 적절한 것을 고르시오.

① 우유 많이 마시기
② 많이 먹기
③ 새 재킷 사기
④ 운동 많이 하기
⑤ 다이어트 하기

W Sangho, you grew very tall. What _____ to you during the vacation?
M I don't know. I didn't do anything special to _____ _____.
W Maybe you drank a lot of milk.
M Actually, I don't like milk, but _____ _____ _____ of it, I did eat a lot. I also _____ a lot of weight.
W Yeah, I guess you should buy a new jacket.
M Right. I _____ _____ _____ at least a little. I should go on a diet now.
W You don't have to. You look pretty good now.

15 다음을 듣고, 방송의 목적으로 가장 적절한 것을 고르시오.

① 학교 매점을 홍보하려고
② 보건실 위치를 안내하려고
③ 새 보건 교사를 소개하려고
④ 손 씻는 방법을 설명하려고
⑤ 바이러스 대응법을 안내하려고

W Hello, students! This is _____ _____ _____ Janet Brown. Recently, a scary virus has been _____ our health. Please wear masks all the time, and wash your hands as _____ _____ _____. You can buy masks, soap, and hand sanitizers at the school store. When you feel sick, please visit my office on the first floor. I hope nobody in this school _____ _____ _____ and everyone stays safe and healthy.

16 대화를 듣고, 남자가 지불할 금액을 고르시오.

① $29   ② $30   ③ $32
④ $40   ⑤ $43

M Excuse me. How much are this calendar and this sketchbook?
W The calendar is $10, and the sketchbook is $3.
M Then I'll buy two calendars and three sketchbooks.
W That will be $29. Do you need a bag to _____ _____ _____? It's $1.
M These look too heavy to carry. _____ _____ _____ have them delivered. Do you offer a delivery service?
W Yes. But you have to pay $3 if you purchase under $40.
M Okay. Then I'll pay $3 more and _____ _____ _____.

17 대화를 듣고, 여자의 마지막 말에 대한 남자의 응답으로 가장 적절한 것을 고르시오.

① I haven't seen it yet.
② I like cats better than dogs.
③ It was hard to get the tickets.
④ Your performance was the best.
⑤ I prefer the musical to the movie.

W Did you watch the musical *Cats*?
M Yes, I watched it twice. I like it very much. _____ _____ _____ really well.
W I know. I watched it too. They move just _____ _____. I really liked the songs, too.
M Then did you also watch the movie *Cats*?
W Well, _____ _____. Did you watch it?
M Yes, I watched it with my family last weekend.
W Then how did you like it _____ _____ the musical?

>> **WORDS**   **go on a diet** 다이어트 하다   **scary** 무서운   **sanitizer** 소독제   **have ~ delivered** ~을 배달시키다   **delivery** 배달
purchase 구입하다

18 대화를 듣고, 남자의 마지막 말에 대한 여자의 응답으로 가장 적절한 것을 고르시오.

① I've just turned it off.
② I want it. Give me a lot.
③ Where are the flashlights?
④ It's because people use a lot of electricity.
⑤ I can't help turning on the air conditioner.

M　Oh my god. It suddenly got so dark. What happened?
W　The lights are _____ _____. Let's look out the window.
M　The whole apartment complex is dark. I guess _____ _____ _____ _____.
W　You're right. What should we do now?
M　We have to finish dinner. I'll _____ _____ the candles.
W　Now I can see my food. But the candlelight is hot.
M　We can't turn on the air conditioner _____ _____. I can give you some ice instead if you want.

19 대화를 듣고, 여자의 마지막 말에 대한 남자의 응답으로 가장 적절한 것을 고르시오.

① I went there already.
② Oh, I shouldn't have.
③ They are looking forward to it.
④ I know nothing about martial arts.
⑤ Can I? That would be really great.

M　Have you been to China?
W　Yes. My grandparents live in China. I've been there many times.
M　I _____ you. I really want to travel to China.
W　Why? Do you like Chinese food?
M　No, I like Chinese _____ _____ _____. I saw the huge mountains of China in those movies. I want to see them _____.
W　You're right. I'll ask my grandparents to _____ me one more time. Do you want to go with me?

20 다음 상황 설명을 듣고, Anne이 Tom에게 할 말로 가장 적절한 것을 고르시오.

① How would I look with a perm?
② I'd like to have a hair cut.
③ I'm sorry, I'll visit you later.
④ A short hair won't look good on you.
⑤ Can you recommend a good hairstyle on me?

M　Tom is a hair designer. One day, Anne visited his hair shop to _____ _____ _____. She wanted to have her long hair _____ _____, so she asked Tom if she would look good with short hair. Tom answered that she _____ _____ _____ long hair. So, she changed her mind and wants to ask him if she should _____ _____ _____ _____. In this situation, what would Anne most likely say to Tom?

01 대화를 듣고, 여자가 구입할 쿠션을 고르시오.

02 대화를 듣고, 호텔에 관해 두 사람이 언급하지 <u>않은</u> 것을 고르시오.

① 가격　　　　② 위치
③ 냉방 시설　　④ 부대시설
⑤ 식사 제공 횟수

03 대화를 듣고, 여자가 남자에게 전화한 목적으로 가장 적절한 것을 고르시오.

① 설문 조사　　② 상품 안내
③ 기부금 요청　④ 기부 물품 독촉
⑤ 경품 당첨 안내

04 대화를 듣고, 회의를 하는 데 걸릴 시간을 고르시오.

① 10분　　② 15분　　③ 20분
④ 30분　　⑤ 45분

05 다음 그림의 상황에 가장 적절한 대화를 고르시오.

①　　　②　　　③　　　④　　　⑤

06 대화를 듣고, 두 사람이 대화하는 장소로 가장 적절한 곳을 고르시오.

① 예식장　　　　② 옷 가게
③ 수선 가게　　　④ 신발 가게
⑤ 기념품 상점

07 다음을 듣고, 그림에 대해 언급하지 <u>않은</u> 것을 고르시오.

① 제작 재료　　② 작가 이름
③ 작품의 크기　④ 제작 연도
⑤ 전시 장소

08 다음을 듣고, 무엇에 관한 설명인지 고르시오.

① 짐을 안전하게 보관하는 방법
② 기내용 가방 크기에 대한 제한
③ 위험한 액체류 사용에 대한 규제
④ 공항 보안 검색대의 수하물 확인 절차
⑤ 보안 검색대를 통과하는 액체류 소지 규정

09 다음을 듣고, 두 사람의 대화가 <u>어색한</u> 것을 고르시오.

①　　　②　　　③　　　④　　　⑤

10 대화를 듣고, 남자가 여자를 위해 할 일로 가장 적절한 것을 고르시오.

① 수업 추천하기
② 숙제 도와주기
③ 간식 사다 주기
④ 친구 소개해 주기
⑤ 스페인어 수업 등록해 주기

11 대화를 듣고, 남자가 여자에게 부탁한 일로 가장 적절한 것을 고르시오.

① 파일 인쇄하기
② 컴퓨터 고치기
③ 프로그램 설치하기
④ 노트북 컴퓨터 빌리기
⑤ 회의를 위한 파일 만들기

12 대화를 듣고, 두 사람이 시험을 치를 요일을 고르시오.

① Monday　② Tuesday　③ Wednesday
④ Thursday　⑤ Friday

13 다음 표를 보면서 대화를 듣고, 여자가 신청할 유학 프로그램을 고르시오.

	Program	Country	Schedule	Housing
①	A	U.S.	Jul. – Nov.	homestay
②	B	Canada	Feb. – Jun.	dormitory
③	C	Canada	Jul. – Nov.	homestay
④	D	England	Jul. – Nov.	dormitory
⑤	E	England	Feb. – Jun.	homestay

14 대화를 듣고, 두 사람이 대화 직후에 할 일로 가장 적절한 것을 고르시오.

① 회의하기　　　② 퇴근하기
③ 야식 먹기　　　④ 사무실 청소하기
⑤ 중국 음식 주문하기

15 다음을 듣고, 방송의 목적으로 가장 적절한 것을 고르시오.

① 주말 날씨를 예보하려고
② 축구 경기 규칙을 설명하려고
③ 경기가 취소된 이유를 알리려고
④ 학교의 방침에 문제를 제기하려고
⑤ 우천 시 행사 장소 변경을 공지하려고

16 대화를 듣고, 여자가 지불할 금액을 고르시오.

① $6　　　② $9　　　③ $11
④ $14　　　⑤ $15

17 대화를 듣고, 남자의 마지막 말에 대한 여자의 응답으로 가장 적절한 것을 고르시오.

Woman: _____

① Sure, the repairman will fix it today.
② Okay. I don't care how much it costs.
③ Right. We'll have to buy a new one.
④ That's all right. We didn't need it anyway.
⑤ I'd better call my parents right now.

18 대화를 듣고, 여자의 마지막 말에 대한 남자의 응답으로 가장 적절한 것을 고르시오.

Man: _____

① I'm just concerned about you.
② I already caught a cold from you.
③ Could you bring me a warm sweater?
④ I have a headache, so I'll see a doctor.
⑤ Here's the medicine you wanted.

19 대화를 듣고, 남자의 마지막 말에 대한 여자의 응답으로 가장 적절한 것을 고르시오.

Woman: _____

① Really? I'm a vegetarian as well.
② Why don't you try this delicious beef?
③ In fact, I don't know how to cook meat.
④ Yeah, I heard you were a vegetarian.
⑤ I'm sorry. I should have checked your taste.

20 다음 상황 설명을 듣고, Amy가 남자친구에게 할 말로 가장 적절한 것을 고르시오.

Amy: _____

① I really like Italian food.
② I hope you like the food I made for you.
③ Why don't we have Korean food this time?
④ Maybe we could eat it next time.
⑤ Sorry, but I don't feel like having Korean food tonight.

---

01 대화를 듣고, 여자가 구입할 쿠션을 고르시오.

① (하트 사각형) ② (점 사각형) ③ (점 하트)

④ (하트 원) ⑤ (검은 사각형)

M May I help you?

W Yes, I need to buy a cushion for my sofa.

M Which do you prefer, a round one or a _____ _____?

W I prefer the square one to the round one.

M Okay. Which do you like better, the one with _____ or the one with hearts?

W I like the one _____ _____ _____ better. I'll take it.

M Good. Here it is.

---

02 대화를 듣고, 호텔에 관해 두 사람이 언급하지 <u>않은</u> 것을 고르시오.

① 가격   ② 위치
③ 냉방 시설   ④ 부대시설
⑤ 식사 제공 횟수

W I got _____ _____ for our trip to Jejudo. If we buy a package tour, our hotel will only cost 200,000 won.

M That's for _____ _____ _____ at the hotel? Wow, where is it?

W It's in the town center, so it's not close to the beach. Here are some pictures.

M It seems fine, but a little old. It will probably have poor air conditioning.

W Don't worry. _____ _____ _____ said the air conditioner works well.

M Good. Well, is there a swimming pool?

W Yes. There are also a gym and a business center.

---

03 대화를 듣고, 여자가 남자에게 전화한 목적으로 가장 적절한 것을 고르시오.

① 설문 조사   ② 상품 안내
③ 기부금 요청   ④ 기부 물품 독촉
⑤ 경품 당첨 안내

[Telephone rings.]

M Hello.

W Mr. James? This is Kate from the Hope Society.

M Yes, I know about the Hope Society. I volunteered there last Christmas.

W Oh, I'm sure everyone at _____ _____ _____ your help.

M It was my pleasure.

W We are trying to help feed hungry children, and _____ _____ will be a great help to them.

M Hmm... I can't afford to make _____ _____ _____, but I guess I can give you $30.

W Oh, thank you.

» WORDS **prefer** 선호하다 **square** 사각형의 **round** 둥근 **dot** 점 **cost** ~의 비용을 부과하다 **town center** 중심가
close to ~에 가까운 **work** 작동하다 **gym** 체육관 **feed** ~에게 먹이다 **afford to** ~할 여유가 있다

04 대화를 듣고, 회의를 하는 데 걸릴 시간을
고르시오.

① 10분 ② 15분 ③ 20분
④ 30분 ⑤ 45분

M Is the schedule for the 2 o'clock meeting ready?

W Yes. What do you want to know?

M I just want to know _____ _____ it will take.

W Well, we're supposed to review the new policies for 10 minutes.

M We also _____ _____ _____ the holiday season project, right?

W Yes, that will take 20 minutes.

M Lisa prepared a 15-minute presentation, too.

W Actually, I asked her to give _____ _____ next week.

M Great. Then, it will be a short meeting.

05 다음 그림의 상황에 가장 적절한 대화를
고르시오.

① ② ③ ④ ⑤

① M What are you doing?

  W I'm drawing people in the park.

② M Where are you in the picture?

  W I'm the person in the middle. I _____ _____ have long hair.

③ M Is it okay to bring food in here?

  W No, you are _____ _____ _____ do that in the museum.

④ M Can I exchange it for a different color?

  W Sure. Do you have _____ _____?

⑤ M Excuse me! Can you take a picture of us?

  W Sure. Strike a pose!

06 대화를 듣고, 두 사람이 대화하는 장소로
가장 적절한 곳을 고르시오.

① 예식장   ② 옷 가게
③ 수선 가게   ④ 신발 가게
⑤ 기념품 상점

W Wow, it looks like everything is on sale!

M Well, not _____ _____. Only the women's items are on sale.

W Why don't we look around?

M Okay, _____ _____ _____ to.

W Hmm, I don't know what I should buy for my cousin's wedding. Look at these white heels. If I wear my green dress, these shoes will be perfect.

M They don't _____ _____ at all. How about the flat ones over there?

W I don't like those. But look at these cute summer sandals. And those boots are _____!

M Well, I think you should choose just one pair.

>> **WORDS** review 검토하다 presentation 발표 in the middle 가운데에 있는 strike a pose 포즈를 잡다 on sale 할인 중인 item 상품
look around 둘러보다 **heel** 굽이 있는 신발; 발꿈치 **flat** 납작한

07 다음을 듣고, 그림에 대해 언급하지 않은 것을 고르시오.

① 제작 재료   ② 작가 이름
③ 작품의 크기   ④ 제작 연도
⑤ 전시 장소

W   *The Starry Night* is an _____ _____ by the Dutch painter, Vincent van Gogh. It was painted in June, 1889, and it shows the view from the window of van Gogh's room just _____ _____. It has been in _____ _____ of the Museum of Modern Art in New York City since 1941. It is one of the most famous paintings in the history of Western culture.

08 다음을 듣고, 무엇에 관한 설명인지 고르시오.

① 짐을 안전하게 보관하는 방법
② 기내용 가방 크기에 대한 제한
③ 위험한 액체류 사용에 대한 규제
④ 공항 보안 검색대의 수하물 확인 절차
⑤ 보안 검색대를 통과하는 액체류 소지 규정

M   To all our passengers. You can help us keep _____ _____ _____ moving faster by following these rules. First, make sure that any liquids you're carrying are in bottles that are 100 ml or less in volume. Anything larger than that isn't allowed on the plane. Second, store all of your 100 ml containers in _____ _____ _____ plastic bag. This bag should _____ _____ _____ of your luggage and placed in the security bin to be _____ _____. Do not leave any liquids inside your luggage. Thank you for your cooperation.

09 다음을 듣고, 두 사람의 대화가 어색한 것을 고르시오.

①   ②   ③   ④   ⑤

① M   Could you drive me home?
　 W   _____ _____.
② M   Why don't we go out and watch a movie?
　 W   I wish I could, but I have an assignment to do.
③ M   How do you like your new school?
　 W   It _____ _____ _____ my expectation.
④ M   How come you're late for the interview?
　 W   I came here by taxi. I am ready for the interview.
⑤ M   Which color _____ _____ _____, purple or red?
　 W   Neither. I like green.

10 대화를 듣고, 남자가 여자를 위해 할 일로 가장 적절한 것을 고르시오.

① 수업 추천하기
② 숙제 도와주기
③ 간식 사다 주기
④ 친구 소개해 주기
⑤ 스페인어 수업 등록해 주기

M   Hi, Kate. Are you taking a language class here?
W   Yes, I _____ in basic Spanish. How about you, Kevin?
M   I'm in _____ _____ _____ now. How do you like it?
W   I enjoy learning Spanish. But I'm worried about one thing.
M   Oh, what's that?
W   We have a _____ _____ coming up, but I don't know any of my classmates.
M   Oh, my friend James is in that class, too. I _____ _____ _____ to him.
W   Thank you!

>> **WORDS**   **starry** 별이 빛나는   **Dutch** 네덜란드의   **western** 서양의   **make sure** ~을 반드시 하다   **liquid** 액체(류)   **volume** 부피
     store 저장하다   **container** 용기   **security bin** 보안 검색용 바구니   **cooperation** 협조   **assignment** 과제   **come up** 다가오다

11 대화를 듣고, 남자가 여자에게 부탁한 일로 가장 적절한 것을 고르시오.

① 파일 인쇄하기
② 컴퓨터 고치기
③ 프로그램 설치하기
④ 노트북 컴퓨터 빌리기
⑤ 회의를 위한 파일 만들기

M   What's wrong with my computer?

W   What happened?

M   I don't know. I tried to open this file, but this message _____ _____.

W   Let me see. [pause] Ah, that's because your computer can't open that type of file.

M   What should I do?

W   You _____ _____ _____ a program first.

M   Oh, I don't have that much time. I need to print it for a meeting in five minutes!

W   I think my computer can open it. I can _____ _____ _____ if you send me the file.

M   That's great! Could you just print _____ _____?

W   Sure. Here is my USB drive.

12 대화를 듣고, 두 사람이 시험을 치를 요일을 고르시오.

① Monday   ② Tuesday
③ Wednesday   ④ Thursday
⑤ Friday

M   Irene, are you studying _____ _____ _____ on Thursday? It's already Monday.

W   Didn't you know? This Thursday we don't have any exams.

M   Really? How come?

W   It's our school's _____ _____.

M   Oh, I forgot. Then, does it mean that I have _____ _____ _____ to study?

W   You're right.

M   Wow! How lucky!

13 다음 표를 보면서 대화를 듣고, 여자가 신청할 유학 프로그램을 고르시오.

	Program	Country	Schedule	Housing
①	A	U.S.	Jul. – Nov.	homestay
②	B	Canada	Feb. – Jun.	dormitory
③	C	Canada	Jul. – Nov.	homestay
④	D	England	Jul. – Nov.	dormitory
⑤	E	England	Feb. – Jun.	homestay

M   Look at this! Erica, _____ _____ will you sign up for?

W   I've already been to the U.S., so I want to try another country.

M   When are you planning to leave?

W   I'm going to finish my first year here in June, so I'd like to leave _____ _____ _____.

M   I see.

W   But I can't decide _____ _____ _____ to do a program with a homestay or with a dormitory.

M   With a homestay, you would have _____ _____ _____ _____ to speak English.

W   That's true. I guess I know what I'm going to do.

>> WORDS   **How come ~?** 어째서 ~인가?   **lucky** 운이 좋은   **sign up for** ~에 등록하다   **homestay** 가정 체류   **dormitory** 기숙사

14 대화를 듣고, 두 사람이 대화 직후에 할 일로 가장 적절한 것을 고르시오.

① 회의하기
② 퇴근하기
③ 야식 먹기
④ 사무실 청소하기
⑤ 중국 음식 주문하기

M Hey, aren't you hungry?

W Yes, it's _____ _____. When did you eat dinner?

M I had Chinese food at five.

W I see. We still have a lot of work to do. So _____ _____ _____ go out and eat something?

M Sure. What would you like to eat?

W How about doughnuts and coffee? There is an Uncle Doughnuts near here.

M Great! _____ _____ _____ now.

15 다음을 듣고, 방송의 목적으로 가장 적절한 것을 고르시오.

① 주말 날씨를 예보하려고
② 축구 경기 규칙을 설명하려고
③ 경기가 취소된 이유를 알리려고
④ 학교의 방침에 문제를 제기하려고
⑤ 우천 시 행사 장소 변경을 공지하려고

W Good morning, students. I know many of you feel disappointed because _____ _____ _____ the football game last Saturday. I've received many emails asking me to explain why this decision was made. The reason was the weather. The Weather Service had issued _____ _____ _____ warning. This meant that there was a chance of dangerous lightning in the area. I'll let you know when the game is _____. Thank you for your understanding.

16 대화를 듣고, 여자가 지불할 금액을 고르시오.

① $6 ② $9 ③ $11
④ $14 ⑤ $15

W Hello. I really like these tulips. How much are they?

M They're one dollar each, or six dollars for seven.

W Hmm. How about _____ _____ _____?

M They're also a dollar each. But a dozen only costs nine _____.

W Okay. And what about these lilies?

M They're a little cheaper. I can give you a dozen for five dollars.

W Great. Then I'd like seven tulips and a _____ _____.

M Okay.

17 대화를 듣고, 남자의 마지막 말에 대한 여자의 응답으로 가장 적절한 것을 고르시오.

① Sure, the repairman will fix it today.
② Okay. I don't care how much it costs.
③ Right. We'll have to buy a new one.
④ That's all right. We didn't need it anyway.
⑤ I'd better call my parents right now.

W Has the repairman fixed the heater yet?

M Unfortunately, he said it _____ _____ _____.

W What? But he said he could fix it last week.

M The heater company was unable to _____ _____ _____ because it is an old model.

W That's terrible news! We don't have enough money.

M I know. What should we do?

W I think my parents have one they're not using right now.

M Oh, great! We could use that heater until we buy a new one.

>> **WORDS**   **disappointed** 실망한   **decision** 결정   **issue** 발표하다   **chance** 가능성   **lightning** 번개   **dozen** 12개의 묶음   **lily** 백합
　　　　　　repairman 수리공   **terrible** 끔찍한, 안 좋은

18 대화를 듣고, 여자의 마지막 말에 대한 남자의 응답으로 가장 적절한 것을 고르시오.

① I'm just concerned about you.
② I already caught a cold from you.
③ Could you bring me a warm sweater?
④ I have a headache, so I'll see a doctor.
⑤ Here's the medicine you wanted.

M Lisa, why are you wearing winter clothes? It's not that cold out today.
W Really? I feel a little cold.
M Hmm…. You _____ _____. You might be getting sick.
W No. I didn't sleep well last night. That's all.
M Are you sure? You look like _____ _____ _____ _____, too. Let me check.
W I'm okay, Tommy. It's just because of lack of sleep.
M It might be more than you think. You _____ _____ the signs your body is sending to you.
W All right, all right. Why do you _____ _____ me?

19 대화를 듣고, 남자의 마지막 말에 대한 여자의 응답으로 가장 적절한 것을 고르시오.

① Really? I'm a vegetarian as well.
② Why don't you try this delicious beef?
③ In fact, I don't know how to cook meat.
④ Yeah, I heard you were a vegetarian.
⑤ I'm sorry. I should have checked your taste.

M Thanks for inviting me, Suji.
W Welcome to my house, Andy! We've _____ _____ _____ you. I cooked roast beef. I'm sure you'll like it.
M Hmm…. It looks good, but is there anything else?
W We also have some meatballs. I made them myself this morning. _____ _____.
M I'm sorry. But actually, I'm a vegetarian. I don't eat meat.
W Oh my! I didn't know that. I didn't make anything without meat except for the _____ _____.
M Don't worry about it. I'll just have some soup.

20 다음 상황 설명을 듣고, Amy가 남자친구에게 할 말로 가장 적절한 것을 고르시오.

① I really like Italian food.
② I hope you like the food I made for you.
③ Why don't we have Korean food this time?
④ Maybe we could eat it next time.
⑤ Sorry, but I don't feel like having Korean food tonight.

M Amy and her boyfriend watched a movie at the theater. Afterwards, they were hungry, so they decided to _____ _____ to eat at a nice restaurant. Amy's boyfriend suggested an Italian restaurant because he knows that Amy likes pasta and pizza. But they go to an Italian restaurant _____ _____ _____ _____. So Amy wants to have _____ _____ today. She is in the mood for Korean food. However, she is not sure if her boyfriend likes Korean food. In this situation, what would Amy most likely say to her boyfriend?

>> WORDS **lack of sleep** 수면 부족 **be concerned about** ~에 관해 걱정하다 **medicine** 약, 약물 **vegetarian** 채식주의자 **meat** 육류
afterwards 그 후에, 나중에 **in the mood for** ~할 생각인

01 대화를 듣고, 여자가 구입할 지갑을 고르시오.

02 대화를 듣고, 베트남 여행에 관해 언급되지 <u>않은</u> 것을 고르시오.

① 해변   ② 음식   ③ 교통수단
④ 숙소   ⑤ 물가

03 대화를 듣고, 남자가 여자에게 전화한 목적으로 가장 적절한 것을 고르시오.

① 음식을 주문하려고   ② 주문을 취소하려고
③ 주소를 확인하려고   ④ 주문을 추가하려고
⑤ 주문을 독촉하려고

04 대화를 듣고, 두 사람이 대화하는 장소로 가장 적절한 곳을 고르시오.

① 주차장   ② 기차역
③ 자동차 대여점   ④ 자동차 판매점
⑤ 자동차 정비소

05 다음 그림의 상황에 가장 적절한 대화를 고르시오.

①   ②   ③   ④   ⑤

06 대화를 듣고, 남자가 여자에게 부탁한 일로 가장 적절한 것을 고르시오.

① 아침에 깨워 주기
② 샌드위치 만들어 주기
③ 학교에 태워다 주기
④ 저녁식사 준비해 주기
⑤ 샤워 수건 가져다주기

07 다음은 십 대들의 고민을 나타낸 도표이다. 도표의 내용과 일치하지 <u>않는</u> 것을 고르시오.

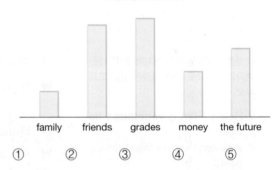

08 다음을 듣고, 기금 마련 행사에 대해 언급되지 <u>않은</u> 것을 고르시오.

① 날짜   ② 장소   ③ 프로그램
④ 출연자   ⑤ 입장료

09 다음을 듣고, 무엇에 관한 설명인지 고르시오.

① 귀마개   ② 목도리   ③ 털장갑
④ 털모자   ⑤ 털부츠

10 대화를 듣고, 남자가 주말에 한 일로 가장 적절한 것을 고르시오.

① 책 읽기
② 외갓집 방문하기
③ 양로원 청소하기
④ 도서관에서 자원봉사 하기
⑤ 어르신들 산책 도와 드리기

11 다음을 듣고, 두 사람의 대화가 <u>어색한</u> 것을 고르시오.

① ② ③ ④ ⑤

12 다음 극장 좌석 배치를 보고, 두 사람이 선택할 구역을 고르시오.

SCREEN			
① A			④ D
② B		③ C	⑤ E
			EXIT

13 대화를 듣고, 두 사람의 부모님의 결혼기념일을 고르시오.

① 11월 11일   ② 11월 12일
③ 11월 13일   ④ 11월 29일
⑤ 11월 30일

14 대화를 듣고, 남자가 대화 직후에 할 일로 가장 적절한 것을 고르시오.

① 교실 청소하기
② 영어 수업 참여하기
③ 아이스크림 만들기
④ 친구에게 전화 걸기
⑤ 아이스크림 가게 가기

15 다음을 듣고, 방송의 목적으로 가장 적절한 것을 고르시오.

① 탑승 시작을 알리려고
② 경유지 변경을 알리려고
③ 탑승 게이트를 안내하려고
④ 탑승하지 않은 고객을 찾으려고
⑤ 새로운 출발 시간을 알리려고

16 대화를 듣고, 남자가 지불할 금액을 고르시오.

① $ 35   ② $ 40   ③ $ 45
④ $ 50   ⑤ $ 55

17 대화를 듣고, 여자의 마지막 말에 대한 남자의 응답으로 가장 적절한 것을 고르시오.

Man: _____

① Will you try it on?
② How much is it?
③ I'd like this backpack.
④ Can I get a discount?
⑤ I can change it for you.

18 대화를 듣고, 여자의 마지막 말에 대한 남자의 응답으로 가장 적절한 것을 고르시오.

Man: _____

① Can I come at 3?
② I have a terrible toothache.
③ We're closed on Thursday.
④ He is a famous dentist.
⑤ Let's go to the convenience store.

19 대화를 듣고, 남자의 마지막 말에 대한 여자의 응답으로 가장 적절한 것을 고르시오.

Woman: _____

① I learn English through movies.
② English is my favorite subject.
③ In fact, I want to be a interpreter.
④ I've been speaking English for about eight years.
⑤ I can teach you how to give a speech in English.

20 다음 상황 설명을 듣고, 민수가 지수에게 할 말로 가장 적절한 것을 고르시오.

Minsu: _____

① How often do you exercise?
② Too much workout isn't good for your health.
③ I think you are pretty enough.
④ I'll treat you to dinner tonight.
⑤ Why don't you eat something and exercise?

01 대화를 듣고, 여자가 구입할 지갑을 고르시오.

① ② ③ ④ ⑤

M How can I help you?

W I'm _____ _____ a wallet. Where are they?

M They are in the corner over there.

W I can see only long ones. Do you have shorter ones, too? I want _____ _____ _____ in my bag.

M The short ones are on the shelf right next to you.

W Oh, there are many cute wallets. I like this black one with white dots.

M OK. _____ _____ _____ at the counter.

02 대화를 듣고, 베트남 여행에 관해 언급되지 않은 것을 고르시오.

① 해변 ② 음식 ③ 교통수단
④ 숙소 ⑤ 물가

M Jina, how was your trip to Vietnam?

W It was fantastic. The beach was so beautiful and the sand was very soft.

M How was the food? Did you eat Vietnamese _____ _____?

W Of course I did. I loved it, but my parents didn't like it because of the smell.

M I see. How did you get around there? Did you take a taxi?

W I was thinking of _____ _____ _____, but I couldn't. There were so many motorcycles on the street. I usually took a taxi.

M Sounds like you had a wonderful time there. I want to go there some day.

W You should. _____ _____ are very _____ and the people are nice. I'm already planning my next visit to Vietnam.

03 대화를 듣고, 남자가 여자에게 전화한 목적으로 가장 적절한 것을 고르시오.

① 음식을 주문하려고
② 주문을 취소하려고
③ 주소를 확인하려고
④ 주문을 추가하려고
⑤ 주문을 독촉하려고

[Telephone rings.]

W Uncle Jim's Hamburger Store. How may I help you?

M Hello. This is Brian Milan. I ordered two hamburgers just before.

W Yeah. You ordered a cheeseburger and a chicken burger. Is it right?

M That's right. Is it _____ _____ _____ the order? Something popped up.

W I'm so sorry. But we already _____ _____.

M Okay. Then please _____ _____ _____ as I ordered.

W It will take about 15 minutes. Is it okay?

M No problem. Thank you.

>> **WORDS** **over there** 저쪽에 **shelf** 선반 **wallet** 지갑 **dot** 점 **order** 주문하다; 주문 **pop up** 갑자기 일어나다

04 대화를 듣고, 두 사람이 대화하는 장소로 가장 적절한 곳을 고르시오.

① 주차장　　　② 기차역
③ 자동차 대여점　④ 자동차 판매점
⑤ 자동차 정비소

M　What seems to be the problem with your car?

W　The steering wheel _____ _____ _____ _____.

M　Oh, I see. Is there any other problem?

W　And sometimes it makes a noise when I start the engine.

M　Umm... I think I should take _____ _____ _____ of the car.

W　_____ _____ will it take?

M　It will take more than three hours.

W　Then, I'll come back tomorrow morning.

M　OK.

05 다음 그림의 상황에 가장 적절한 대화를 고르시오.

①　②　③　④　⑤

① W　Can you help me move this box?
　 M　Of course I can.
② W　I'd like to send this package _____ _____.
　 M　OK. Place it on the scale.
③ W　How much is it all together?
　 M　It's 10,000 won.
④ W　Will you _____ _____ _____ or by credit card?
　 M　I'll pay in cash.
⑤ W　Can you _____ _____ _____?
　 M　I'm afraid I can't.

06 대화를 듣고, 남자가 여자에게 부탁한 일로 가장 적절한 것을 고르시오.

① 아침에 깨워 주기
② 샌드위치 만들어 주기
③ 학교에 태워다 주기
④ 저녁식사 준비해 주기
⑤ 샤워 수건 가져다주기

M　Oh, no! It's already 7:30! I'm going to be late.

W　I tried to wake you up, but you kept sleeping. So, _____ _____ me.

M　No, I won't. I'll take _____ _____ _____ and leave for school.

W　Aren't you hungry? You skipped dinner yesterday.

M　Actually, _____ _____. But I don't have time for breakfast.

W　That's too bad.

M　Mom. Can you make a sandwich while I'm taking a shower? I think I _____ _____ _____ on my way to school.

W　OK, I can do that.

M　I love you, Mom.

>> **WORDS**　**steering wheel** 핸들　**scale** 저울　**in cash** 현금으로　**leave for** ~을 향해 떠나다　**skip** ~을 거르다

07 다음은 십 대들의 고민을 나타낸 도표이다. 도표의 내용과 일치하지 <u>않는</u> 것을 고르시오.

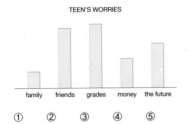

TEEN'S WORRIES

family friends grades money the future
①   ②   ③   ④   ⑤

① M Teens' _____ _____ is their grades.
② M Friends are the second biggest worry for teens.
③ M There are more teens who worry about their future than _____ _____ _____ their friends.
④ M The fourth top ranked problem for teens is money.
⑤ M There are _____ _____ _____ have family problems than those who have money problems.

08 다음을 듣고, 기금 마련 행사에 대해 언급되지 않은 것을 고르시오.

① 날짜   ② 장소   ③ 프로그램
④ 출연자   ⑤ 입장료

W Hello, I'm Park Mina, the president of the student council. Our school is holding a _____ _____ for people in need. It will _____ _____ in the Community Center, on Saturday, May 9th. For the event, we are planning _____ _____ _____, food booths, and a concert. There's no entrance fee for the flea market and food booths, but you need to pay ten dollars for the concert. The profits from this event will _____ _____ _____. Thank you.

09 다음을 듣고, 무엇에 관한 설명인지 고르시오.

① 귀마개   ② 목도리   ③ 털장갑
④ 털모자   ⑤ 털부츠

M These are one of _____ _____ _____ winter accessories. These are a pair of small pieces of material like fur with a strap that goes over the head. Little children wear these items _____ _____ _____ _____. But these days, we can see women wearing these for their fashion. With these items, we can _____ _____ _____ from the cold.

10 대화를 듣고, 남자가 주말에 한 일로 가장 적절한 것을 고르시오.

① 책 읽기
② 외갓집 방문하기
③ 양로원 청소하기
④ 도서관에서 자원봉사 하기
⑤ 어르신들 산책 도와 드리기

M What did you do during the weekend?
W Nothing special. I just read books at home. What about you?
M I did _____ _____.
W Where did you go?
M I went to _____ _____ _____.
W You went there before. Did you clean their room this time, too?
M No, this time I talked with the elderly people and _____ _____ _____ in the garden.
W How was it?
M It was very rewarding. They looked happy.

>> **WORDS** **grade** 성적, 학점 **rank** 순위를 차지하다 **student council** 학생회 **entrance fee** 입장료 **flea market** 벼룩시장 **profit** 수익금
accessory 액세서리 **fur** 털 **strap** 띠 **cold** 추위 **elderly** 나이가 있는 **rewarding** 보람 있는

11 다음을 듣고, 두 사람의 대화가 **어색한** 것을 고르시오.

① ② ③ ④ ⑤

① W How have you been?

M I've _____ _____ there.

② W You have a long face. What's wrong?

M My pet dog is very sick.

③ W How often do you eat out?

M About once a month.

④ W Do you have _____ _____ _____ our talent show?

M How about dancing together?

⑤ W How do you go to school?

M I _____ _____ _____.

12 다음 극장 좌석 배치를 보고, 두 사람이 선택할 구역을 고르시오.

SCREEN			
① A			④ D
② B		③ C	⑤ E
			EXIT

W Let's choose where to sit in the theater.

M I usually sit in the middle of _____ _____ _____ _____.

W Is there any reason?

M I can enjoy _____ _____ _____ there.

W But it's difficult to get out of the seat if we sit there. I have to visit the restroom _____ _____ _____ while the movie is showing.

M Then let's sit on the back seat of the corner. I can still enjoy the full screen there.

W Thanks. _____ _____ do you _____? Right or left?

M I prefer the right one near the exit.

13 대화를 듣고, 두 사람의 부모님의 결혼 기념일을 고르시오.

① 11월 11일　② 11월 12일
③ 11월 13일　④ 11월 29일
⑤ 11월 30일

M You know what? Our parents' _____ _____ is coming.

W You're right. It's on November 30th.

M Yeah. What shall we do for them? Last year, we bought some flowers and a bottle of wine for them.

W Yeah, they loved our present. I remember. Oh, wait! What's _____ _____ _____?

M It's November 12th. Why?

W Oh my god! Their anniversary is tomorrow.

M Oh, you're right. It is November 13th, not 30th.

W We _____ _____ _____. Let's think about what to do for them.

>> WORDS　**talent show** 장기 자랑　**in the middle of** ~의 가운데에　**reason** 이유　**exit** 출구　**anniversary** 기념일

14 대화를 듣고, 남자가 대화 직후에 할 일로 가장 적절한 것을 고르시오.

① 교실 청소하기
② 영어 수업 참여하기
③ 아이스크림 만들기
④ 친구에게 전화 걸기
⑤ 아이스크림 가게 가기

W What took you so long, Jake? Did the class finish late?
M No, the English class finished on time. But _____ _____ on my way home.
W What is it?
M My cellphone _____. I looked for it everywhere, but I couldn't find it. So I couldn't contact you, either.
W I see. Where did you look for it?
M I went back to the street again. And I searched the classroom, too.
W Didn't you _____ _____ _____ on your way home?
M Oh, I stopped at the ice cream store! I didn't think about it.
W Maybe you dropped your phone there. Let's _____ _____ _____ together.
M Okay. Thanks, Mom.

15 다음을 듣고, 방송의 목적으로 가장 적절한 것을 고르시오.

① 탑승 시작을 알리려고
② 경유지 변경을 알리려고
③ 탑승 게이트를 안내하려고
④ 탑승하지 않은 고객을 찾으려고
⑤ 새로운 출발 시간을 알리려고

W This is _____ _____ for _____ on flight 123 to Helsinki, with a stop in Istanbul. The flight has been delayed _____ _____ _____ _____ conditions. The flight crew has arrived at the gate, but the ground crew is still de-icing the wings of the aircraft in preparation for departure. Our _____ _____ _____ is 10:50 a.m. Thank you for your patience.

16 대화를 듣고, 남자가 지불할 금액을 고르시오.

① $ 35   ② $ 40   ③ $ 45
④ $ 50   ⑤ $ 55

M Excuse me, I want to buy those postcards.
W They're 5 dollars per box.
M Five dollars? How many cards are there in the box?
W _____ _____ _____ 10 different cards. And if you buy more than 10 boxes, you can get a ten percent discount.
M Hmm ... If I buy ten boxes, _____ _____ _____ to 50 dollars. Then I can get a ten percent discount on it. Am I right?
W Yeah. You're right.
M Then it's a _____ _____. I'll take ten boxes.
W Thanks a lot.

>> **WORDS** **on time** 제시간에 **contact** 연락하다 **search** 수색하다 **stop** 정거, 착륙 **delay** 지연시키다 **flight crew** 비행 승무원
de-icing 제빙 작업 **in preparation for** ~의 준비로 **departure** 출발 **patience** 참을성, 인내력 **get a discount** 할인을 받다

17 대화를 듣고, 여자의 마지막 말에 대한 남자의 응답으로 가장 적절한 것을 고르시오.

① Will you try it on?
② How much is it?
③ I'd like this backpack.
④ Can I get a discount?
⑤ I can change it for you.

W How may I help you?
M I want _____ _____ _____ _____ _____. Is it possible?
W Let me see. It's our product. Do you have _____ _____?
M No, I don't. Actually, I got it as a gift.
W I'm afraid we can't _____ _____ _____ _____ if you don't have the receipt.
M I see. Then, can I _____ it for something else?
W Of course you can. What you do want to exchange it for?

18 대화를 듣고, 여자의 마지막 말에 대한 남자의 응답으로 가장 적절한 것을 고르시오.

① Can I come at 3?
② I have a terrible toothache.
③ We're closed on Thursday.
④ He is a famous dentist.
⑤ Let's go to the convenience store.

[Telephone rings.]
W Doctor Lee's dental clinic. What can I do for you?
M Hello. I _____ _____ _____ for this Wednesday, but I want to change it.
W OK. Can I have your name?
M It's John Brown.
W Yes, you're _____ _____ _____ the doctor at 2 p.m. this Wednesday. How do you want to change it?
M I have _____ _____ _____ on that day. Can I come on Thursday _____?
W Sure. What time is convenient for you?

19 대화를 듣고, 남자의 마지막 말에 대한 여자의 응답으로 가장 적절한 것을 고르시오.

① I learn English through movies.
② English is my favorite subject.
③ In fact, I want to be a interpreter.
④ I've been speaking English for about eight years.
⑤ I can teach you how to give a speech in English.

M Mina, that was _____ _____ _____. I didn't know you were so good at English.
W Thanks. I was very nervous, but at least I didn't forget my lines.
M You _____ _____ _____ hard.
W Yes, I've been practicing for this speech contest for more than two months.
M I'm sure you will _____ _____ _____ _____. By the way, how come your pronunciation is so perfect? How long have you been speaking English?

20 다음 상황 설명을 듣고, 민수가 지수에게 할 말로 가장 적절한 것을 고르시오.

① How often do you exercise?
② Too much workout isn't good for your health.
③ I think you are pretty enough.
④ I'll treat you to dinner tonight.
⑤ Why don't you eat something and exercise?

M Minsu's friend Jisu thinks she is too fat. She decided to _____ _____ _____ and stopped eating. She looks pale and _____ _____ _____. Minsu is worried that Jisu is _____ _____ _____. He thinks it is much better to have a good diet and do some exercise than to go hungry. In this situation, what would Minsu most likely say to his friend, Jisu?

>> **WORDS** **product** 제품 **gift** 선물 **receipt** 영수증 **exchange** 교환하다 **dental clinic** 치과 **nervous** 긴장한 **at least** 최소한 **line** 대사 **practice** 연습하다 **speech** 연설 **pronunciation** 발음 **diet** 식단

05회 » 듣기 실전 모의고사

01 대화를 듣고, 남자가 만든 컵을 고르시오.

02 대화를 듣고, 운동화에 관해 언급되지 <u>않은</u> 것을 고르시오.

① 용도　　② 무게　　③ 사이즈
④ 색상　　⑤ 가격

03 대화를 듣고, 남자가 여자에게 전화한 목적으로 가장 적절한 것을 고르시오.

① 커피를 주문하려고
② 파일 전송을 부탁하려고
③ 문서 출력을 부탁하려고
④ 컴퓨터 수리를 부탁하려고
⑤ 보고서 작성을 부탁하려고

04 대화를 듣고, 두 사람이 대화하는 장소로 가장 적절한 곳을 고르시오.

① 병원　　② 약국　　③ 미용실
④ 가발 가게　　⑤ 모자 가게

05 다음 그림의 상황에 가장 적절한 대화를 고르시오.

①　　②　　③　　④　　⑤

06 대화를 듣고, 남자가 여자에게 부탁한 일로 가장 적절한 것을 고르시오.

① 책 빌려주기　　② 교실 청소하기
③ 도서관 문 잠그기　　④ 교실 창문 닫기
⑤ 우산 빌려주기

07 다음을 듣고, 여자가 축제에 대해 언급하지 <u>않은</u> 것을 고르시오.

① 날짜　　② 장소
③ 시작 시간　　④ 행사 내용
⑤ 종료 시간

08 대화를 듣고, 영화에 대해 언급되지 <u>않은</u> 것을 고르시오.

① 감독　　② 수상 여부
③ 소재　　④ 출연 배우
⑤ 상영 시간

09 다음을 듣고, 무엇에 관한 설명인지 고르시오.

① air　　② water　　③ earth
④ food　　⑤ house

10 대화를 듣고, 남자가 대화 직후에 할 일로 가장 적절한 것을 고르시오.

① 카드 사 오기
② 음식 준비하기
③ 탁자 세팅 하기
④ 거실 장식하기
⑤ 할머니 모셔 오기

11 다음을 듣고, 두 사람의 대화가 <u>어색한</u> 것을 고르시오.

①   ②   ③   ④   ⑤

12 다음 영화 상영표를 보고, 두 사람이 볼 영화를 고르시오.

	Title	Time	Type
①	*Spiderman*	11:00 ~ 13:00	3D
②	*My Pet*	11:00 ~ 13:00	2D
③	*Spiderman*	14:00 ~ 16:00	2D
④	*My Pet*	14:00 ~ 16:00	3D
⑤	*Spiderman*	16:00 ~ 18:00	3D

13 대화를 듣고, 두 사람이 만날 시각을 고르시오.

① 5시 45분   ② 6시   ③ 6시 15분
④ 6시 30분   ⑤ 7시

14 대화를 듣고, 여자가 어제 한 일로 가장 적절한 것을 고르시오.

① 산책하기
② 병원 가기
③ 얼음 얼리기
④ 친구 병문안 가기
⑤ 강아지 산책시키기

15 다음을 듣고, 방송의 목적으로 가장 적절한 것을 고르시오.

① 쇼핑센터의 개장을 안내하려고
② 쇼핑센터를 층별로 안내하려고
③ 쇼핑센터 내 미아를 찾으려고
④ 쇼핑센터의 폐점 시간을 알리려고
⑤ 재고 정리 세일에 대해 안내하려고

16 대화를 듣고, 남자가 지불할 금액을 고르시오.

① $12   ② $13   ③ $14
④ $15   ⑤ $16

17 대화를 듣고, 여자의 마지막 말에 대한 남자의 응답으로 가장 적절한 것을 고르시오.

Man: _____

① It was on sale.
② I can fix it for you.
③ I bought it last Saturday.
④ You can find it on our website.
⑤ I'll pick up some paper for you.

18 대화를 듣고, 남자의 마지막 말에 대한 여자의 응답으로 가장 적절한 것을 고르시오.

Woman: _____

① I prefer math to history.
② History is my favorite subject.
③ Can you teach me how to do it?
④ The history test is one week later.
⑤ Try to understand the flow of history.

19 대화를 듣고, 여자의 마지막 말에 대한 남자의 응답으로 가장 적절한 것을 고르시오.

Man: _____

① It's next to the park.
② The parking fee is 5,000 won.
③ I had to pay the penalty for it.
④ It's in the second basement level.
⑤ You can take the car elevator over there.

20 다음 상황 설명을 듣고, 미라가 남자에게 할 말로 가장 적절한 것을 고르시오.

Mira: _____

① Let's set the date.
② Is your leg hurt?
③ Can I sit next to you?
④ Would you please call me later?
⑤ I'm sorry, but you're distracting me.

01 대화를 듣고, 남자가 만든 컵을 고르시오.

① ② ③ ④ ⑤

W Wow! There are so many cups! Where did they come from?

M My classmates and I made them in our art class.

W That's amazing. Where's yours?

M Why don't you find it yourself?

W Umm. You're _____ _____ _____. So maybe that one with the stars?

M That was close. But mine is that one with the moon and the stars.

W Oh, there's _____ _____.

M No, I don't _____ _____ _____. Actually, I made it to use as a pen holder.

02 대화를 듣고, 운동화에 관해 언급되지 않은 것을 고르시오.

① 용도 ② 무게 ③ 사이즈
④ 색상 ⑤ 가격

W How may I help you?

M I'm looking for a pair of sneakers.

W Are they for you?

M Yes, I'm going _____ _____ them when I _____ _____ at the gym.

W What's your size?

M I wear a size ten.

W Would you try these on? They're _____ _____.

M These are very light. How much are they?

W They're _____ _____ now. They are 40 dollars now.

M That's a good price. I'll take them.

03 대화를 듣고, 남자가 여자에게 전화한 목적으로 가장 적절한 것을 고르시오.

① 커피를 주문하려고
② 파일 전송을 부탁하려고
③ 문서 출력을 부탁하려고
④ 컴퓨터 수리를 부탁하려고
⑤ 보고서 작성을 부탁하려고

[Telephone rings.]

M Hello, honey. It's me. Are you busy now?

W No, I'm not. I was just having _____ _____ _____. What's up?

M I left an important file on my computer. Can you send it to me?

W Ok. Please wait. I'm _____ on the computer. Where did you _____ it?

M It's in my document file folder. And the name is Annual Report 2019.

W I found it. Do you _____ _____ _____ _____ it to your email?

M Yes. Thanks.

》 WORDS **amazing** 놀라운 **pen holder** 연필꽂이 **sneakers** 운동화 **try on** 착용해 보다 **light** 가벼운 **document** 문서 **annual** 연간의

04 대화를 듣고, 두 사람이 대화하는 장소로 가장 적절한 곳을 고르시오.

① 병원　　② 약국
③ 미용실　　④ 가발 가게
⑤ 모자 가게

M　How would you like your hair done?
W　I want it trimmed a little and _____ _____.
M　Oh, I see. But before the perm, I strongly _____ _____ some nutrition to your hair. Your hair is very dry now.
W　Okay. And is it possible to change the hair color, too?
M　It would be better to _____ _____ _____ later. Having the two procedures at the same time _____ _____ your hair.
W　Then I'll follow your advice. I don't want my hair damaged.
M　All right. I'll wash your hair first. Follow me this way.

05 다음 그림의 상황에 가장 적절한 대화를 고르시오.

①　②　③　④　⑤

① W　How do you usually go to school?
　 M　I take the bus.
② W　I can't find my transportation card.
　 M　But you're _____ _____ now.
③ W　Does this bus go to the City Hall?
　 M　I'm _____ _____. Take the green bus.
④ W　Here comes the bus.
　 M　Let's _____ _____ it!
⑤ W　How long does it take to get there by bus?
　 M　It takes only ten minutes.

06 대화를 듣고, 남자가 여자에게 부탁한 일로 가장 적절한 것을 고르시오.

① 책 빌려주기
② 교실 청소하기
③ 도서관 문 잠그기
④ 교실 창문 닫기
⑤ 우산 빌려주기

[Cellphone rings.]
M　Mina, it's me, Minsu. Are you still at school?
W　Yes, I'm reading a book in the library.
M　Can I _____ _____ _____ _____?
W　Tell me. What is it?
M　I left the classroom last, but I'm _____ _____ _____ I closed the windows.
W　But you can close them tomorrow morning.
M　It's going to rain tonight, so the windows should be closed.
W　Oh, I see. Then, I will go to the classroom and make sure the windows _____ _____ before I go home. Don't worry.
M　Thanks a lot, Mina.

>> WORDS　trim 다듬다, 잘라 내다　**perm** 파마　**nutrition** 영양　**dry** 건조한　**procedure** 시술　**damage** 해를 끼치다
transportation 교통　**city hall** 시청

07 다음을 듣고, 여자가 축제에 대해 언급하지 <u>않은</u> 것을 고르시오.

① 날짜　　　② 장소
③ 시작 시간　　④ 행사 내용
⑤ 종료 시간

W Hello, everyone. This is your student leader Lee Yuna. I'm happy to tell you about _____ _____ _____. It is going to be held next Friday, November 6th. It will begin at 4 p.m., so please come to _____ _____ by 3:40. There will be _____ _____ by the school band and the dance group. Also, there will be a prize lottery with various kinds of gifts. Don't miss this exciting event!

08 대화를 듣고, 영화에 대해 언급되지 <u>않은</u> 것을 고르시오.

① 감독　　　② 수상 여부
③ 소재　　　④ 출연 배우
⑤ 상영 시간

W Did you see the famous movie _____ _____ Mr. Bong?
M Are you talking about the movie that won the best movie award last week?
W That's right.
M Unfortunately, I didn't see the movie yet. What's it about?
W It's about _____ _____ _____ the rich and the poor.
M Oh, I see. Is it long?
W Kind of. _____ _____ _____ is about 130 minutes. But it's _____ _____ at all.
M I think I should watch it.

09 다음을 듣고, 무엇에 관한 설명인지 고르시오.

① air　　② water　　③ earth
④ food　　⑤ house

M This is everywhere _____ _____ to the human _____. Without this, no living thing can _____ _____ _____. In the past, people didn't really care about the quality of this. These days, however, people are _____ _____ _____ the quality of this. There are applications to show the quality of this, and there are home appliances to purify this. What is this?

10 대화를 듣고, 남자가 대화 직후에 할 일로 가장 적절한 것을 고르시오.

① 카드 사 오기
② 음식 준비하기
③ 탁자 세팅 하기
④ 거실 장식하기
⑤ 할머니 모셔 오기

M Mom, I think we're all set for the welcome home party for grandma.
W Great! She will be very surprised to see all of this.
M You know, _____ _____ _____ in the hospital for about a month. I really want to make her happy.
W Right. She will be very moved. The food is ready and we decorated the living room and the table.
M Oh, we _____ _____ _____ the card.
W You're right. Do we have a card at home?
M I don't think so. I will go to _____ _____ _____ and buy one. We still have some time.
W Okay. But please hurry.

>> WORDS　**hold** 개최하다　**prize lottery** 경품 추첨　**award** 상　**yet** 아직　**past** 과거　**quality** 품질　**application** 응용 프로그램
home appliances 가전제품　**purify** 정화하다　**set** 준비가 된　**moved** 감동한　**decorate** 장식하다

11 다음을 듣고, 두 사람의 대화가 <u>어색한</u> 것을 고르시오.

① ② ③ ④ ⑤

① **W** Do you _____ _____ I open the windows?

  M Please don't. There's yellow dust today.

② **W** _____ _____ will you be arriving from the trip?

  M I'll be arriving at around 5 p.m.

③ **W** Can I bring Susan to your birthday party?

  M Why not? _____ _____, _____ _____.

④ **W** Did you watch the soccer game yesterday?

  M I missed it because of an important meeting.

⑤ **W** Have you _____ _____ _____ Spain?

  M Yes, I went there five years ago.

12 다음 영화 상영표를 보고, 두 사람이 볼 영화를 고르시오.

	Title	Time	Type
①	Spiderman	11:00 ~ 13:00	3D
②	My Pet	11:00 ~ 13:00	2D
③	Spiderman	14:00 ~ 16:00	2D
④	My Pet	14:00 ~ 16:00	3D
⑤	Spiderman	16:00 ~ 18:00	3D

W We have two movies showing now. One is *My Pet* and the other is *Spiderman*. _____ _____ _____ _____?

M I don't like animation movies. Let's watch *Spiderman*.

W _____ _____ _____ for me. Shall we watch the 2 o'clock movie?

M But it's 2D. I want to watch the 3D movie. It's a little expensive, but _____ _____ _____.

W I've never watched a 3D movie. We still have two options.

M Let's watch the movie in the afternoon. How about meeting 30 minutes earlier in front of the theater?

W Okay.

13 대화를 듣고, 두 사람이 만날 시각을 고르시오.

① 5시 45분 ② 6시
③ 6시 15분 ④ 6시 30분
⑤ 7시

M Do you have any idea about our team project for science class? I think we should get started.

W You're right. Can we talk about this now?

M Sorry. I have to leave now. I have _____ _____ _____.

W When does it finish?

M It starts at five and finishes at six.

W Hmm. _____ _____ _____ then. What about talking about the project over some snacks?

M Okay.

W Then, let's meet in front of the swimming pool.

M Good. Please give me fifteen more minutes to take a shower and change clothes.

W All right. _____ _____ _____ six then.

>> WORDS **yellow dust** 황사 **miss** 놓치다 **showing** 상영 중인 **option** 선택권 **get started** 시작하다

14 대화를 듣고, 여자가 어제 한 일로 가장 적절한 것을 고르시오.

① 산책하기
② 병원 가기
③ 얼음 얼리기
④ 친구 병문안 가기
⑤ 강아지 산책시키기

M Jisu, you don't look well. Is anything wrong?

W Actually, I _____ _____ _____ while taking a walk yesterday.

M Did you go see a doctor?

W No, I thought it was not _____ _____ _____. So, I just put ice on it.

M Can I see it? *[pause]* Oh, it's swollen. I think you really need to go see a doctor.

W You're right. It _____ _____ now.

15 다음을 듣고, 방송의 목적으로 가장 적절한 것을 고르시오.

① 쇼핑센터의 개장을 안내하려고
② 쇼핑센터를 층별로 안내하려고
③ 쇼핑센터 내 미아를 찾으려고
④ 쇼핑센터의 폐점 시간을 알리려고
⑤ 재고 정리 세일에 대해 안내하려고.

W Hello, shoppers. May I have your attention, please? We would like to _____ _____ _____ about a special offer. We will be having _____ _____ _____ starting from tomorrow to next Monday. We will have _____ _____ of up to 70% on some of the selected merchandise in our company. The products _____ _____ clothing to accessories. For more information, please visit our website, www.bestgoods.com. We hope you will enjoy your shopping. Thank you.

16 대화를 듣고, 남자가 지불할 금액을 고르시오.

① $12 ② $13 ③ $14
④ $15 ⑤ $16

M Excuse me, I want to buy some fruits.

W How about some apples? They're very fresh.

M How much are they?

W Two dollars for each one. But if you buy a bag of six apples, _____ _____ ten dollars.

M Then I'll take a bag. And how much are those oranges? They look delicious.

W They are very _____ _____ _____. Only one dollar for each one. How many do you want?

M I'd like five oranges.

W One bag of apples and five oranges. _____ _____ _____.

M Thank you.

>> **WORDS** see a doctor 진찰 받다 swollen 부은 shopper 쇼핑객 offer 할인; 제안 up to ~까지 selected 엄선된
merchandise 상품 fresh 신선한

17 대화를 듣고, 여자의 마지막 말에 대한 남자의 응답으로 가장 적절한 것을 고르시오.

① It was on sale.
② I can fix it for you.
③ I bought it last Saturday.
④ You can find it on our website.
⑤ I'll pick up some paper for you.

M It's Ace Electronics service center. May I help you?
W I _____ _____ _____ from your online store last week, but there's a problem.
M What's the problem?
W The paper is constantly getting jammed.
M I'm so sorry _____ _____ _____. If you fill out the service form, we will pick it up and repair it.
W Where can I _____ _____ _____?

18 대화를 듣고, 남자의 마지막 말에 대한 여자의 응답으로 가장 적절한 것을 고르시오.

① I prefer math to history.
② History is my favorite subject.
③ Can you teach me how to do it?
④ The history test is one week later.
⑤ Try to understand the flow of history.

W How was your test today?
M I did pretty well on math, but I _____ _____ the history test.
W I'm sorry to hear that. You studied hard for the history test.
M That's what I'm saying. Maybe there's _____ _____ with my study methods.
W Tell me. How do you study history?
M I just _____ _____ _____ all the important information.
W Umm... I don't think that's a good way to study history.
M Then how should I study?

19 대화를 듣고, 여자의 마지막 말에 대한 남자의 응답으로 가장 적절한 것을 고르시오.

① It's next to the park.
② The parking fee is 5,000 won.
③ I had to pay the penalty for it.
④ It's in the second basement level.
⑤ You can take the car elevator over there.

M Excuse me, ma'am. You _____ _____ _____.
W Why is that? It's empty.
M Look at the sign. It's for _____ _____.
W Oh, I'm so sorry. I didn't see that. Is there anywhere to park around here?
M _____ _____ _____ is full now, but there is some space in the underground parking lot.
W Thank you. How can I get down to the underground parking lot?

20 다음 상황 설명을 듣고, 미라가 남자에게 할 말로 가장 적절한 것을 고르시오.

① Let's set the date.
② Is your leg hurt?
③ Can I sit next to you?
④ Would you please call me later?
⑤ I'm sorry, but you're distracting me.

W Mira is studying at the library. The final exam is tomorrow and the library _____ _____ _____ students. Soon, a boy comes and sits right next to her. He starts to _____ _____ _____. Mira tries to ignore it and _____ _____ her studies. But his shaking doesn't stop. To make it worse, now he starts to tap his pen. Finally, Mira _____ _____ _____ him to stop distracting her concentration. In this situation, what would Mira most likely say to the boy?

>> **WORDS** constantly 지속적으로 jammed 걸린 fill out (양식에) 기입하다 method 방법 empty 비어 있는 underground 지하의
parking lot 주차장 ignore 무시하다 tap 톡톡 두드리다 distract 분산시키다 concentration 집중(력)

Memo

중학 영어의 모든 것

VISANG

all
that

중학 영어 3-2

Answers

visang

우리는 남다른 상상과 혁신으로
교육 문화의 새로운 전형을 만들어
모든 이의 행복한 경험과 성장에 기여한다

ABOVE IMAGINATION

우리는 남다른 상상과 혁신으로
교육 문화의 새로운 전형을 만들어
모든 이의 행복한 경험과 성장에 기여한다

PART I 실력 다지기

Lesson 01 비교 구문

▶▶ Grammar Practice   pp. 12~15

Ⓐ1 (1) fast (2) not as (3) as

Ⓐ2 (1) doesn't, as (2) less, than (3) as, tall

Ⓑ1 (1) more carefully than (2) less expensive
  (3) even more, than (4) senior to

Ⓑ2 (1) better (2) bigger (3) much(even, a lot, still, far)
  (4) to

Ⓒ1 (1) other material, other, than
  (2) the most, of, Nothing, more
  (3) No other, hot, any other, all, months

Ⓓ1 (1) could (2) twice (3) possible (4) three times as

Ⓓ2 (1) possible(I could) (2) three times
  (3) twice heavier (4) twice as

Ⓔ1 (1) The higher, the more (2) no more (3) least
  (4) smaller, smaller

Ⓔ2 (1) not more (2) no less (3) better, better (4) less

Ⓕ1 (1) boy, boys (2) more, the most
  (3) happier, happiest
  (4) I ever saw, I've ever seen

Ⓕ2 (1) the strongest man that I've ever met
  (2) one of the most famous

▶▶ Grammar Test   pp. 16~17

01 ①   02 ③   03 no more than the alphabet
04 math is much easier   05 ④   06 as long as,
longer than, longer than any other bridge   07 ②
08 ①   09 three times   10 ③   11 The more, the
more   12 ①   13 (1) taller than (2) less heavy than

01 〈as+원급+as〉의 형태로 빈칸에는 원급이 와야 한다.
02 '시간이 갈수록 일 때문에 점점 더 바빠진다'의 의미가 되도록
  〈비교급+and+비교급〉의 형태를 쓰므로 busier가 알맞다.
03 '겨우(only)'의 의미로 no more than을 쓴다.
04 비교급을 강조할 때는 비교급 앞에 much, even, a lot,
  still, far 등을 쓴다.

05 ④ 〈one of the+최상급+복수 명사〉이므로 city를 cities
  로 고쳐야 한다.
06 최상급은 〈부정 주어 ~ as(so)+원급+as〉, 〈부정 주어 ~
  비교급+than〉, 〈비교급+than any other+단수 명사〉로
  바꿔 쓸 수 있다.
07 ② 외출했다가 귀가한 아들에게 '적어도(최소한) 30초 이상
  손을 씻어라'라고 하는 말이 되도록 not less than이 쓰인
  문장으로 완성하는 것이 알맞다.
08 〈not as(so)+원급+as〉는 〈less+원급+than〉과 바꿔 쓸
  수 있다.
09 엄마가 여동생보다 세 배 더 무거우므로 〈배수사+비교급+
  than〉을 활용하여 '~보다 …배 더 ~한(하게)'의 의미를 완
  성한다.
10 ③ 최상급의 의미가 되려면 〈부정 주어+as(so)+원급+as〉
  로 써야 하므로 not 없이 써야 한다.
11 '~하면 할수록 점점 더 …하다'의 의미는 〈The+비교급 ~,
  the+비교급 …〉으로 나타낸다.
12 ① 〈as+원급+as+주어+can(could)〉이므로 비교급
  louder를 원급의 부사 loud로 고쳐야 한다.
13 (1) Lisa는 Kate보다 키가 크기 때문에 〈비교급+than〉 구
  문을 이용한다. (2) Kate는 Lisa보다 몸무게가 덜 나가므로
  〈less+비교급+than〉을 이용한다.

▶▶ Reading   pp. 18~19

1 ④   2 The more people get   3 ②   4 ④

[1~2]

우리가 사는 것을 구매하는 이유
  여러분은 여러분이 원하거나 필요로 하지조차 않는 것을
여러분이 구매하는 이유를 궁금해한 적이 있습니까? 물건을
사는 것에 있어서 무엇이 우리에게 영향을 끼치는지 생각해
봅시다.

나는 왜 내 친구가 산 것을 사고 싶은가?
  Jeff는 쇼핑센터에 가서 진열된 축구화 한 켤레를 본다. 그
는 그 신발을 한눈에 알아보는데, 그 이유는 그의 축구팀에
있는 남자아이들의 반 이상이 그것을 착용하기 때문이다. 그
는 이미 여러 켤레의 축구화를 가지고 있지만, 그는 새로운
축구화 한 켤레를 결국 사고 만다. 우리는 Jeff의 행동을 설명
하기 위해 '악대차 효과'를 쓸 수 있다. 악대차는 사람들이 올
라타고 음악을 즐기도록 독려하는, 퍼레이드에 쓰는 차이다.
더 많은 사람들이 악대차에 탈수록 다른 이들은 그것을 타거
나 따라갈 가능성이 더 크다. 이런 식으로, 사람들은 다른 사
람들이 그것을 샀다는 이유만으로 뭔가를 사는 경향이 있다.

1 ⓓ: Jeff가 가지고 있는 축구화 ⓐ, ⓑ, ⓒ, ⓔ: Jeff의 축구부원들이 많이 신어서 Jeff가 쇼핑센터에서 한눈에 알아보고 새로 사게 된 축구화

2 (A)의 주절이 the more likely로 시작하는 문장으로 바뀐 것으로 보아, 종속절(As more and more people ~)을 〈the + 비교급 + 주어 + 동사〉 형태로 바꿔 써서 비교급 구문인 〈the + 비교급 + 주어 + 동사, the + 비교급 + 주어 + 동사〉 형태로 문장을 완성하는 것이 알맞다.

3
> 지구 위로 떠다니는 수백만 개의 쓰레기가 있다. 그들 대부분은 콩보다 크지 않다. 하지만, 어느 덩어리는 다른 것보다 훨씬 더 크다. 그 중에 Vespa라고 불리는 쓰레기 조각이 있다. 그것은 한때 로켓의 일부분이었는데 무게가 약 100킬로그램에 달한다. 그것은 현재 활동 중인 인공위성이나 우주선에게는 위험스럽다. 유럽 우주 기구는 그것을 없애기 위해 프로젝트를 곧 시작할 것이다. 그들은 수집용 우주선을 발사할 계획인데, 그것은 우주에 떠다니는 Vespa를 잡을 것이다. 수집선이 Vespa와 함께 지구로 돌아오면, 그 둘은 지구의 대기 중에서 불타게 될 것이다.

② Vespa는 다른 것보다 큰 덩어리인 우주 쓰레기라고 했다.

4
> 여러분의 몸은 체온을 가능한 한 섭씨 37도에 가깝게 유지하기 위해 항상 노력하고 있다.
> (C) 그러나, 체온이 섭씨 29.5도보다 낮아지거나 섭씨 40도보다 더 높아지면 그것은 여러분의 건강을 위협하게 되고 응급 상황이 될 수 있다. 적절한 체온을 유지하기 위해, 여러분의 몸은 다양한 방식으로 반응한다. (A) 예를 들어, 여러분이 춥다고 느끼면, 여러분은 떨기 시작한다. 그것은 여러분의 몸이 근육을 빠르게 수축하고 이완시킴으로써 열을 발생시키기 때문이다. (B) 반면에 여러분이 덥다고 느끼면, 여러분은 땀을 흘리기 시작한다. 땀은 대부분 물인데, 땀 속의 물이 증발하면서 몸은 식게 된다.

주어진 문장에서 신체는 체온을 섭씨 37도에 가깝게 유지하려 한다는 서술에 이어 (C) 체온이 지나치게 낮거나 높은 경우 위험하므로 몸이 반응하게 된다는 것을 말한 후에, (A) 그 예로 추울 때 떠는 경우와 (B) 더울 때 땀을 흘리는 경우를 예시와 대조의 구조로 제시하고 있다.

>> **Expression Test** p. 21

1 ③　　**2** be discouraged　　**3** ③　　**4** ④　　**5** ③
6 ⓓ → ⓑ → ⓒ → ⓐ

1 I prefer ~.(나는 ~을 더 좋아해.)라는 B의 대답으로 보아 A의 말은 빨간 차와 녹색 차 중 선호하는 것을 묻는 표현인 Which do you prefer, ~?를 이용하여 완성하는 것이 알맞다.

2 A가 시험을 망쳤다고 했으므로 B의 말로는 '실망하지 마.'의 의미로 상대방을 위로할 때 쓰는 표현인 Don't be discouraged.를 쓰는 것이 알맞다.

3 ③은 '고의가 아니었어.'라는 변명하는 표현이고, 나머지는 모두 안심시키거나 격려하는 표현이다.

4 '나는 B보다 A를 더 좋아해.'라는 뜻으로 선호하는 것을 표현할 때 I prefer A to B. / I like A better than B. 등으로 말한다.

5 A가 B에게 왜 시무룩해 있는지 물었고 B는 엄마가 입원해 있다고 답하는 것으로 보아, 빈칸에는 걱정을 나타내는 표현인 I'm concerned(anxious, worried) about ~.이 빈칸에 알맞다.

6 무슨 일이야? 걱정이 있어 보여. – ⓓ 나는 내 성적이 걱정스러워. 나는 시험에 대비해서 충분히 공부하지 못했어. – ⓑ 너는 공부할 수 있는 한 주가 온전히 있었잖아. – ⓒ 너는 나를 알잖아. 마지막 순간에서야 비로소 시작하는 거. – ⓐ 네가 시험을 망쳐도 너 자신 외에는 누구도 탓할 사람이 없어.

>> **서술형 평가** p. 22

1 (1) Which do you prefer?　(2) I'm worried about that.
2 (1) more　(2) greatest　(3) more interesting, other
3 (1) as beautiful as　(2) No, smarter than　(3) the saddest story　**4** (1) the more　(2) shorter, the less
5 (1) older than　(2) much(even, a lot, far, still) older
(3) the tallest　(4) much(even, a lot, far, still) taller

1 (1) 선호에 대해 물을 때 which do you prefer?의 표현을 사용한다. (2) 걱정하는 표현을 할 때는 I'm worried about ....을 쓴다.

2 (1) many의 비교급은 more (2) 〈one of + 최상급〉은 '가장 ~한 것들 중 하나'라는 의미로 최상급의 의미이다. (3) 〈비교급 + than any other + 단수 명사〉는 '다른 ~보다 가장 …한'의 의미로 최상급의 의미를 가진다.

3 (1) 'A는 B만큼 ~하다'라는 원급 비교이다. (2) 〈부정 어 ~ 비교급 + than〉은 '누구도 ~보다 더 …하지 않은'의 의미로 최상급의 의미이다. (3) '지금까지 ~한 것들 중에서 가장 …한'은 〈the + 최상급(+ that) + 주어 + have ever + 과거분사〉로 나타낸다.

4 〈the 비교급＋주어＋동사, the 비교급＋주어＋동사〉는 '~할수록, 더욱 …하다'의 의미를 가진다.

5 (1) 〈비교급＋than＋비교 대상〉의 형태로 두 대상을 비교한다. (2), (4) much, even, a lot 등은 비교급 앞에서 '훨씬'의 뜻으로 쓰인다. (3) '(셋 이상) ~중에서 가장 …하다'라고 표현할 때는 〈the＋최상급＋(명사)＋of/in ~〉의 형태를 쓴다.

▶▶ Final Test
pp. 23~27

01 ④　**02** (1) ⓑ (2) ⓓ　**03** ②　**04** ④　**05** ②　**06** ④
07 I prefer going to the movies to going to the mountains.　**08** ④　**09** ②　**10** ①　**11** ③　**12** ④
13 ①　**14** The older, the more confident　**15** ④
16 and　**17** ①　**18** three times more (money)
19 ②, ④　**20** ①　**21** (1) time → times (2) my → mine 〔my bicycle〕　**22** No, old as, older than, women
23 ①　**24** the most interesting book that I have ever read　**25** ②　**26** 새장의 구조가 (책의) 무거운 무게를 지탱할 수 있다는 것　**27** ③　**28** ①　**29** ③　**30** ⑤

01 ①, ②, ③, ⑤는 반의어 관계이고, ④는 서로 무관한 단어이다.

02 (1) 할 수 있는 힘 또는 상황: 능력(ability) (2) 사람들이 어떤 것을 건널 수 있도록 그 위에 지어진 구조물: 다리(bridge)

03 • 기술은 우주에 가는 것을 <u>가능하게</u> 했다.
• <u>가능한 한</u> 깨끗하게 네 손을 씻어라.

04 ④는 걱정하는 표현이고, 나머지는 안심시키거나 격려하는 표현이다.

05 자신의 능력에 대해 낙담하고 비관하는 말에 대한 답변이므로 ② Don't be positive.는 안심시키는 표현인 Be positive로 쓰는 것이 알맞다.

06 영화보다 뮤지컬을 더 좋아한다는 대답으로 보아 빈칸에는 더 선호하는 것을 묻는 질문이 알맞다. ④는 영화와 뮤지컬에 대한 의견을 묻는 표현이므로 알맞지 않다.

07 prefer to를 활용해 to 앞에 더 선호하는 대상을 써서 문장을 완성한다.

08 뒤에 비교급 faster가 있으므로 비교급을 강조하는 부사인 still이 알맞다. very는 원급 강조에 쓰인다.

09 쓰는 것보다 더 적은 칼로리를 섭취해야 살이 빠지게 된다는 내용이다. 빈칸에는 '더 적은'의 의미로 few의 비교급 fewer가 알맞다.

10 as ~ as 사이에는 형용사, 부사의 원급을 쓰는데, 동사 draws를 수식하므로 부사 well을 쓴다.

11 '가능한 한 …한'은 〈as＋원급＋as＋possible〔주어＋can/

could〕〉을 써서 나타낸다. 현재 시제이므로 I could는 알맞지 않다.

12 Sally는 Sam보다 20분 더 일찍 도착했으므로 early의 비교급 earlier가 빈칸에 알맞다.

13 ①은 '미란이가 다른 소녀들만큼 참을성 있다'라는 동등한 비교의 의미이고, 나머지는 '미란이가 이 학교에서 가장 참을성 있다'라는 최상급의 의미이다.

14 〈The＋비교급 ~, the＋비교급 …〉은 '~하면 할수록 점점 더 …하다'의 의미를 나타낸다.

15 ④ 〈one of the＋최상급＋복수 명사〉로 most는 the most가 되어야 한다.

16 ⓐ 점점 더 …한: 〈비교급＋and＋비교급〉 ⓑ 단어의 비교급이 〈more＋원급〉이면 〈비교급＋and＋비교급〉 대신 〈more and more＋원급〉으로 쓴다.

17 ① Andrew가 Jane보다 키가 작으므로 표의 내용과 일치하지 않는다.

18 Joe가 Kevin보다 세 배 더 많은 돈을 소비하므로 〈배수사＋비교급＋than〉으로 표현할 수 있다.

19 〈보기〉의 문장이 최상급이므로 ② 〈비교급＋than any other＋단수 명사〉: 다른 어느 ~보다 더 …한 ④ 〈부정 주어 ~ as＋원급＋as〉를 이용하여 최상급을 나타낼 수 있다.

20 비교급 강조 표현으로는 much, even, far still, a lot 등이 있다. ① very는 원급을 강조하는 표현이다.

21 원급을 이용한 배수 표현은 〈배수사＋as＋원급＋as〉로 써야 한다. '두 배'는 two times〔twice〕이고, 비교 대상이 그녀의 자전거와 내 자전거이므로 my는 mine 또는 my bicycle로 써야 한다.

22 〈the＋최상급〉 = 〈부정 주어 ~ as＋원급＋as〉 = 〈비교급＋than all the other＋복수 명사〉

23 주어진 문장은 'Lois가 단어를 200개나 외웠다'의 의미이므로 as many as를 no less than으로 바꿔 쓸 수 있다.

24 '지금까지 ~한 것들 중에서 가장 …한'은 〈the＋최상급＋that＋주어＋have ever＋과거분사〉의 표현을 사용한다.

25
> 가게 밖에 서 있는 한 소년을 가리키며, 가게 주인은 그의 손님에게 말한다. "저 아이만큼 어리석은 사람은 없어요. 이것 보세요." 가게 주인은 1달러짜리 지폐와 5달러짜리 지폐를 꺼내어 그 소년이 어느 것을 원하는지 그에게 묻는다. 그는 1달러짜리 지폐를 가진다. 그 손님은 나중에 그 소년에게 "너는 왜 5달러짜리 지폐를 가지지 않았니?"라고 묻는다. 소년은 "내가 5달러짜리 지폐를 선택하는 그 날, 게임은 끝나기 때문이에요. 1달러가 아닌 5달러를 선택하면 그는 내가 다시 이곳에 서지 못하게 할 테니까요."라고 답한다.

소년은 가게 주인으로부터 공짜 돈을 계속 받기 위해 5달러짜리가 아닌, 1달러짜리 지폐를 받아온 것이므로 가게 주인보다 더 지혜롭다고 할 수 있다.

26
　　Home Insurance Company는 William LeBaron Jenney에게 다른 건물들보다 더 크고 더 안전한 건물을 지어 달라고 요청했다. 어느 날, Jenney는 그의 아내가 작은 새장 위에 무거운 책을 올려놓은 것을 보고, 그 새장이 그 무게를 지탱할 수 있다는 것을 알았다. 그 발견에서 영감을 얻어서, Jenney는 Home Insurance Building의 강철 구조를 디자인 했다. 1885년에 지어진 이 건물은 골조에 강철을 사용한 최초의 건물이며, 세계 최초의 초고층 건물들 중 하나로 여겨진다.

새장이 무거운 책의 무게를 지탱할 수 있다는 것을 발견한 후 그 점에 착안하여 건물을 디자인했다.

[27~28]
　　크리스마스 전에, 온라인 쇼핑은 어느 때보다 더 인기가 많다. 이는 배달원들에게 가장 중요한 때이다. 그러나 1월 2일의 배달 또한 크리스마스의 그것만큼이나 엄청나다. (그것은 사람들이 원하지 않는 물건을 반품하거나 교환하기 때문이다.) 그래서 그 날은 반품의 날이라고 불리기까지 한다. 배달 서비스는 그날 수백만 개의 물건들을 다루어야 한다. 반품은 사업가와 쇼핑객 모두에게 많은 비용을 지불하게 하므로 그들은 지혜롭게 팔고 사는 방법을 찾을 필요가 있다.

27 ③ 주어진 문장의 내용(그것은 사람들이 원치 않는 물건들을 반품하거나 교환하기 때문이다.)으로 보아, 앞에는 그 결과에 해당하는 '1월 2일의 배달도 크리스마스만큼이나 엄청나다'가 와야 한다. 이런 이유로 '그날(1월 2일)이 반품의 날로 불린다'라는 말이 주어진 문장 뒤에 이어지는 것이 자연스럽다.

28 ⓐ 다음에 than이 있으므로 popular의 비교급인 more popular를 쓰고, ⓑ 앞뒤에 원급 비교를 나타내는 as ~ as 가 있으므로 원급인 huge가 적절하다.

[29~30]
　　얼음으로 연주하는 것이 가능할까? 얼음 음악 콘서트가 북 스웨덴에서 열린다. 모든 악기는 얼음으로 만들어졌고, 콘서트장 안의 온도는 약 섭씨 영하 5도이다. 관객들은 매우 따뜻한 옷과 모자, 그리고 장갑까지 껴야 한다. 얼음 악기는 어느 악기들보다 더 날카로운 소리를 만들어낸다. 그리고 그 소리는 악기가 연주됨에 따라 더 크고 더 듣기 좋아진다. 그것은 얼음 악기가 진동을 흡수하기는 하지만, 나무로 만든 악기보다는 많이 흡수하지 않기 때문이다.

29 얼음으로 만든 악기로 연주되는 음악 콘서트를 소개하는 내용이므로 ③이 적절하다.

30 (A) 다음에 than이 있으므로 비교급인 sharper, (B) 〈become + 비교급〉은 '더 ~하게 되다'의 의미이며 and 다음에 비교급 sweeter가 있으므로 louder, (C) 앞뒤에 원급 비교를 나타내는 as ~ as가 있으므로 원급인 much가 적절하다.

Part I 실력 다지기

Lesson 02　분사, 분사구문

▶▶ Grammar Practice
pp. 32~35

A1 (1) fixing (2) running (3) stolen (4) given (5) taught

A2 (1) sleeping (2) used (3) rolling (4) broken
(5) taken

B1 (1) saw him dancing (2) that standing cat
(3) the novel written by me
(4) I like running shoes

B2 (1) falling rocks (2) wounded soldiers
(3) a letter written in English
(4) The boy reading a book

C1 (1) satisfied (2) exciting (3) tired

C2 (1) interested (2) satisfied (3) disappointing
(4) shocked

D1 (1) Getting (2) Having walked
(3) Not(Never) having

D2 (1) Sam being absent (2) Having lost the key
(3) Not having learned to swim

E1 (1) ⓓ (2) ⓔ (3) ⓒ (4) ⓑ (5) ⓐ

E2 (1) If (2) Because (3) Though(Although) (4) with

F1 (1) It raining (2) Judging (3) Frankly

F2 (1) Not having enough money
(2) There being no food (3) Frankly speaking

▶▶ Grammar Test
pp. 36~37

01 (1) playing (2) broken (3) standing **02** Though
(Although) he gets **03** (1) Coming (2) Not having
04 ① **05** closed **06** ③ **07** Generally speaking
08 ② **09** ③ **10** ② **11** (1) Seeing a police officer, she ran away. (2) It being rainy tomorrow, I think the picnic will be canceled. **12** ④ **13** (1) Considering her age, she looks very old. (2) Frankly speaking, I'm not interested in him.

01 (1), (3) 분사와 그 수식하는 명사의 관계가 능동, 진행의 의미이면 현재분사를 쓴다. (2) 수동의 의미이면 과거분사를 쓴다.

02 분사구문의 의미상 양보를 나타내는 접속사 Though(Although)를 써야 한다.

03 (1) 부사절과 주절의 주어와 시제가 같으므로 접속사와 주어를 생략하고 동사 came을 〈동사원형+ing〉 형태인 Coming으로 바꾼다. (2) 부사절과 주절의 시제가 같으며 부정의 의미를 나타내야 하므로 현재분사 앞에 Not을 쓴다.

04 주어가 감정을 유발하는 주체이므로 현재분사로 고쳐야 한다.

05 〈with+명사+분사〉의 형태에서 명사와 분사의 관계가 '감긴'이라는 수동의 의미가 되어야 하므로 closed로 써야 한다.

06 ③ that boy가 휴대 전화를 사용하는 중이라는 진행의 의미이므로 현재분사로 쓰는 것이 알맞다. (→ using)

07 '일반적으로 말해서'는 비인칭 독립분사구문의 관용적 표현인 Generally speaking으로 표현한다.

08 ② my watch가 수리의 대상이 되는 수동의 의미이므로 과거분사가 알맞다. (→ repaired)

09 분사구문이 되는 부사절의 시제와 주절의 시제가 같으므로 be동사는 현재분사 Being으로 쓴다.

10 완료분사구문이므로 부사절로 바꿔 쓸 때 부사절의 동사는 주절의 동사의 시제보다 앞선 시제인 과거 시제로 써야 한다.

11 (1) 주절과 부사절의 시제가 같으므로 Seeing으로 시작하는 분사구문으로 완성한다. (2) 부사절의 주어가 주절의 주어와 다르므로 부사절의 주어 it은 분사구문에서 생략하지 않는다.

12 두 문장 모두 분사구문의 시제가 주절의 시제보다 이전의 일이므로 완료분사구문 〈having+과거분사〉를 쓴다. 부정을 나타낼 때는 having 앞에 not을 쓴다.

13 '~을 고려해 보면'과 '솔직히 말해서'는 각각 비인칭 독립분사구문 Considering과 Frankly speaking을 써서 표현한다.

▶▶ Reading

pp. 38~39

1 seeing me in the village　**2** ⑤　**3** ③　**4** ①

[1~2]

나의 아버지의 비밀 (I)
　1920년대에, 사람들이 동네에서 나를 봤을 때, 그들은 "파락호의 딸이 간다."라고 말하곤 했다. 나의 아버지, 김용환은 매우 부유한 가문의 아들이었으나, 그는 항상 도박장에 있었다. 그것이 그가 파락호라고 불렸던 이유인데, 그것은 그 가족의 재산을 탕진한 사람을 의미한다.

　내가 16살이었을 때, 나의 가족은 이미 내가 서씨와 결혼하도록 약속을 했었다. 결혼 풍습에 따라 서씨 가문은 나의 가족에게 새 옷장을 살 약간의 돈을 보냈다.
　결혼식 날 직전에 나의 엄마는 내 방으로 들어오셔서 말씀하셨다. "네 아버지가 옷장 살 돈을 가져갔다. 우리는 선택의 여지가 없어. 너는 네 이모의 오래된 옷장을 가져가야겠구나."
　"가족들은 얼마나 속상할까,"라고 사람들은 내 뒤에서 속삭이곤 했다. 결혼 첫날 이후로 시댁에서의 삶은 내게 힘들었다.

1 부사절의 주어(people)와 주절의 주어(they)가 같으므로 부사절의 접속사(when)와 주어(people)를 삭제하고, 동사를 현재분사 seeing으로 쓴다.

2 ⓔ 결혼 전에 시댁으로부터 받은 옷장 살 돈을 도박꾼인 아버지가 가져갔으므로 사람들이 가족들의 심정에 관해 할 말로는 delightful(기분 좋은)이 아닌 embarrassing(당황스러운, 참담한)이 알맞다.

3

　나의 아버지와 나는 집으로 운전을 해서 가는 중이었는데, 갑자기 어느 트럭이 우리 바로 앞으로 뛰어들었다. 아버지는 브레이크를 밟으며, 가까스로 그 트럭을 피했다. 그 운전수는 우리에게 소리 지르기 시작했다. 그러나 아버지는 그 남자에게 손을 흔들며 그냥 웃었다. "아버지, 이건 아버지 잘못이 아니잖아요. 아버지는 왜 그렇게 하셨어요?" 아버지가 대답하셨다. "어느 사람들은 분노와 실망으로 가득한 쓰레기 차 같단다. 그들의 쓰레기가 쌓이면, 그들은 그것을 너에게 쏟아부을 수도 있어. 그런 일이 일어났을 때, 그것을 기분 나쁘게 생각하지 말고, 그냥 웃고, 손을 흔들며, 그들이 잘 되기를 기원해 주어라. 그들의 쓰레기를 받아서 그들에게 돌려주지 마라. 그건 그들에게 상처만 줄 뿐이야."

마지막 말에서 아버지는 남들이 자신의 기분을 상하게 할지라도, 그들과 맞붙어 싸우지 말고 그들이 잘 되기를 기원해 주라고 했다.

4

　뒷걸음질 하는 행동의 효과를 보여 주는 재미있는 실험이 있다. 세 개 집단의 사람들에게 연출된 범죄 영상을 보여 주었다. 첫 번째 집단은 그 영상을 보면서 앞이나 뒤로 걷는 상상을 했다. 두 번째 집단은 실험하는 동안에 실제로 앞이나 뒤로 걸었다. 마지막 집단은 가만히 앉아 있었다. 그 결과 − 실제로 행동하든지 상상하든지 − 뒤로 움직이는 것이 가만히 앉아 있거나 앞으로 움직이는 행동보다 사람들이 정보를 더 잘 기억해내는 데 도움이 되었다. 아마도 뒤로 움직이는 것이 우리가 정보를 얻었던 과거의 그 시점으로 우리가 되돌아갈 수 있도록 정신적으로 우리에게 도움을 주는 것 같다. 다음번 당신이 무언가를 기억하려고 노력한다면, 뒤로 걸어라.

실제로 뒤로 걷거나 뒤로 걷는 것을 상상하는 것이 과거의 일을 기억하는 데 도움이 된다고 했으므로 빈칸에 적절한 말은 ①이다.

1 ⑤   2 ⑤   3 ①   4 ③   5 ③   6 I can't thank you
enough. / I'm thankful for your help. / I really
appreciate your help. 등

1 ⑤는 감사를 표현하는 말에 대한 응답이고, 나머지는 감사하
   는 표현이다.

2 B가 겨울 캠프에 가서 주말을 잘 보냈다고 하고 빈칸 뒤에서
   긍정의 대답과 함께 스키 타는 법을 배우고 이글루를 만들었
   다고 했으므로 빈칸에는 캠프의 프로그램에 만족했는지 묻는
   ⑤가 가장 알맞다.

3 밑줄 친 부분은 감사하는 표현인데, ① it's my pleasure는
   감사 표현에 답하는 말이다.

4 ③ 시험 결과가 만족스럽지 않다는 말에 대해 칭찬한 후, 감
   사 표현에 답하는 말인 It's my pleasure.(천만에요.)로 답
   하는 것은 어색하다.

5 ⓒ 네가 휴대전화를 샀다고 들었어, Joyce. - ⓑ 맞아. 여기
   있어. 멋있어 보이지 않니? – ⓓ 그래, 멋있어. – ⓐ 나는 색
   이 아주 마음에 들어.

6 빈칸 뒤에 A가 감사 표현에 답하는 말을 하므로 빈칸에는 고
   마움을 나타내는 표현이 들어가야 한다.

1 How do you like the cap?   2 (1) Though (2) Because
(3) When   3 (1) surprising news (2) Frankly speaking
(3) boiled egg   4 (1) Opening the box, I found an old
letter in it. (2) Having no money, my friend bought a
train ticket for me. (3) Dad went out of the house
saying "Good-bye." (4) Tom arriving, we started for
home.   5 (1) waving her hands (2) wearing a blue
cap (3) broken shovel (4) following a cat

1 만족 여부에 대해 물을 때 How do you like ~?를 써서 묻
   는다.

2 분사구문은 양보, 이유, 원인, 시간 등의 다양한 뜻을 가진
   다. 주절과 부사절 내용의 문맥을 통해 알맞은 접속사를 알
   수 있다.

3 (1), (3) 분사와 그 수식하는 명사의 관계가 능동이면 현재분사
   를, 수동이면 과거분사를 쓴다. (2) 비인칭 독립분사구문은 분
   사구문의 주어가 일반인일 경우 이를 생략하고 쓰는 분사구
   문이다.

4 부사절을 분사구문으로 바꿔 쓸 때 부사절의 접속사를 없애
   고 그 주어가 주절의 주어와 같으면 부사절의 주어를 생략하
   고 동사를 현재분사로 고친다. 부사절의 주어와 주절의 주어
   가 다를 경우에는 분사 앞에 주어를 생략하지 않는다.

5 분사와 그 수식하는 명사의 관계가 능동이면 현재분사를, 수
   동이면 과거분사를 쓴다.

01 ④   02 ⑤   03 Are you satisfied with the color?
04 ⓒ → ⓑ → ⓓ → ⓐ   05 ③   06 ④   07 ④   08 ②
09 closing → closed   10 Lived → Living   11 ③
12 ②   13 ④   14 giving   15 ②   16 ③   17 ②   18 ②
19 (1) I saw (2) I had seen   20 ④   21 Briefly
speaking   22 ⑤   23 reduce → reducing   24 ⑤
25 ①   26 ②   27 ⓐ called ⓑ Finding   28 ③   29 ②
30 ③

01 ④는 반의어 관계이고, 나머지는 유의어 관계이다.

02 '~을 뒤쫓다'는 run after로, '이륙하다'는 take off로 쓴다.

03 만족 여부를 묻는 표현은 Are you satisfied with ~?이다.

04 ⓒ 나는 이 팩스 기계 사용하는 방법을 몰라. → ⓑ 여기에 종
    이를 넣고 번호를 눌러. 그리고 마지막으로 이 녹색 단추를
    눌러. → ⓓ 아, 정말 되네! 도와줘서 고마워. → ⓐ 천만에.

05 만족하는지 묻는 말에 긍정의 대답을 했으므로 뒤에는 만족
    을 나타내는 말이 이어지는 것이 알맞다.

06 빈칸에는 B가 도움을 줘서 고맙다는 말이 오는 것이 자연스
    럽다. ④는 도울 수 있어서 기쁘다는 말로 B가 할 수 있는 말
    이다.

07 만족 여부를 묻는 표현 Are you happy with ~?는 Are
    you satisfied with ~?로 바꿔 쓸 수 있다.

08 부사절은 분사구문으로 바꿔 쓸 수 있다. 접속사와 주어를 생
    략하고, 부사절의 동사를 Turning으로 써서 문장을 바꿔 쓴
    다. 조건을 나타내는 부사절에서는 현재 시제로 미래 시제를
    표현하므로, 부사절에 쓰이는 turn도 주절에 쓰인 미래 시제
    와 같다고 볼 수 있다.

09 명사 your book은 분사와 수동의 관계이므로 closing을
    과거분사 closed로 써야 한다.

10 주어 Emma와 분사 Lived가 능동의 관계이므로 현재분사
    Living으로 써야 한다.

11 주절의 시제는 현재이지만 어제 휴대 전화를 잃어버렸다는
    부사절의 내용은 주절보다 과거의 일이므로 완료분사구문
    Having lost가 알맞다.

12 ⓐ, ⓒ, ⓓ는 밑줄 친 부분과 수식하는 대상이 진행, 능동의 관계이므로 현재분사, ⓑ, ⓔ는 각각 수동, 완료의 관계이므로 과거분사를 써야 한다.

13 첫 번째 문장에서는 stand가 앞의 woman과 능동, 진행의 관계이므로 현재분사 standing으로, 두 번째 문장에서는 my name과 call이 수동의 관계이므로 called로 써야 한다.

14 연속된 상황을 하나의 문장으로 표현할 경우 분사구문을 쓸 수 있다.

15 ② Judging from(~으로 판단하건대)

16 ⓐ 자고 있는 (동작) → 현재분사 ⓑ 빨기 위한 (용도) → 동명사 ⓒ 수집하는 것(주격보어 my hobby = collecting wrapping paper) → 동명사 ⓓ 축구를 하고 있는 → 현재분사 ⓔ 만들고 있는 → 현재분사

17 ①, ③ 능동, 진행의 의미로 명사를 수식 → 현재분사 ④, ⑤ 수동, 완료의 의미로 명사를 수식 → 과거분사

18 ① 주어(Jenny)와 watch의 관계가 능동, 진행 → 현재분사 ③ 목적어(a stranger)와 walk의 관계가 능동, 진행 → 현재분사 ④ 주어(the door)와 lock의 관계가 수동 → 과거분사 ⑤ 목적어(someone)와 approach의 관계가 능동, 진행 → 현재분사

19 Having seen이 쓰였으므로 (1) 부사절이 주절보다 한 시제 앞선 과거 시제로 쓰여 saw가 알맞고, (2) 부사절이 과거 시제인 주절보다 한 시제 앞이므로 과거완료가 알맞다.

20 ⓒ 주절의 주어인 it과 분사구문의 주어가 다르므로 분사 앞에 주어를 써 주어야 한다. ⓔ '파티에 초대된'이라는 수동의 의미이므로 과거분사를 써야 한다.

21 비인칭 독립분사구문인 Briefly speaking으로 '간단히 말해서'의 의미를 나타낼 수 있다.

22 밑줄 친 분사구문은 '쥐 때문에 놀라서'라는 의미로 앞에 Being이 생략되었다. 이유를 나타내는 Because가 이끄는 부사절로 바꿔 쓸 수 있다.

23 접속사가 남겨져 있는 분사구문으로 현재분사가 와야 한다.

24 신용카드가 사람들을 더 소비하게 만든다고 했으므로 밑줄 친 using을 문맥상 '~하지 않는다면'의 의미인 ⑤ Unless가 이끄는 절로 바꿔 쓰는 것은 알맞지 않다.

25
> 꿈꾸는 동안의 뇌 활동은 우리가 깨어 있을 때처럼 증가한다. 사실, 꿈꾸는 것은 스트레스를 다루면서 여러분이 문제를 해결하는 것을 도울 수 있다. 하버드 의대의 어느 연구에 따르면, 자면서 꿈을 꾸는 사람들은 다른 사람들로부터 긍정적인 감정을 더 잘 감지할 수 있다고 했다. 그러나 꿈을 꾸지 않는 사람들은 부정적인 감정에 더 예민했다. 일반적으로 말해서, 꿈은 뇌가 부정적인 감정을 안전하게 놓아 주는 데 도움을 준다.

자면서 꿈을 꿀 때 뇌의 활동과 꿈을 꾸는 사람들의 긍정적인 면을 소개했다.

26
> 어느 날 저녁, 식사를 하면서, 아들이 그의 아버지에게 물었다. "아빠, 벌레는 먹기에 좋아요?" 아들이 그 질문을 하는 이유를 이해하지 못한 채, 아버지는 대답했다 "그건 더럽구나. 우리가 먹으면서 그런 것은 얘기하지 않는 거야." "알았어요, 죄송해요." 아들이 답했다. 저녁 식사 후에 아버지는 물었다. "자, 아들아. 왜 갑자기 벌레 질문을 했던 거니?" "아, 신경 쓰지 마세요." 아들이 말했다. "아빠 수프에 벌레가 있었는데, 이제 없어졌어요."

아들은, 아빠 수프에 벌레가 있는 것을 보고 벌레가 먹기에 좋은지 질문한 것인데, 문맥상 마지막에 벌레가 없어졌다는 것은 아버지가 그 벌레를 먹었다는 ②의 의미이다.

[27~28]
> 실패 박물관이라고 불리는 독특한 전시회가 있다. 혁신 연구가인 Samuel West 박사가 자신이 수집한 실패 사례들로 그 전시회를 처음 시작했다. 산업 프로젝트의 80에서 90퍼센트가 실패한다는 것을 알았을 때, 그는 사람들이 그 안에 담긴 실패와 교훈의 이야기를 들을 필요가 있다고 생각했다. 작품 중에 플라스틱으로 만든 자전거와 Amazon Fire 전화기가 있다. 그 자전거는 일반 자전거보다 2배 비싸지만 부서지기가 쉬웠다. Amazon Fire 전화기는 '구매' 버튼이 있었지만, 사람들은 그것을 싫어했다.

27 ⓐ '실패 박물관이라고 불리는'이라는 수동의 의미이므로 call의 과거분사 형태를 써야 하고, ⓑ '알았을 때'라는 의미로 분사구문이므로 find의 현재분사 형태를 써야 한다.

28 ③ 어떻게 실패 작품들을 수집했는지에 대한 내용은 없다.

[29~30]
> 여러분은 더 똑똑해 보이고 싶은가? 다른 사람들의 똑똑한 점을 요약하라! 다른 사람들이 말한 좋은 점을 단순히 다시 진술하는 사람은 흔히 더 잘 기억될 수 있다. 비슷한 방식으로, 회의에서 끼어들 기회를 찾는 것이 힘들 때는, 다른 사람들이 말한 가장 좋은 말들을 메모하는 것이 좋다. 회의가 끝나갈 때, 그 아이디어들을 간단명료하게 요약하라. 다른 사람들을 칭찬할 때조차도 여러분의 말은 더 똑똑하게 들릴 것이다. 기억하라! 똑똑하게 보이기 위해, 여러분이 항상 훌륭한 아이디어를 발표할 필요는 없다.

29 ⓑ는 접속사와 주어가 생략된 분사구문이므로, have를 현재분사의 형태 having으로 써야 한다.

30 똑똑해 보이기 위해 ③ 다른 사람들이 말한 훌륭한 점을 다시 진술하라는 방법이 제시되었다.

Grammar Practice

pp. 52~55

A1 (1) ⓐ (2) ⓑ (3) ⓐ (4) ⓒ

A2 (1) It's true that we're late
(2) (that) I should escape
(3) that you have long experience
(4) certain that plants need water

B1 (1) ○ (2) × (3) ○

B2 (1) Whether (2) whether(if) (3) whether (4) whether

C1 (1) While you are eating
(2) Unless you are careful with it / If you are not careful with it
(3) after the water is boiled
(4) since I met him at his graduation

D1 (1) Because (2) though (3) so that (4) so, that
(5) so, that, can (6) Even though

E1 (1) However (2) Otherwise (3) Thus (4) Besides
(5) Nevertheless

F1 (1) and (2) but (3) Either (4) but

F2 (1) 너와 네 남동생 둘 다 잘못했다.
(2) 나는 오후에 축구나 야구를 할 것이다.
(3) 남자들뿐만 아니라 여자들도 자전거 타는 법을 배워야 한다.
(4) Judith가 아닌 네가 그 트럭을 운전해야 한다.
(5) Linda와 Kyle 둘 다 회의에 참석하지 않았다.
(6) 소방관들뿐만 아니라 경찰관들도 다쳤다.

Grammar Test

pp. 56~57

01 ⑤ **02** Mr. Baker but (also) Mr. Smith seems to know the news **03** ② **04** ② **05** ③ **06** ④ **07** ④ **08** Unless you stop **09** ④ **10** ③ **11** whether Albert likes the present or not / whether or not Albert likes the present **12** ⑤ **13** neither, nor

01 문맥상 '게다가'의 의미로 첨가를 나타내는 Besides가 알맞다.

02 B as well as A는 not only A but (also) B로 바꿔 쓸 수 있다.

03 because 뒤에는 절이 오며 because of 뒤에는 명사(구)가 온다.

04 〈보기〉와 ②의 that은 목적어로 쓰인 명사절을 이끄는 접속사이다. ① 지시대명사 ③ 주격 관계대명사 ④ 목적격 관계대명사 ⑤ 지시형용사

05 '만약 ~하지 않는다면'이라는 의미가 되어야 하므로 Unless가 알맞다.

06 첫 번째 문장에는 상관접속사 both A and B가, 두 번째 문장에는 not only A but also B가 쓰였다.

07 첫 번째 문장의 so that은 '~하기 위해서'의 의미로 목적을 나타내며, 두 번째 문장의 〈so+형용사+that+주어+can't〉는 '너무 ~해서 …할 수 없다'의 의미이다.

08 If ~ not은 '만약 ~하지 않는다면'이라는 뜻으로, Unless로 바꿔 쓸 수 있다.

09 ④의 if는 '~인지 아닌지'라는 의미로 명사절을 이끄는 접속사로 쓰였다. 나머지 문장의 if(If)는 조건의 부사절을 이끄는 접속사로 '만약 ~한다면'의 의미이다.

10 ③ until은 시간을 나타내는 접속사로, '짐을 쌀 때까지 일찍 출발할 것이다.'라는 의미는 어색하다.

11 whether나 if는 '~인지 아닌지'라는 뜻으로 동사 know의 목적어 역할을 하는 명사절을 이끈다. if 바로 뒤에는 or not을 쓸 수 없다.

12 Unless는 '만약 ~하지 않는다면'의 의미로 If ~ not과 같은 의미이다.

13 '요구르트와 아이스크림을 둘 다 좋아하지 않는다.'라는 의미가 되어야 하므로 〈neither A nor B〉가 알맞다.

Reading

pp. 58~59

1 (A) because (B) if (C) that **2** ⑤ **3** ⑤ **4** ④

[1~2]

나의 아버지의 비밀

1946년에 낯선 사람이 나를 찾아와서 "당신이 김용환 선생님의 딸입니까?"라고 물었다. 내게 그것은 이상한 질문이었는데, 왜냐하면 나는 파락호의 딸로 불리는 데 더 익숙했기 때문이었다. 그 남자는 "저는 당신의 아버지의 친구입니다."라고 말했다. 나는 나의 아버지에 관한 좋은 기억이 없었기 때문에, 그 순간에 나는 실망스러운 소식을 예상하고 있었다.

아버지의 친구는 그의 이야기를 계속했다. "그는 도박꾼이 아니었습니다. 당신의 아버지는 가족의 돈을 만주의 독립군들에게 보냈습니다. 그는 일본 경찰들로부터 이것을 비밀로 하기 위해 스스로를 도박꾼으로 보이게 했습니다." 처음에 나는 그가 사실을 말하고 있는지 확신할 수 없었다. 하지만 나중에, 나는 나의 아버지에 관한 진실을 발견했고 나는 내가 아버지에 대해 잘못 생각하고 있었음을 깨달았다. 그 순간 이후로 이제껏, 내가 자신의 인생을 독립 운동에 바쳤던 파락호의 딸인 것을 나는 자랑스럽게 여겨 왔다.

1 (A) 빈칸 뒤에서 낯선 이의 질문이 이상하게 여겨진 이유가 나오므로 because가 알맞다. (B) 아버지가 독립군 활동 자금을 보냈다는 남자의 말이 사실인지 확신할 수 없었다는 말이 되도록 if(~인지 아닌지)를 쓰는 것이 알맞다. (C) 빈칸 뒤의 내용은 필자가 깨달은 내용이므로 명사절을 이끄는 that이 빈칸에 알맞다.

2 ⓐ, ⓑ, ⓓ, ⓔ는 모두 파락호 김용환을 가리키고, ⓒ는 김용환의 친구를 가리킨다.

3

> 인공 지능(AI)은 진찰을 해주고, 피부암을 탐지하거나 전문가 수준의 정확성으로 수술을 하기도 한다. 인공 지능이 곧 현재 의사들이 하고 있는 일의 80퍼센트만큼을 대체할 것이라고 일컬어진다. 환자들은 인간 의사들보다 인공 지능을 더 좋아할까? 최근 연구는 환자들이 인공 지능을 선택하는 데 주저한다는 것을 보여준다. 환자들은 자신을 특별하다고 보지만, 그들은 인공 지능이 자신들을 특별한 환자가 아닌, 보통의 환자로 대할 것이라고 믿는다. 환자들은 그냥 '감기' 대신에 '내' 감기라고 말하고 싶어 하며, '내' 감기는 특별한 병이라고 생각하고 싶어 한다. (그러므로 그들은 그들의 병이 보통의 경우로 치료되어지기를 원한다.)

자신과 자신의 병이 특별하게 대우 받기를 원하는 환자들이 인공 지능에게 진찰 받기를 주저한다는 내용이므로, ⓔ는 글 전체의 흐름과 어울리지 않는다. (ⓔ average → special)

4

> 여러분이 거울로 자신을 볼 때, 여러분은 그 상이 또 다른 자신의 모습이라는 것을 안다. 다른 동물들도 똑같을까? 1970년대, Gordon Gallup 박사는 동물들의 지능 수준을 알기 위해 거울 검사를 만들었다. 그는 더 높은 지능이 있는 동물은 그들의 상이 그들 자신을 보여 준다는 것을 알 것이라고 생각했다. 그 이후로 연구자들은 많은 종류의 동물들에게 그 검사를 시행했다. 지금까지 인간과 침팬지, 돌고래, 코끼리를 포함한 오직 여덟 종류만이 그 검사를 통과했다. 그들 모두는 많은 공통점을 가지고 있다. 크고 복잡한 뇌를 가지고 있을 뿐만 아니라, 서로를 도우면서 사회적인 무리 속에서 산다.

④ 동물들에게 어떻게 거울 검사를 실행하는지에 대한 언급은 없다.

1 ② **2** What's the matter **3** ③ **4** Can you tell me (the reason) why **5** ④ **6** ③

1 우산을 왜 가져왔는지 묻는 말이므로 그 이유로 비가 올 가능성에 대해 답하는 것이 자연스럽다. ②는 '오늘 비가 올 리가

없어.'라는 뜻이므로 알맞지 않다.

2 A의 질문에 대해 B가 화가 난 이유를 들어 답하므로, A의 질문으로는 '무슨 문제가 있니?'의 의미인 What's the matter with you?가 알맞다.

3 ⓑ 나는 오늘 매우 슬퍼. - ⓒ 무엇 때문에 그러니? - ⓐ Mike가 다음 주에 한국을 떠나야 하기 때문이야. - ⓓ 아, 정말 슬플 수밖에 없겠다.

4 원인을 물어보는 말로 '나에게 ~한 이유를 말해 줄 수 있습니까?'는 Can you tell me the (reason) why ~?로 나타낼 수 있다.

5 B가 할 수 없다고 답했으므로 A의 빈칸에는 가능성을 묻는 Is it possible(likely, probable) to ...?이 알맞다.

6 ③은 '그는 다음 달에 영국에 가는 게 좋겠다.'의 의미로 충고하는 표현이고, 나머지는 모두 '그는 다음 달에 영국에 갈지도 모른다.'의 의미로 추측 및 가능성을 나타내는 표현이다.

1 (1) Why do you say so? (2) Is it possible (for us) to grow vegetables in the space station? **2** (1) that we don't know as much as we think (2) That Beckett is actually a Mexican **3** (1) though it snowed heavily (2) Whether the rumor is true or not **4** (1) Both Tom and Minsu(Jina) (2) swim but can skate(ride a bike) (3) Neither Jina nor Minsu (4) Not only Jihoon but also Tom **5** (1) that she visited her grandmother (2) if she went to watch musicals (3) because her grandmother wanted her to spend time with her

1 (1) 이유를 물을 때 why do you say so?의 표현을 사용한다. (2) 맥락상 가능성을 묻는 표현이 들어간다. 가능성을 물을 때는 Is it possible to ~? 표현을 이용한다.

2 (1) 접속사 that을 이용하여 주격보어 역할을 하는 명사절을 만든다. (2) 접속사 that이 이끄는 명사절이 주어 역할을 한다.

3 though는 '비록 ~하지만', whether는 '~인지 아닌지'라는 뜻의 접속사이다.

4 ⟨both A and B⟩는 'A와 B 둘 다', ⟨not A but B⟩는 'A가 아니라 B', ⟨neither A nor B⟩는 'A와 B 둘 다 아닌', ⟨not only A but also B⟩는 'A뿐만 아니라 B도'인데, 표의 내용과 주어진 단어를 확인 후, 내용에 맞게 문장을 완성한다.

5 if, that은 명사절을 이끄는 접속사이고 because는 이유를 나타내며 부사절을 이끄는 접속사이다.

Lesson 03 접속사 **9**

01 ④   **02** (1) fiction (2) delay   **03** ③   **04** Is it possible
to live   **05** ②   **06** ⑤   **07** ②   **08** ①   **09** ②   **10** since
11 Not, but   **12** ⑤   **13** ③   **14** ①   **15** ④   **16** ①
17 ④   **18** ①   **19** Besides   **20** therefore   **21** though
22 ②   **23** ⑤   **24** ②   **25** ①   **26** ③   **27** ②   **28** ⑤
29 so that we can distinguish each one   **30** ③

01 ④는 '부러움, 질투'라는 유의어 관계이지만, 나머지는 모두 반의어 관계이다.

02 (1) '가상의 사람과 사건에 관한 책과 이야기'는 fiction(소설)을 의미한다. (2) '사물이나 인물이 계획보다 더 시간이 걸리게 하다'는 delay(지연시키다)를 의미한다.

03 ③ 명사 interest는 '관심사; 이자'라는 뜻으로 쓰인다.

04 '~이 가능할까?'라고 가능성 정도를 물어볼 때 〈Is it possible to+동사원형 ~? / Is it possible(likely) that+주어+동사 ~?〉 등의 표현을 쓸 수 있다.

05 A의 대답으로 보아 A의 친구가 A와 얘기하지 않으려는 원인을 묻는 표현이 와야 한다. ②는 원인을 묻기는 하지만, 의미상 '왜 그녀에게 말하지 않았니?'라는 질문이기 때문에 상황에 알맞지 않다.

06 ⑤ Is it necessary to ~?는 '~하는 것이 필요하니?'라는 뜻으로 의무 여부를 묻는 표현이고, ①, ②, ③, ④는 모두 가능성 정도(~하는 것이 가능할까?)를 묻는 표현이다.

07 네 음식은 어떠니? – ⓐ 나는 여기 음식에 정말 만족해. 너는 어떠니? – ⓓ 사실 나는 내 음식이 전혀 마음에 들지 않아. – ⓒ 왜 마음에 들지 않니? – ⓑ 왜냐하면 음식이 너무 기름져. 나는 기름진 음식을 좋아하지 않아.

08 ① if 바로 뒤에는 or not을 쓸 수 없다. (→ whether or not)

09 첫 번째 빈칸은 '~인지 아닌지'라는 의미의 명사절을 이끄는 if를 쓰고, 두 번째 빈칸은 '만약 ~하면'이라는 의미의 조건 부사절을 이끄는 if를 쓴다.

10 빈칸 뒤의 절이 앞의 절에 대한 이유이므로 '~ 때문에'라는 의미의 접속사 since를 쓴다. in order to는 '~하기 위해서'라는 뜻이다.

11 〈B as well as A〉는 'A뿐만 아니라 B도'라는 의미로 〈not only A but also B〉와 바꿔 쓸 수 있다.

12 〈보기〉와 ⑤의 that은 명사절을 이끄는 접속사로 목적절을 이끄는 역할을 한다. ①, ③ 앞 문장의 내용을 받는 지시대명사 ②, ④ 관계대명사

13 ③ or not과 함께 쓰여 '~인지 아닌지'라는 의미를 나타내려면 either 대신 명사절을 이끄는 접속사 whether를 쓴다.

14 ①에서는 '언제'라는 의미의 의문사로 쓰였고, 나머지 문장에서는 '~할 때'라는 의미로 시간의 부사절을 이끄는 접속사로

쓰였다

15 문맥상 'Elena는 숙제를 다 했지만 그녀는 외출하는 것이 허락되지 않았다.'의 의미로 양보의 접속사 although(though)가 알맞다.

16 ① since가 '~ 이래로'의 의미인 시간의 접속사로 쓰였고, 나머지는 모두 '~ 때문에'를 의미하는 이유의 접속사로 쓰였다.

17 ④ '나는 댄스음악을 좋아한다. 반면에, 내 여동생은 재즈를 좋아한다.'의 의미가 자연스럽다.

18 ① 상관접속사는 동일한 문법 성분을 이어 준다. dance와 sing이 동사원형의 형태로 바르게 이어져 있다. ② also → but (also) ③ run → running ④ and → or ⑤ or → nor

19 빈칸 뒤에서 접착 노트의 장점을 추가로 설명하고 있으므로 첨가의 의미를 가진 Besides가 알맞다.

20 뒷 문장이 앞 문장에 대한 결과를 나타내므로 결과의 의미를 지닌 접속부사 therefore가 알맞다.

21 '로마 제국의 많은 업적은 여전히 존재한다. 로마 제국은 천 년 이상 전에 막을 내렸다.'라는 내용이므로 양보의 의미를 가진 접속사 though가 알맞다.

22 ⓒ 상관접속사로 〈not A but B〉의 형태가 알맞다. ⓓ 접속사 if는 바로 뒤에 or not을 쓸 수 없다.

23 첫 번째 문장에서는 '너무 ~해서 …할 수 있다'의 의미로 〈so+부사+that+주어+can〉의 형태가 쓰였으며, 두 번째 문장은 시간의 부사절이 미래를 나타낼 때 현재 시제를 사용하므로 stops가 알맞다.

24 ⓑ what이 아니라 the fact와 동격인 절을 이끄는 접속사 that이 와야 한다.

25

> 만약 당신이 여행을 가는 것과 최신 휴대전화 사는 것 중에서 결정을 고민하고 있다면, 여행을 선택하라. 몇몇 연구에 따르면, 물리적 물체에 돈을 쓰는 것보다는 경험에서 더 많은 행복을 얻을 수 있다. 왜 그런가? 연구들은 우리가 새로운 제품에 익숙해짐에 따라 즐거움은 사라진다는 것을 보여 준다. 그러나 경험은 그것을 기억할 때마다 작은 기쁨을 계속 가져다준다.

마지막 문장에서 경험을 기억해낼 때마다 그것이 계속 작은 기쁨을 가져다주므로, 물질에 돈을 쓰는 것보다 '경험'으로부터 더 많은 행복을 얻을 수 있다는 것을 알 수 있다.

26

> 여러분은 지금 어떻게 앉아 있는가? 어깨와 머리를 구부린 채 앉아 있다면, 여러분은 명확하게 생각하지 못하거나 무언가를 잘 기억하지 못할지도 모른다. (B) 게다가 이런 패배한 듯한 자세는 실제로 불안함과 좌절감을 가져온다. (C) 반면에 여러분이 꼿꼿한 자세로 앉는다면, 그것은 뇌로 향하는 혈액과 산소의 흐름을 40퍼센트까지 향상시킨다. (A) 그러므로 어려운 수학 문제를 푸는 데 어려움을 겪고 있다면, 꼿꼿한 자세로 앉아라.

(B) 구부정한 자세의 또 다른 부정적인 효과를 이야기한 후, (C) 바른 자세의 긍정적인 효과를 제시하여, (A) 결론적으로 평소에 어려운 문제를 풀 때 바르게 앉으라고 마무리하고 있다.

[27~28]

> 1차 세계 대전 동안에 몇몇 동물들은 군사들을 도왔다. 말들은 군사들을 태웠을 뿐 아니라 거대한 총과 구급차를 끌기도 했다. 그들의 배설물에서 나온 가스는 전등을 켜는 데 이용되었다. 애완견과 애완 비둘기는 너무 빨라서 총에 잘 맞지 않았기 때문에 메시지를 전달하였다. 금붕어도 그들의 역할을 했다. 어떻게? 가스 공격 후에, 군사들은 물에 방독면을 씻고 나서 금붕어를 물에 넣었다. 만약 금붕어가 죽었다면, 그것은 방독면에 아직도 독이 있다는 의미였다.

27 ⟨not only ~ but also...⟩는 '~뿐만 아니라 …도 역시'라는 의미이고, ⟨both ~ and ..⟩는 '~와 … 둘 다'라는 의미이다.

28 방독면을 물로 씻은 후에 금붕어를 씻은 물에 넣어 금붕어가 죽는지 보는 방법으로 방독면에 독이 남아 있는지 여부를 판단했다고 했다.

[29~30]

> 매년 많은 새로운 허리케인 소식이 TV에서 보인다. 여러분은 그들이 어떻게 이름을 얻는지 궁금해한 적이 있는가? 세계기상기구(WMO)는 우리가 각각의 허리케인을 구별할 수 있도록 허리케인의 이름을 부여한다. 세계기상기구는 이름 목록을 만들고 허리케인은 알파벳 순서로 이름을 부여받는다. 그러므로 그 해의 첫 번째 폭풍은 A, 두 번째는 B로 시작하는 이름을 부여받는 식이다. 그 이름은 폭풍이 허리케인으로 발전할 때까지 유지된다.

29 ⟨so that＋주어＋can ~⟩구문을 이용하여 '우리가 각각의 허리케인을 구별할 수 있도록'의 의미가 되도록 문장을 완성한다.

30 이 글은 '허리케인에 이름을 부여하는 방법'에 대해 말하고 있으므로 ③이 제목으로 알맞다.

Lesson 04 가정법

▶▶ Grammar Practice
pp. 72~75

Ⓐ1 (1) can't (2) encourage, can (3) As, doesn't accept

Ⓐ2 (1) were (2) had (3) could

Ⓑ1 (1) had studied (2) had agreed (3) had drunk
(4) would have gone

Ⓑ2 (1) would have gone (2) had, have
(3) hadn't been

Ⓒ1 (1) Were you (2) Had Owen helped
(3) Had I known

Ⓒ2 (1) Were today (2) Were Joseph (3) Had I been

Ⓓ1 (1) were (2) had been (3) could (4) had told

Ⓓ2 (1) 내가 하루 종일 일하지 않아도 되면 좋을 텐데.
(2) 그가 지난밤 파티에 왔다면 좋을 텐데.
(3) 내가 과거에 공부를 열심히 했다면 좋을 텐데.

Ⓔ1 (1) were (2) had been (3) took (4) had been

Ⓔ2 (1) knew (2) had been (3) were (4) had visited

Ⓕ1 (1) Without (2) were not (3) But

Ⓕ2 (1) With → Without (2) But → But for
(3) were for → were not for

▶▶ Grammar Test
pp. 76~77

01 ④   **02** ④   **03** ③   **04** ⑤   **05** ①   **06** ⑤
07 (1) doesn't have a key, can't unlock (2) you saw the fire, the house didn't burn down   **08** ⑤   **09** ⑤
10 ④   **11** (that) you had joined the club meeting
12 ③   **13** If I had been able to speak French, I could have shown him the way.

01 last night으로 보아 과거의 일에 대한 유감을 나타내는 ⟨I wish＋가정법 과거완료(주어＋had＋p.p.)⟩의 형태로 문장을 완성하는 것이 알맞다.

02 조건절로 보아 가정법 과거이므로 주절의 동사는 ⟨조동사의 과거형＋동사원형⟩의 형태로 문장을 완성하는 것이 알맞다.

03 '지금 시간이 없다'라는 문장 뒤에 '내가 그들과 함께 테니스를 칠 수 있다면 좋을 텐데.'의 의미로 현재의 실현 불가능한 소망을 나타내도록 ⟨I wish＋가정법 과거⟩의 형태로 문장을 완성하는 것이 알맞다.

04 과거를 나타내는 부사 yesterday가 있는 것으로 보아 과거에 있었던 일에 대한 가정을 나타내는 가정법 과거완료가 쓰여야 하므로 주절은 ⟨조동사의 과거형＋have＋p.p.⟩가 되

어야 한다. ⑤ → have missed

05 '만약 ~했다면, …했을 텐데'의 의미로 과거 사실에 반대되는 가정을 나타내므로 가정법 과거완료 〈If+주어+had+p.p. ~, 주어+조동사의 과거형+have+p.p. ...〉로 쓴다.

06 〈Without ~, 가정법 과거〉일 때 Without ~는 If it were not for ~로 바꿔 쓸 수 있다.

07 ⑴ 가정법 과거이므로 현재 사실과 반대의 일을 가정하고 있다. 따라서 직설법에서는 현재 시제를 쓴다. ⑵ 가정법 과거완료이므로 과거 사실과 반대의 일을 가정하고 있다. 따라서 직설법에서는 과거 시제를 쓴다.

08 ⑤ 조건절은 가정법 과거의 형태이고, 주절은 가정법 과거완료의 형태이므로 어색하다. 주절을 가정법 과거(would take)로 고치거나 조건절을 가정법 과거완료(had had)로 고쳐야 한다.

09 ⑤ 가정법 과거완료는 과거 사실과 반대되는 가정을 나타내므로 직설법 과거로 바꿔 쓰는 것이 알맞다. (→ she couldn't finish it in time)

10 〈as if+가정법 과거〉는 주절의 시제와 같은 시점의 사실과 반대되는 가정을 나타낸다. 따라서 In fact와 함께 현재 시제를 쓰는 것이 알맞다.

11 〈보기〉처럼 유감을 표현한 직설법 문장을 〈I wish+가정법〉 표현을 이용한 문장으로 바꿔 쓰며, that절의 시제가 과거이므로 〈I wish+가정법 과거완료〉로 바꿔 쓴다.

12 〈as if+가정법 과거〉는 직설법으로 바꿀 때 주절의 시제와 같은 시제로 쓰므로 첫 번째 문장은 〈In fact, 직설법 현재〉로 바꿔 쓰는 것이 알맞다. 〈I wish+가정법 과거완료〉는 〈I am sorry (that)+직설법 과거〉로 바꿔 쓸 수 있다. 이때, 긍정문은 부정문으로, 부정문은 긍정문으로 쓴다.

13 과거에 하지 못했던 일에 관한 가정을 표현하고 있으므로 가정법 과거완료를 써야 한다.

> Reading

1 existed, could get　**2** ④　**3** effort　**4** ④

[1~2]

웜홀: 실제인가, 이론인가?

안녕하세요, 과학 애호가분들. 저는 Sci 박사입니다. 오늘 저는 우주 여행에 관해 얘기하겠습니다. 우리가 광속으로 여행한다면, 우리는 다른 행성에 매우 빨리 도착할 수 있을 것입니다. Einstein은 공간과 시간이 연결되어 있다는 것을 알아냈습니다. 그는 그것을 시공간이라고 불렀습니다. 그는 시공간이 실제로 휘어질 수 있다고 생각했습니다. 그것이 휘어질 때, 서로 멀리 떨어져 있는 부분들이 더 가까워집니다. 제가 종이 한 장을 가지고 이렇게 설명하겠습니다. 종이의 윗

부분과 아랫부분에 각각 작은 점을 그리세요. 그리고 점들이 만나도록 그것을 접으세요. 종이의 점 위에 구멍을 뚫으면 그것은 연결될 것입니다. 웜홀이라고 불리는 그런 지름길이 우주에 존재한다면, 우리는 수백만 광년 떨어진 곳에 빠르게 도착할 수 있을 것입니다.

하지만 축하하기에 이릅니다. 웜홀은 이론상으로만 존재합니다. 우리가 그것을 발견하더라도 웜홀은 매우 불안정할 것입니다. 우주선이 그 안으로 날아 들어간다면, 그것은 찌그러지거나 부서져서 산산조각 날지도 모릅니다. 저는 우리가 언젠가 그것을 발견하고 그것을 통해 여행할 방법을 얻기를 바랍니다.

1 우리말의 내용과 문맥을 볼 때, 현재 상황과 반대되는 내용의 문장이므로 가정법 과거의 문장으로 완성하는 것이 알맞다. 가정법 과거의 조건절의 동사는 과거형 동사를 쓰고, 주절의 동사에는 〈과거형 조동사+동사원형〉 형태를 쓰므로 각각 existed, could, get이 알맞다.

2 ④ 앞에서 웜홀은 이론상으로만 존재하며, 뒤에 이어지는 문장에서 우주선이 웜홀로 들어가면 찌그러지거나 산산조각 날 것이라고 했으므로 stable은 unstable로 쓰는 것이 알맞다.

3

새들은 왜 V 형태로 날까? V 형태는 효율과 많은 관련이 있음이 밝혀졌다. 새들이 V 형태로 날 때 그들은 노력을 최소화할 수 있다. V의 앞부분에 있는 선두 새가 가장 열심히 일하는 반면, 그 뒤에 있는 나머지 새들은 더 수월한 시간을 보낸다는 것을 과학자들이 발견했다. 그 이유는 날개를 퍼덕거리는 것이 위로 향하는 작은 공기의 흐름을 만들어서 그 흐름을 타고 나는 새들은 유익한 추진력을 얻기 때문이다. 만약 선두 새가 없다면, 나머지는 날기 위해 더 많은 노력을 들여야 할 것이다. 선두의 새는 지치기 때문에 새들은 번갈아가며 선두에 선다.

글 전반부에 새들은 V 형태로 날 때, 가장 적은 노력을 들일 수 있다고 언급했다.

4

〈Allegri's Miserere〉는 가장 아름다운 성가 음악 작품들 중 하나이지만, 모차르트가 없었다면 여러분은 그것을 들을 수 없었을지도 모른다. 그것은 1년에 한 번씩 바티칸에서만 연주되곤 했는데, 그 작품은 철저하게 지켜졌다. 그것은 복제되는 것이 금지되어서 거의 150년 동안 비밀로 지켜졌다. 그러나 14살의 모차르트가 바티칸에서 그것을 한 번 들었을 때, 그는 악보를 보지 않고 그것을 적었다. 바티칸이 그 사실을 알게 되었을 때, 그들은 그 복제본이 정확한 정도에 놀랐다. 그렇게 해서 오늘날까지 우리가 그 음악을 알게 되고 사랑하게 된 것이다.

④ 모차르트는 〈Allegri's Miserere〉를 한 번 듣고 그 악보를 적었다.

12　Part I 실력 다지기

1 I wish I could   **2** ②   **3** ①   **4** ④   **5** ③   **6** ⑤

1 I wish I could ~는 '~할 수 있으면 좋을 텐데'라고 소망을 말하는 표현이다.

2 한가하면 하고 싶은 것을 상상하여 묻고 있으므로 I would 〔could〕 ....를 이용하여 상상하는 것을 표현한다.

3 밑줄 친 문장은 '내가 너와 함께 역사 박물관에 갈 수 있으면 좋을 텐데.'의 의미로 현재 사실과 반대되는 소원을 말하는 표현으로 ①의 갈 수 없다는 의미이다.

4 I would like to는 '나는 ~하고 싶다'라는 의미로 바람, 소망을 표현한다. ④의 used to는 '~하곤 했다'의 의미이다.

5 상상하여 묻는 표현은 What would you do if you ...? 이고, 이에 대한 대답은 I would ....로 한다.

6 ⓓ 너는 남동생이 있니? – ⓑ 아니, 난 외아들이어서 내게 남동생이 있으면 좋겠어. – ⓒ 만약 네게 남동생이 있다면, 너는 무엇을 할 거니? – ⓐ 나는 남동생과 캐치볼을 할 거야.

>> **서술형 평가** p. 82

1 (1) I wish I could see the earth from space.   (2) I would float around like an astronaut.   **2** (1) were not so far away, we would buy it   (2) were taller, I could be a basketball player   (3) If I had been you, I would not have bought that coat   **3** (1) he were a bus driver   (2) my daughter had not lost   (3) as if they had much time   **4** (1) could buy that car   (2) we couldn't have gone camping   (3) could have enjoyed skating   **5** (1) could win the science contest   (2) could get an electric car

1 (1) 바람, 소원을 말할 때 I wish I could ~.의 형태로 표현하고, (2) 상상한 내용을 묻는 What would you do if ~? 에 대한 답이므로 I would ...로 답한다.

2 (1), (2) 가정법 과거는 〈If+주어+동사의 과거형, 주어+조동사의 과거형+동사원형〉의 형태로 현재의 사실과 반대되는 일을 가정하거나 소망할 때 쓴다. (3) 가정법 과거완료는 〈If+주어+had+p.p., 주어+조동사의 과거형+have+ p.p.〉의 형태로 과거의 사실과 반대되는 일을 가정할 때 사용된다.

3 (1), (3) 〈as if+가정법〉은 '마치 ~인 것처럼'의 뜻으로, '사실은 그렇지 않다'라는 의미를 나타낸다. (2) 〈I wish+가정법〉은 이룰 수 없는 소망이나, 현재(가정법 과거) 또는 과거(가정법 과거완료) 사실에 대한 아쉬움을 나타낼 때 쓴다.

4 (1) 가정법 과거는 〈If+주어+동사의 과거형, 주어+조동사의 과거형+동사원형〉의 형태로, (2), (3) 가정법 과거완료는

〈If+주어+had+p.p., 주어+조동사의 과거형+ have +p.p.〉의 형태로 쓴다.

5 가정법 과거는 〈If+주어+동사의 과거형, 주어+조동사의 과거형+동사원형〉의 형태로 '만약 ~하다면 …할 텐데'라는 의미로, 현재의 사실과 반대되는 일을 가정하거나 소망할 때 쓴다.

>> **Final Test** pp. 83~87

01 ④   **02** ③   **03** ④   **04** ①   **05** ⑤   **06** ③   **07** ⓒ – ⓓ – ⓑ – ⓐ   **08** ③   **09** ③   **10** ③   **11** had not neglected   **12** ③   **13** ④   **14** ③   **15** had not done   **16** ⑤   **17** ①, ⑤   **18** If it were not for sneakers   **19** Had Sujin been more diligent   **20** ④   **21** ⑤   **22** ②   **23** I wish I had had   **24** I were taller, I would be   **25** ①   **26** ③   **27** ⑤   **28** ⑤   **29** had been   **30** ④

01 ④는 유의어 관계이며, 나머지는 반의어 관계이다.

02 '우주로 사람들을 실어 나르기 위한 탈것'은 ③ spaceship (우주선)이다.

03 '진흙이나 물 등의 표면 아래로 내려가다'는 ④ sink(가라앉다)이다.

04 I'd like to는 '~하고 싶다'라는 의미로 소망을 말하는 표현이다.

05 A의 말에 대해 B가 '아마도 나는 전 세계를 여행할 거야.'라고 답하는 것으로 보아 '만약 네가 부자라면 너는 무엇을 할 거니?'라는 뜻의 상상하여 묻는 표현이 알맞다.

06 ③ 소망을 말하는 표현에 대해 동정하는 말을 하는 것은 어색하다.

07 ⓒ 만약 네가 역사 속 어떤 인물을 만날 수 있다면, 너는 누구를 만날 거니? – ⓓ 나는 Newton을 만날 거야. – ⓑ 너는 왜 그를 만나려고 하니? – ⓐ 나는 그가 생각했던 방식이 궁금해.

08 조건절이 가정법 과거이므로 주절에는 〈조동사의 과거형+동사원형〉이 온다.

09 주절이 〈조동사의 과거형+have+p.p.〉로 가정법 과거완료이므로 조건절에도 과거완료형 〈had+p.p.〉로 쓴다.

10 의미상 'Jude는 마치 나를 위해 뭔지든 할 것처럼 말한다.'라는 의미가 되도록 as if를 쓰는 것이 알맞다.

11 주절의 형태가 가정법 과거완료이므로 조건절에도 가정법 과거완료의 형태가 와야 하는데 의미상 '공부를 소홀히 하지 않았더라면'이므로 had not neglected가 되어야 한다.

12 과거를 나타내는 부사 yesterday와 함께 쓰인 것으로 보아 주절보다 더 과거 시점의 가정이므로 as if 다음에는 가정법 과거완료 형태가 와야 한다. (→ had seen)

13 주어진 우리말이 현재이므로 가정법 과거로 표현한 ④가 알

맞다.

14 주절의 동사(wish)와 같은 시제인 현재 상황에 대한 바람을 표현하므로 wish 뒤의 동사로는 가정법 과거 문장의 형태인 could go가 알맞다.

15 우리말 내용과 last night이라는 부사구로 보아 과거에 대한 내용이므로 과거 사실의 반대를 나타내는 가정법 과거완료 (had+p.p.)로 쓴다.

16 ⑤ 가정법 과거완료의 문장이므로 주절의 동사는 〈조동사의 과거형+have+p.p.〉가 되어야 한다. (→ have gone)

17 〈Without(But for)+가정법〉은 가정법의 조건절을 대신할 수 있는데 주절의 형태가 〈조동사의 과거형+have+p.p.〉이므로 가정법 과거완료임을 알 수 있다. 따라서 조건절은 If it had not been for로 바꿔 쓸 수 있다.

18 '~이 없다면'은 〈without(but for)+가정법 과거〉, 또는 if it were not for 등으로 나타낼 수 있다.

19 우리말 내용상 If Sujin had been more diligent인데, 주어진 단어 중에 If가 없으므로 주어와 동사를 도치하여 배열하는 것이 알맞다.

20 ④ 주절의 시제가 〈조동사의 과거형+have+p.p.〉의 형태이므로 가정법 과거완료라는 것을 알 수 있다. 따라서 조건절의 동사는 〈had+p.p.〉의 형태가 알맞다. (→ had met)

21 ⑤ 〈주어+wish〉 다음에 문맥상 가정법 과거가 와야 하므로 lives는 lived로 써야 한다.

22 ⓒ, ⓔ는 주절의 문장이 〈조동사의 과거형+동사원형〉의 형태이므로 가정법 과거임을 알 수 있다. 따라서 조건절의 동사는 과거형이 알맞다. 나머지는 가정법 과거완료이므로 빈칸에 had가 알맞다.

23 과거의 아쉬운 부분을 말할 때에는 〈I wish+가정법 과거완료〉를 써서 말할 수 있다. 직설법의 부정문은 조건절에서 긍정문으로 쓴다.

24 현재 사실에 대한 반대의 가정이므로 가정법 과거인 〈If+주어+동사의 과거형 ~, 주어+조동사의 과거형+동사원형 ⋯.〉으로 쓴다.

25
> Steve Jobs는 그의 컴퓨터 회사의 이름을 뭐라고 지을지 생각하고 있었다. 그 일이 있었을 때, Steve는 어느 농장에서 막 사과나무의 가지를 잘랐다. 그의 동료가 Matrix와 같은 많은 이름을 내놓기 시작했을 때, Steve는 Apple Computer라는 이름을 제안했다. "나는 사과 농장에서 일하는 것이 무척 즐거워. Apple은 재미있고 무섭지 않게 들리잖아."라고 그는 말했다. 만약 그가 사과나무가 있는 곳에서 일하지 않았다면, 우리는 세계적으로 가장 유명한 컴퓨터 회사의 로고를 볼 기회가 없었을 것이다.

회사 이름을 결정해야 하는 시기에 Steve Jobs가 사과 농장에서 일하는 것을 좋아해서, 회사 이름으로 Apple을 제안했다는 내용이다. 따라서 빈칸에 들어갈 말은 apple trees이다.

26
> 어느 남자가 이발소에 들어가기 전에 문에서 "위험. 개 조심!"이라고 쓰인 표지판을 보았다. 그는 조심스럽게 문을 열었지만, 그가 볼 수 있는 것이라고는 바닥에 누워 자고 있는 살찐 늙은 개였다. "사람들이 조심해야 하는 개가 이 개인가요?" 그가 이발사에게 물었다. "네, 맞아요." "그런데, 내게는 이 개가 위험해 보이지 않는데요." 이발사가 답했다. "내가 그 표지판을 붙이지 않았다면, 손님도 그 개에게 걸려 넘어졌을 겁니다."

마지막에서 당신도 개에 걸려 넘어졌을 거라고 말하는 것으로 보아 많은 손님들이 개에 걸려 넘어졌었다는 것을 유추할 수 있다.

[27~28]
> 모두가 두려움을 가지지만, 너무 많은 두려움은 우리에게 해로울 수 있는데, 그것이 우리가 새로운 것을 시도하지 못하도록 막기 때문이다. 우리가 두려워하는 것은 학습된 것이며, 우리 자신의 두려움을 이길 수 있는 방법이 한 가지 있다. 우리가 상상한 것을 듣는 대신에, 우리는 우리가 두려워하게 만드는 것에 관한 사실을 배울 수 있다. 지식은 사람이 두려움을 덜 느끼도록 도울 수 있다. 여러분은 개를 두려워하는가? 그들에 관해 공부하라. 만약 여러분이 개로부터 여러분 자신을 지키는 방법을 확실히 안다면, 여러분은 두려움을 느끼지 않을 것이다.

27 가정법 과거에서 주절은 〈주어+would (not)+동사원형〉을 써야 하므로, ⓔ는 felt가 아니라 feel이 알맞다.

28 두려움은 학습된 것이므로, 두려움을 유발하는 것에 관해 공부하고 연구하면 두려움을 덜 느낀다고 했다.

[29~30]
> "당신의 열정을 따르라." 내가 이 조언을 읽었을 때, 나는 그것이 멋지다고 생각했다. 내가 타고난 내 열정을 발견한다면, 나는 인생에서 성공할 것 같았다. 그래서 나는 그것을 찾아보기로 결심했다. 나는 많은 곳으로 여행을 다녔고 새로운 것들을 경험했다. 하지만, 나는 수많은 세월을 보냈고, 결국 소중한 시간과 돈을 낭비했다. 이제야 나는 열정이 타고나는 것이 아님을 깨달았다. 그것은 당신이 개발하는 것이다. 내가 처음부터 "당신의 열정을 개발하라."라는 조언을 받았다면 좋았을 것이다.

29 처음부터 열정을 개발하라는 조언을 들었다면 좋았으리라는 과거 사실에 대한 아쉬움을 나타내는 표현이므로 〈I wish+가정법 과거완료(주어+had+p.p.)〉를 써야 한다. (be → had been)

30 열정이라는 것은 타고 나는 것이 아니라, 자신이 개발하는 것임을 나중에서야 깨달은 글쓴이는 애초에 "열정을 개발하라"라는 조언을 들었더라면 소중한 시간과 돈을 낭비하지 않았을 것이라고 아쉬워하고 있다.

Lesson 05 일치, 화법, 특수 구문

▶▶ Grammar Practice

pp. 92~95

(A1) (1) is (2) is (3) is (4) are (5) is

(A2) (1) ○ (2) ○ (3) is (4) is (5) ○ (6) vet (7) was

(B1) (1) was (2) had done (3) wrote (4) starts (5) was

(B2) (1) invented (2) boils (3) saw

(C1) (1) said, she (2) told, I (3) had come, there

(C2) (1) solved this (2) not(never) to be
(3) What is your

(D1) (1) the very (2) does practice (3) that(when)
(4) planet that(which)

(D2) (1) ⓒ (2) ⓐ (3) ⓑ (4) ⓓ (5) ⓒ

(E1) (1) Never did I expect (2) stood a strange man
(3) can I (4) did I

(E2) (1) leaves the bus (2) stood Jack
(3) shone the sun (4) neither did

(F1) (1) go (2) I was (3) he is (4) wear (5) was happy

(F2) (1) take a walk (2) went (3) I was

▶▶ Grammar Test

pp. 96~97

01 ④　02 ②　03 ④　04 (1) are → is (2) were → was
05 ③　06 go camping　07 (1) do (2) did (3) does
08 ②　09 ⑤　10 ④　11 It was in September that
(when)　12 ④　13 It is my English teacher that(who)
will visit Canada next week.

01 ④ 역사적 사실은 시제 일치와 관계없이 항상 과거 시제를 쓴다. (→ hosted)

02 the rest of와 half of는 뒤에 오는 명사의 수에 따라 동사의 수를 결정한다. 첫 번째 문장의 food는 단수이고 과거형 문장이므로 was, 두 번째 문장의 boys는 복수이고 현재형 문장이므로 are가 알맞다.

03 ④ 주절의 시제가 과거이므로 종속절의 시제는 과거나 과거 완료가 되어야 한다. (→ printed(had printed))

04 (1) 관계대명사 What이 이끄는 명사절이 문장에서 주어로 쓰이면 단수 취급한다. (2) 〈not A but B〉 구문이 주어이면 동사는 B의 수에 일치시킨다.

05 ③ 〈분수+of〉가 주어로 쓰이면 그 뒤에 오는 명사의 수에 따라 동사의 수가 결정되는데 the nations가 복수이므로 are를 써야 한다.

06 반복되는 어구는 생략이 가능한데, B의 말에서 go camping이 A의 말과 동일하게 반복되므로 생략할 수 있다.

07 (1), (2) 동사를 강조하는 경우 〈조동사 do/does/did+동사원형〉을 쓴다. (3) '~도 그렇다'라는 긍정의 동의 표현은 〈so+조동사+주어〉를 쓴다.

08 ② 주절의 동사가 과거이면 종속절의 동사는 과거 또는 과거 완료로 써야 한다. (do → did(had done))

09 ⑤ the very는 명사를 강조할 때 쓰며, 동사 know를 강조할 때는 조동사 do를 쓴다. (the very know → do know)

10 장소 부사구가 문장의 앞으로 오면 〈장소 부사구+동사+주어〉의 어순으로 문장을 쓴다.

11 시간 부사구를 강조할 때는 〈It was ~ that(when) ...〉 강조 구문을 쓴다.

12 전달 동사가 과거이므로 will은 과거형 would가 되어야 하며, 직접화법의 tomorrow는 간접화법에서 the next (following) day로 바꾼다.

13 〈It is ~ that...〉 강조 구문에서 강조하고 싶은 말인 My English teacher를 It is와 that 사이에 넣는다.

▶▶ Reading

pp. 98~99

1 모든 도시에 머물 곳을 마련해라.　2 told(asked, ordered) us to build a house　3 ③　4 ②

[1~2]

아버지의 지혜
　부유하고 지혜로운 아버지에게 Puru와 Puneet이라는 두 아들들이 있었다. 그가 세상을 떠나기 전에 그는 그의 두 아들을 불렀고 그들에게 마지막 지혜의 말을 전했다. "내 사랑하는 아들들아. 모든 도시에 집을 지어라. 편하게 자라. 네 음식을 즐겨라. 마지막으로, 부자처럼 돈을 써라." 그의 죽음 이후, 그의 아들들은 아버지 재산의 각자 몫을 가졌고 다른 도시에 정착해서 그들의 아버지의 말을 따랐다. 5년이 흘렀고 Puru에게는 남은 돈이 없었다. 그러나 Puneet은 어느 때보다 더 부유했다. Puru는 자신이 어디부터 잘못됐는지 알기 위해서 Puneet을 찾아갔다. "Puneet, 너는 우리 아버지의 조언을 따르지 않았니?"

Puneet은 이렇게 말했다. "나는 아버지의 말씀을 따랐어. 우리 아버지께서 모든 도시에 집을 지으라고 우리에게 말할 때, 나는 그것을 머물 곳을 마련하라는 것으로 여겼어. 그래서 나는 모든 도시에서 친구를 사귀었어. 또, 나는 열심히 일하고 피곤했기 때문에, 밤마다 잠을 편하게 잤어. 나는 내가 배고플 때만 먹어서 아주 간단한 끼니라도 훌륭한 맛이었어. 부자처럼 돈을 쓰라고? 나는 내게 더 많은 돈을 가져다줄 곳에 돈을 쓰려고 애썼어. 내게는 이것이 우리의 아버지가 설명하려고 하셨던 바로 그 지혜였어."

1 아버지의 유언이었던 모든 도시에 집을 지으라는 아버지의 유언을, Puneet은 모든 도시에 머물 곳을 마련하라는 것으로 여기고, 모든 도시에서 친구를 사귀었다고 했다.

2 인용문이 명령문인 직접화법의 문장을 간접화법으로 바꿀 때, 전달 동사로 tell, ask, order 등을 쓸 수 있고, 명령문은 to부정사로 쓴다.

3
> 성미가 고약한 어린 소년이 있었다. 그가 화를 낼 때마다 그의 아버지는 그에게 울타리에 못을 박게 했다. 마침내 소년이 화를 내지 않는 날이 왔다. 이번에는 그가 화를 참을 수 있을 때마다 아버지는 그에게 못을 하나씩 뽑게 했다. 그는 드디어 못을 모두 뽑았다고 그의 아버지께 말씀드렸다. 그러자 아버지는 그를 울타리로 데리고 가서 "아들아, 울타리의 구멍들을 봐라. 울타리는 절대 똑같아지지 않을 거란다. 네가 여러 번 사과하더라도, 그 상처는 여전히 거기 있어."라고 말했다.

타인에게 화를 낸 후 미안하다고 말해도 그 상처는 지워지지 않는다고 했으므로 아버지의 마지막 말은 ③ '다른 사람들에게 상처를 주지 않도록 절대 화를 내지 마라.'의 의미이다.

4
> 인터넷에는 수천 개의 영상이 있고, 여러분이 그 영상에서 보는 것이 사실이라고 여러분은 생각할지도 모른다. 그러나 첨단 기술을 이용해서, 사람들은 많은 새로운 방식으로 영상을 편집할 수 있다. 예를 들어, 영상은 존재하지 않는 사람들을 창조하고, 사람들이 말한 적이 없는 것을 그들이 말한 것으로 만들 수 있다. 이러한 영상들은 deepfake라고 불린다. 이것을 퇴치하기 위해 중국이 새로운 법을 적용하려는 것은 바로 deepfake 때문이다. 새로운 법이 적용되면, 인공지능이나 가상현실을 이용한 영상이나 오디오에는 반드시 표시를 해야 한다. 베이징의 관리들은 이 법이 거짓 뉴스의 확산을 막는 데 도움이 될 것이라고 말했다.

② 뒤의 Those clips는 주어진 문장에 소개된 예를 가리키며, 이것이 deepfake로 불린다고 했으므로 ②가 적절하다.

> **Expression Test**

1 ②   **2** should have put   **3** ①   **4** ①   **5** I should have done them   **6** ⑤

1 나머지는 제안하는 표현이고, ②는 이유를 묻는 표현이다.

2 〈should have+p.p.〉는 '~했어야 했는데 (하지 않았다)'라는 의미로 과거 일에 대한 후회를 나타낸다.

3 산에 오르는 데 필요한 것으로 편안한 옷과 신발을 착용할 것을 제안하는 말이 알맞다. 제안하거나 권유하는 표현으로 I suggest (that) ...., You'd better ...., I think you should .... 등이 있다.

4 밑줄 친 문장은 과거에 하지 않았던 일에 대해 후회를 나타내는 표현이다. ①은 '우리가 지하철을 탔었음에 틀림없다.'라는 뜻으로 과거 일에 대한 강한 확신을 나타내는 표현이다.

5 〈should have+p.p.〉는 '~했어야 했는데 (하지 않았다)'라는 의미로 과거 일에 대한 후회를 나타낸다.

6 ⓓ Sandy, 이 사진 멋있다. 이게 너니? – ⓑ 그래. 그것은 정말로 재미있었어. 나는 내가 하늘의 새인 것 같은 느낌을 받았어. – ⓐ 신나 보인다. 나도 이것을 해 보고 싶어. 내가 그것을 할 수 있을 거라고 생각하니? – ⓒ 물론이야. 전문가에게 배우기를 권할게.

> **서술형 평가**

1 (1) I should have tried it on. (2) Why don't you get a refund?   **2** (1) are (2) were (3) invented (4) was   **3** (1) It was Alice that(who) I saw in the bakery this morning. (2) It was in the bakery that(where) I saw Alice this morning. (3) It was this morning that(when) I saw Alice in the bakery.   **4** (1) did Jack eat (2) has Larry been (3) stood an old building   **5** (1) I asked Mom if(whether) there was anything to eat. (2) She told me that she could make some omelet for me. (3) She took out a frying pan and told me to bring some eggs from the refrigerator.

1 (1) 후회, 안타까움을 표현할 때 〈I should have+p.p.〉를, (2) why를 써서 제안할 때는 Why don't you ...?로 표현한다.

2 (1) 〈most of+복수 명사〉와 (2) 〈a number of+복수 명사〉가 주어이면 동사의 수를 복수로 쓴다. (3) 역사적 사실은 항상 과거 시제로 쓴다. (4) 주절이 과거이므로 that절의 동사도 과거 시제로 쓴다.

3 〈It ~ that ...〉 강조 구문을 사용하여 강조할 때는 문장에서 강조하고자 하는 말을 It is/was와 that 사이에 쓰고, 강조하는 말을 제외한 나머지를 that 뒤에 쓴다.

4 의미를 강조하기 위해 도치할 경우, (1) 〈부정어+조동사+주어+본동사〉, (2) 〈부정어+동사+주어〉, (3) 〈장소 부사구+동사+주어〉의 어순으로 쓴다.

5 직접화법을 간접화법으로 바꿀 때, (1) 인용문이 의문문이므로 전달 동사 say to를 ask로 바꾸고, 의문사가 없는 경우 if/whether를 쓰고 어순을 〈의문사+주어+동사〉로 쓴다. (2) 인용문이 평서문이므로 전달 동사 say to를 tell로 쓰고 접속사 that을 쓴 뒤, 듣는 이의 입장에 맞게 전달 내용의 인칭대명사를 바꾸고 시제도 일치시킨다. (3) 인용문이 명령문이므로 전달 동사를 tell, order, ask 등을 쓰고 to부정사를 써서 바꾼다. 모든 경우에 주절의 시제에 맞춰 시제를 일치시킨다.

≫ Final Test
pp. 103~107

01 ③ **02** ④ **03** ④ **04** ⓒ → ⓐ → ⓑ **05** ⑤ **06** ③
07 how(what) about **08** ④ **09** were **10** ② **11** ②
12 ③ **13** ③ **14** ⑤ **15** am **16** ③ **17** ② **18** are
19 ③ **20** ② **21** ⑤ **22** has Max thought about immigrating to America **23** ① **24** ③ **25** ② **26** ②
27 Not only does the rink save tons of water to make ice **28** ④ **29** to, him, he sees **30** ②

---

01 '아픈 동물을 치료하는 사람'은 ③ '수의사'이다.

02 injured는 '부상당한'이라는 의미로 hurt와 같은 의미이다.

03 ④는 '곤충'이라는 뜻으로 나머지 ① 개미 ② 벌 ③ 나비 ⑤ 귀뚜라미를 포함한다.

04 ⓒ 봐. 비가 오고 있어. − ⓐ 아, 안 돼! 나는 우산 가져오는 것을 잊었어. − ⓑ 나도 없어. 우리는 일기 예보를 기억했어야 했는데.

05 A는 강해지고 싶다며 어떻게 해야 하는지 B에게 조언을 요청하고 있으므로, 이에 대한 대답으로는 I suggest that ~.을 써서 제안하는 ⑤ '역도를 하라고 제안할게.'가 알맞다.

06 '너는 수업에 늦었어.'라는 A의 말에 B가 동의하므로 ③ '나는 더 일찍 일어났어야 했어.'라는 뜻의 후회를 나타내는 표현이 이어지는 것이 알맞다.

07 A가 B에게 전문 수영 강사에게 배울 것을 제안하고 있다. 빈칸 뒤에 learning이 있으므로 제안하는 표현인 How about ~?이나 What about ~?을 쓰는 것이 알맞다.

08 ④는 establish(설립하다)의 부정을 나타내기 위해 쓰인 과거 시제의 조동사 did이고, 나머지는 강조를 나타내기 위해

쓰인 조동사 do이다.

09 주어로 쓰인 some of의 뒤에 오는 명사에 따라 동사의 수를 결정하는데 apples는 복수이고 내용상 과거이므로 were를 써야 한다.

10 첫 번째 문장에는 동사 want를 강조하는 조동사 do가, 두 번째 문장에는 부정문에 동의할 때 쓰이는 조동사 do가 온다.

11 첫 번째 문장은 불변의 진리이므로 현재 시제를, 두 번째 문장은 역사적 사실이므로 과거 시제를 쓴다.

12 ③에서 did는 '설거지를 하다'라는 뜻인 do the dishes의 과거로 쓰였다. ① does가 동사 expand를 강조한다. ② at the park를 〈It was ~ that(where) ...〉 강조 구문으로 강조하고 있다. ④ Julie를 강조하는 〈It was ~ that ...〉 강조 구문 ⑤ the very가 명사를 강조한다.

13 간접화법에서 said to는 told로, this는 that으로, you는 전달 동사 뒤의 목적어인 me로 바꾼다. 종속절의 조동사는 주절의 told에 맞춰 would로 쓴다.

14 ⑤ 부사절에서 〈주어+be동사〉는 주절의 주어와 같을 때만 생략할 수 있다.

15 〈B as well as A〉가 주어이면 B에 동사의 수를 일치시킨다.

16 빈칸 뒤의 내용으로 보아 '민호도 그렇다'라는 긍정의 동의의 표현 〈So+조동사+주어〉이 알맞다.

17 ② 직접화법의 인용문이 부정 명령문이면 간접화법에서는 〈not+to+동사원형〉의 어순으로 쓴다. (→ not to touch)

18 〈A number of+복수 동사〉와 〈Both A and B〉가 주어이면 동사는 복수로 일치시키고, now로 보아 현재형이 와야 하므로 are가 적절하다.

19 주절의 동사가 과거일 때 종속절에는 과거나 과거완료가 올 수 있는데, 불변의 진리는 시제 일치의 예외 상황으로 주절이 과거여도 올 수 있으므로 ⓐ, ⓒ, ⓔ가 빈칸에 알맞다.

20 의문사 없는 의문문이 인용문인 직접화법 문장을 간접화법으로 바꿔 쓸 때 접속사로 if 또는 whether를 쓴다.

21 의문사가 있는 의문문이 인용문인 문장을 간접화법으로 바꿀 때 인용문의 어순은 〈의문사+주어+동사〉이고 전달 동사가 과거일 때 인용문의 동사도 과거로 바꾼다. 주어 we는 Eva와 Gabriel이 모두 포함된 말이므로 간접화법 문장에서는 they를 쓴다.

22 부정어인 never를 강조하기 위해 문장 앞에 두면 〈부정어+has+주어+p.p.〉의 어순으로 문장을 완성해야 한다.

23 ⓒ, ⓔ 주절과 부사절의 주어가 다른 경우에는 부사절의 〈주어+be동사〉를 생략할 수 없다.

24 (a)는 〈It was ~ that ...〉 강조 구문에서 강조되고 있는 것이 Mike로 사람이므로 that 대신 who를 쓸 수 있다. (b)는 강조되고 있는 것이 at the park로 장소 부사구이므로 that 대신 where를 쓸 수 있다. (c)는 강조되고 있는 것이 last Sunday로 시간 부사구이므로 that 대신 when을 쓸 수 있다.

25

> 여러분은 카메라 플래시가 터진 후에 점들을 보고 나서 왜 그런지 궁금해 한 경험이 있는가? 그것은 여러분의 광수용체들 때문이다. 그것은 여러분의 눈 뒤쪽에서 여러분이 빛을 볼 수 있게 하는 특수 세포들이다. 그것은 빛을 뇌로 전달되는 전기 신호로 바꾼다. 여러분이 보는 이미지를 만드는 것은 바로 뇌이다. 그러나 카메라 플래시가 터지고 나면, 그것이 너무 밝아서 광수용체가 잘 작동하지 못한다. 광수용체가 회복되는 동안에 여러분의 뇌는 아무것도 "보지" 못하고 그 여백을 점으로 채운다.

광수용체는 빛을 전기 신호로 바꾸고, 그 전기 신호가 뇌로 보내진다고 했으므로 ②는 일치하지 않는다.

26

> 여러분은 흰 무지개를 본 적이 있는가? 그것은 안개가 있는 동안에 나타난다. 안개가 그 안에 매우 작은 물방울들을 머금을 때, 놀라운 흰 무지개가 나타난다. 여러분이 태양을 등지고 서서 안개 쪽을 보면 그것을 쉽게 발견할 수 있다. 그것은 밤에, 하늘에 뜬 달이 매우 밝을 때 나타나기도 한다. 그 경우, 그것은 흰 무지개가 아니라 달무지개라고 불린다.

ⓐ, ⓒ, ⓓ, ⓔ는 white rainbow를 가리키고 ⓑ는 fog를 가리키는 It이다.

[27~28]

> 멕시코시티는 따뜻한 곳으로 일 년 내내 추워지지 않지만, 시민들은 빙상 스케이트를 즐길 수 있다. 어떻게 그런가? 표면이 얼음으로 덮여 있지 않은 커다란 실외 스케이트장이 있다. 그것을 덮은 것은 플라스틱이다. 스케이트를 타는 사람들은 그들이 얼린 스케이트장에 있는 것처럼 느낀다고 말한다. 이 스케이트장은 얼음을 만들기 위한 수천 톤의 물을 절약할 뿐만 아니라, 그 얼음을 언 상태로 유지하는 데 필요한 에너지도 절약한다. 그 도시의 시장은 "우리의 친환경 스케이트장은 환경을 해치지 않고 빙상 스케이트의 즐거움을 제공한다."라고 말한다.

27 부정을 나타내는 부사구가 문장의 맨 앞에 쓰였으므로 〈부사구＋조동사＋주어＋동사원형〉의 어순이 알맞다.

28 ④ 하루에 몇 명이 스케이트장을 이용하는지에 대한 답변을 위 글에서 찾을 수 없다.

[29~30]

> Sherlock Holmes와 Watson박사가 캠핑을 간다. 그들은 맛있는 저녁식사와 와인 한 병을 마시고 나서, 잠을 자기 위해 그들의 텐트로 들어간다. 몇 시간 후에 Holmes가 Watson을 깨운다. (B) 그는 Watson에게 말한다. "하늘을 보고 보이는 것을 말해 봐." Watson이 "수백만 개의 별이 보이네, Holmes."라고 답한다. (A) "그것으로 무엇을 추론할 수 있나?" Watson은 수백만 개의 은하계와 수십억 개의 행

> 성이 있는 것이라고 말했다. (C) Holmes는 말한다. "Watson, 이 바보야! 누군가 우리 텐트를 훔쳐 갔다고!"라고 말한다.

29 직접화법을 간접화법으로 바꿀 때, 전달동사 say to는 tell로 바꾸고, 명령문은 to부정사로 바꾸며, 대명사 me, you 등은 모두 전달자의 입장에 맞게 바꿔 준다.

30 잠을 자기 위해 텐트에 들어간 이후 눈을 떴을 때 하늘의 별이 보이는 것을 보고 Holmes는 텐트가 도둑맞았다는 것을 바로 알았지만, Watson은 이를 몰랐던 상황이다.

01 ④	02 ②	03 ⑤	04 ④	05 ①	06 ②	07 ④	08 ①
09 ③	10 ①	11 ③	12 ②	13 ③	14 ⑤	15 ②	16 ③
17 ②	18 ④	19 ①	20 ⑤				

— Dictation Test —

01 umbrella, plain black, folding, pouch, leaving, counter   **02** a book titled, 10-year-old, main character overcomes, That's because   **03** made a reservation, a twin room, better suit, cancel, book a family room   **04** ends at, wait until, the school librarian, offer, won't be late   **05** seashells, along the beach, go hiking, make a plan   **06** I've lost, carry alone, made of, alright, Long time no see   **07** the deliveryman, return, packed it, give it, on the way home   **08** due to, the schedule, be served, the entrance gate   **09** all of you, check out, forget to bring, up to   **10** romantic comedies, fit me well, in the hallway, Have you seen   **11** my eyesight has gotten worse, wearing eyeglasses, to check, get an eye examination   **12** the cheapest one, both of them, a bag charm, the same thing   **13** open a savings account, fill out, deposit, next year, January 22nd   **14** television dramas, play computer games, play soccer, skied, I'd better   **15** all wrinkled, Once, on sale, appliances section   **16** a pair of pants, on shirts, your change   **17** in the same direction, didn't I, take the bus   **18** will be canceled, fine dust, have classes   **19** let out, purchase, have them done, lengthen   **20** were supposed to, forgot, either, if she remembers

01 ④

W   Excuse me, have you seen an umbrella around here?

M   What does it look like?

W   It's just a plain black umbrella.

M   Is it a folding umbrella?

W   Yes. It's inside a black pouch. I remember leaving it on this counter about 10 minutes ago.

M   Then this might be yours. I found it on this counter.

W   Yes, this is mine. Thank you very much.

여   실례합니다. 이 주변에서 우산 보셨나요?

남   그것은 어떻게 생겼나요?

여   그것은 그냥 무늬 없는 검은색 우산이에요.

남   그것은 접이식 우산인가요?

여   네. 그것은 검정색 주머니에 들어 있어요. 제가 그것을 10분 정도 전에 이 계산대 위에 둔 걸로 기억해요.

남   그럼 이것이 당신의 것일지도 모르겠네요. 이 계산대 위에서 그것을 발견했어요.

여   네, 이것이 제 것이에요. 대단히 감사합니다.

02 ②

W   Can you recommend me a good book?

M   I've read a book titled *Wonder* recently. I enjoyed it very much.

W   Who is the main character?

M   The main character is a 10-year-old boy with a rare disease.

W   I see. So, what's the story about?

M   It's about how the main character overcomes his situation and achieves success in his school life.

W   That sounds interesting. Why did you like the book?

M   That's because it was very thought provoking. In addition, it was easy to relate to because it dealt with teenagers.

W   That's good to hear. Maybe I should try reading it too.

여   내게 좋은 책 한 권 추천해줄 수 있니?

남   나는 최근에 〈Wonder〉라는 제목의 책을 읽었어. 나는 그 책이 무척 좋았어.

여   주인공은 누구니?

남   주인공은 희귀한 병에 걸린 열 살짜리 소년이야.

여   그렇구나. 그러면 그 이야기는 무엇에 관한 거니?

남   주인공이 그의 상황을 극복하고 학교생활에서 성공을 거두는 것에 관한 것이야.

여   재미있겠다. 너는 그 책을 왜 좋아하니?

남   왜냐하면 그 책은 많이 생각하게 만들었기 때문이야. 또, 십 대에 관한 것이어서 공감하기도 쉬웠어.

여   그랬구나, 나도 그 책을 한번 읽어봐야겠다.

03 ⑤

[Telephone rings.]

W Good morning, BS Hotel. How can I help you?

M Hello. I made a reservation for this Friday.

W May I have your name, sir?

M My name is Mark Smith.

W Hold on, please. Yes, we have a reservation under that name. It's a twin room for one night.

M Right. Can four people stay in the room?

W A twin room is for two people. A family room would better suit four people.

M Then can I cancel the twin room and book a family room instead?

W Of course. I'll change the reservation it right away.

[전화벨 소리가 올린다.]

여 안녕하세요, BS 호텔입니다. 무엇을 도와 드릴까요?

남 안녕하세요. 제가 이번 금요일에 예약을 했는데요.

여 성함을 여쭤도 될까요, 손님?

남 저는 Mark Smith입니다.

여 잠깐만 기다려주세요. 네, 그 이름으로 예약이 있습니다. 2인실 1박이네요.

남 맞습니다. 네 명이 그 방에 묵을 수 있나요?

여 2인실은 두 명을 위한 방입니다. 네 명에게는 패밀리룸이 더 잘 맞으실 겁니다.

남 그러면 2인실을 취소하고, 대신에 패밀리룸을 예약할 수 있나요?

여 물론입니다. 지금 바로 예약을 바꿔 드리겠습니다.

04 ④

W Tom, did you see the new pizza place in front of the school?

M Yes. Why don't we visit there sometime?

W School ends at 12:30 today. We should go there today.

M Great. Let's meet there at 1.

W Sorry, but can you wait until 1:30? I have to help the school librarian after school.

M No problem. But we should hurry. I saw that they offer the lunch special set until 2.

W I won't be late. See you there at 1:30.

M Okay.

여 Tom, 너 학교 앞에 있는 새 피자 가게 봤니?

남 응. 우리 언제 거기 가 보지 않을래?

여 학교가 오늘 12시 30분에 마치잖아. 오늘 거기 가야겠다.

남 좋아. 거기서 1시에 만나자.

여 미안한데, 1시 30분까지 기다려줄 수 있어? 나는 방과 후에 사서 선생님을 도와 드려야 해.

남 괜찮아. 하지만 서둘러야 해. 거기서 런치 스페셜 세트를 두 시까지만 제공한다는 걸 내가 봤거든.

여 늦지 않을게. 거기에서 1시 30분에 만나자.

남 그래.

05 ①

M Look at that! Those seashells are very pretty.

W I know. I wish I had some at home.

M It feels great walking along the beach.

W Right. The weather is really nice, too.

M We should take breaks like this more often.

W Why don't we go hiking on a mountain next time?

M Good idea. Let's make a plan for it. Oh and by the way, what do you want for lunch?

W Let's try the famous Chinese restaurant near here.

남 저것 봐! 저 조개들은 정말 예쁘다.

여 맞아. 집에 몇 개 두고 싶다.

남 해변을 따라 걸으니까 기분이 정말 좋아.

여 맞아. 날씨도 정말 좋아.

남 우리는 더 자주 이런 휴식을 취해야 해.

여 다음에는 산으로 하이킹을 가는 게 어떠니?

남 좋은 생각이야. 그것을 위한 계획을 세우자. 아, 그런데, 너는 점심으로 무엇을 먹고 싶니?

여 이 근처의 유명한 중식당에 가 보자.

06 ②

① M Have you seen my bag? I think I've lost it.

 W I think I saw your bag on the bench.

② M This bag is too heavy to carry alone.

 W Let me help you.

③ M What is this table made of?

 W It is made of wood.

④ M Are you feeling alright?

 W No, I think I have a fever.

⑤ M Long time no see. How have you been?

 W I've been doing very well.

① 남 너 내 가방 봤니? 내가 그것을 잃어버렸나봐.
　여 내가 네 가방을 벤치 위에 있는 걸 본 것 같아.
② 남 이 가방은 너무 무거워서 혼자 옮길 수가 없어.
　여 내가 너를 도와줄게.
③ 남 이 탁자는 무엇으로 만들어졌니?
　여 그것은 목재로 만들어졌어.
④ 남 너 괜찮니?
　여 아니, 나는 열이 있는 것 같아.
⑤ 남 오랜만이다. 너는 어떻게 지냈니?
　여 나는 아주 잘 지내고 있어.

07 ④

W　Dad, you're having dinner with mom tonight, right?

M　Yes, we're about to go out. Then can I ask a favor?

W　Sure. Is there anything I can do for you?

M　Yes. Actually, the deliveryman is coming to get my book any time soon.

W　Oh, I see that you decided to return it. Do you want me to put it in a package for you?

M　No, you don't have to. I packed it and put it on the table. Please give it to the deliveryman.

W　Okay. No problem. Oh, and can you buy me strawberry ice cream on the way home?

M　No problem.

───────────

여 아빠, 오늘밤에 엄마랑 저녁 드시는 거 맞죠?

남 그래, 우리는 이제 나가려고 한다. 근데 부탁 하나 해도 되니?

여 물론이죠. 제가 해 드릴 게 있어요?

남 응. 사실은, 배달원이 곧 내 책을 가지러 올 거야.

여 아, 그것을 반품하기로 결정하셨군요. 제가 아빠 대신 그것을 포장할까요?

남 아니, 그럴 필요 없어. 내가 그것을 포장해서 탁자 위에 두었어. 그것을 배달원에게 주렴.

여 네, 그럴게요. 아, 그리고 집에 오시는 길에 딸기 아이스크림 좀 사다 주실래요?

남 그래.

08 ①

M　Attention, everyone. I guess you're very tired due to the tight schedule today. Let me briefly tell you the schedule for tomorrow. We are going to visit the National Palace Museum. Breakfast will be served from 6:30 at the restaurant on the first floor. We're planning to leave at 8:20, so please finish your meals by 8:00 and get on the tour bus by 8:10. The bus will be waiting at the entrance gate. Any questions?

───────────

남 주목해주세요, 여러분. 오늘의 빡빡한 일정 탓에 여러분들이 매우 피곤할 것 같네요. 제가 여러분들에게 내일 일정을 간단하게 말씀드릴게요. 우리는 국립고궁박물관에 방문할 것입니다. 아침 식사는 6시 30분부터 1층의 식당에서 제공될 예정입니다. 우리는 8시 20분에 떠날 예정이니, 여러분은 식사를 8시까지 마치고 8시 10분까지 관광버스에 탑승하세요. 버스는 정문에서 대기할 예정입니다. 질문 있으세요?

09 ③

W　So, have all of you found the books you want to read? To check out the books, take them to Ms. Kim, the school librarian. She will help you check them out. Don't forget to bring your student ID, too. You can borrow up to three books but you have to return them in two weeks.

───────────

여 그럼, 여러분은 모두 여러분이 읽고 싶은 책을 찾았나요? 그 책들을 대출하려면 그것을 사서 교사인 김 선생님께 가져가세요. 그 분이 여러분이 그것들을 대출하는 것을 도와주실 거예요. 여러분의 학생증도 가져가는 것을 잊지 마세요. 여러분들은 3권까지 빌릴 수가 있지만 2주 안에 그것들을 반납해야 합니다.

10 ①

① M　What's the weather like today?
　W　No, I don't like rainy days. I should stay at home today.
② M　What kind of movies do you like?
　W　I like romantic comedies. What about you?
③ M　Does the T-shirt fit me well?
　W　I think it's too tight.
④ M　Where shall we hang this picture?
　W　We should put it on the wall in the hallway.
⑤ M　Have you seen this man in the picture?
　W　Yes. This is the man I saw at the hospital.

───────────

① 남 오늘 날씨 어떠니?
　여 아니, 나는 비 오는 날을 좋아하지 않아. 나는 오늘은 집에 있어야 되겠다.

② **남** 너는 어느 종류의 영화를 좋아하니?

여 나는 로맨틱 코미디를 좋아해. 너는 어때?

③ **남** 티셔츠가 나한테 잘 어울리니?

여 너무 꽉 끼는 것 같아.

④ **남** 우리 이 그림을 어디에 걸까?

여 복도의 벽에 걸어야 할 것 같아.

⑤ **남** 당신은 사진 속의 이 남자를 본 적이 있습니까?

여 네. 이 사람이 제가 병원에서 본 그 남자예요.

---

11 ③

M Anne, can you read what it says on the blue sign?

W Yes, it says 'Olympic Expressway.'

M Oh, my. I can't see it. It seems that my eyesight has gotten worse.

W I think you are using your cellphone too much nowadays.

M Maybe I am. I guess I should start wearing eyeglasses now.

W Why don't' you go see the doctor to check your eyesight

M You're right. I'll get an eye examination at the hospital.

남 Anne, 너는 파란 표지판에 쓰인 것을 읽을 수 있니?

여 응, '올림픽대로'라고 적혀 있어.

남 세상에. 나는 그것이 안 보여. 내 시력이 나빠진 것 같아.

여 나는 네가 요즘 휴대전화를 너무 많이 사용하고 있는 것 같아.

남 그런지도 몰라. 나는 이제 안경을 쓰기 시작해야 할 것 같아.

여 혹시 네 시력을 확인하기 위해 진찰을 받는 게 어때?

남 맞아. 병원에서 눈 검사를 받아야겠어.

---

12 ②

M Amy, what are you going to make?

W I'm going to make the cheapest one and buy some snacks with the money left over. How about you?

M I want to make a candle or a clock, but both of them take too long.

W Well, maybe I'll also make a bag charm instead of buying snacks.

M Can I make the same thing? I need something to decorate my bag.

W Sure. It only takes 30 minutes, so let's go eat something after that.

M That'll be great.

남 Amy, 너는 무엇을 만들 거야?

여 나는 제일 싼 것을 만들고 남은 돈으로 간식을 좀 살 거야. 너는 어때?

남 나는 초나 시계를 만들고 싶은데, 둘 다 너무 오래 걸리네.

여 음, 나도 간식을 사는 대신 가방 장식품을 만들래.

남 나도 똑같은 거 만들어도 되니? 나는 내 가방을 꾸밀 뭔가가 필요해.

여 물론이지. 30분밖에 안 걸리니까 그거 만들고 나서 뭐 먹으러 가자.

남 그거 좋겠다.

---

13 ③

W Good morning. How can I help you?

M I'd like to open a savings account and make a deposit of 50,000 won a month, for one year.

W Okay. Let me help you. Please fill out these forms.

M Today is January 20th, so I have to deposit 50,000 won every 20th.

W You are right. Visit us back on January 20th next year to get your money back.

M But, I checked the calendar and that day is Saturday. Then when should I come?

W Then you should come on Monday, January 22nd.

M Oh, I see. Thank you.

여 안녕하세요. 무엇을 도와 드릴까요?

남 예금 계좌를 개설해서 1년 동안 한 달에 5만원씩 저금하고 싶습니다.

여 알겠습니다. 제가 도와드릴게요. 이 양식들을 작성해주세요.

남 오늘이 1월 20일이니까, 매 20일에 제가 5만원을 입금해야 하는군요.

여 맞습니다. 내년 1월 20일에 저희 은행에 다시 방문하셔서 고객님의 돈을 되돌려 받으세요.

남 하지만, 제가 달력을 확인해 보니 그 날이 토요일이에요. 그럼 제가 언제 와야 하나요?

여 그러면 1월 22일 월요일에 오시면 됩니다.

남 아, 알겠습니다. 감사합니다.

---

14 ⑤

W Mark, you look very tired today.

M I do feel very tired. Maybe I spent too much energy yesterday.

W Let me guess. Did you watch television dramas all night?

M No, not yesterday. I couldn't even play computer games yesterday.

W Did you play soccer with your friends outside?

M Well, actually, I skied all day long.

W So that's why you feel tired. I'm going to get some coffee. Will you go with me?

M No, I'd better get some sleep before class. Thanks anyway.

여 Mark, 너 오늘 되게 피곤해 보인다.

남 나 정말로 너무 피곤해. 아마 내가 어제 에너지를 너무 많이 소비했나 봐.

여 내가 맞춰 볼게. 너 밤새 TV 드라마를 봤니?

남 아니, 어제는 아니었어. 나는 어제 컴퓨터 게임은 하지도 못했어.

여 바깥에서 친구들이랑 축구했니?

남 음, 사실은, 나는 하루 종일 스키를 탔어.

여 그래서 네가 피곤한 거구나. 나는 커피를 좀 가지러 가는 중이야. 나랑 같이 갈래?

남 아니, 나는 수업 전에 조금 자는 것이 더 나을 것 같아. 어쨌든 고마워.

---

15 ②

M You come back home from work and your clothes are all wrinkled and dirty. However, you don't have time to wash them. What do you do? Just leave them to the Fashion Styler. Once you put them in, it'll make your clothes so clean as if they were freshly washed. It not only saves your money and cleans your clothes, but it also improves your style. In addition, it's on sale. We're giving a 30% discount until this Sunday. You can find the Fashion Styler in the appliances section.

남 여러분이 퇴근하여 귀가했는데 여러분의 옷은 온통 구겨지고 더럽습니다. 하지만, 여러분에게 그것을 세탁할 시간이 없습니다. 여러분은 무엇을 하시겠어요? 그것을 Fashion Styler에 맡기세요. 여러분이 옷을 그것에 일단 넣으면, 그것은 여러분의 옷을 방금 세탁한 것처럼 깨끗하게 만들어 줄 것입니다. 그것은 여러분의 돈을 절약하고 옷을 깨끗하게 할 뿐만 아니라, 여러분의 스타일도 개선할 것입니다. 게다가 그것은 할인 중입니다. 저희가 이번 일요일까지 30퍼센트를 할인해 드립니다. 여러분은 Fashion Styler를 가전제품 구역에서 보실 수 있습니다.

---

16 ③

M Next, please.

W Okay. I have three shirts and two pairs of pants. How much do I have to pay?

M These shirts are 1,200 won each, and it's 2,000 won for a pair of pants.

W So it will be 7,600 won, right?

M Yes, but we are giving a discount on shirts now. So, each shirt costs 1,000 won.

W That sounds great. Here's 10,000 won. When does the discount end?

M This Friday. Here's your change.

W Thank you.

남 다음 분이요.

여 네. 셔츠 세 장과 바지 두 벌이 있습니다. 제가 얼마를 지불해야 하나요?

남 이 셔츠들은 각각 1,200원이고요, 바지는 한 벌에 2,000원입니다.

여 그래서 7600원이죠, 맞죠?

남 네, 그런데 지금 셔츠는 할인해 드리고 있습니다. 셔츠는 한 장에 1,000원입니다.

여 잘됐네요. 여기 만 원이 있어요. 언제까지 할인해 주시나요?

남 이번 금요일까지요. 잔돈 여기 있습니다.

여 감사합니다.

---

17 ②

W Jake, are you going home?

M Yes. I am. Are you going home, too?

W Yes. It seems like we are going in the same direction. Where do you live?

M I live in the Castle apartment. How about you?

W Me, too. Why didn't I see you on the bus this morning?

M That's because I don't take the bus to school.

W Really? Then how do you go to school?

여 Jake, 너 집에 가는 중이니?

남 응, 그래. 너도 집에 가는 중이니?

여 응. 우리가 같은 방향으로 가고 있는 것 같네. 너는 어디 사니?

남 나는 Castle 아파트에 살아. 너는?

여 나도. 왜 내가 너를 오늘 아침에 버스에서 못 봤지?

남 왜냐하면 나는 학교에 버스를 타고 가지 않아서야.

여 정말? 그럼 너는 학교에 어떻게 가니?

18 ④

M I'm so excited. Sports Day is finally tomorrow.

W Yeah, but I'm worried that it will be canceled.

M Why would it be canceled? Is it going to rain tomorrow?

W No, I'm worried about fine dust. I read it could be bad tomorrow.

M But we can still have Sports Day in the gym.

W Mr. Kim said if the fine dust is too bad, we would have classes instead of Sports Day.

M No way. I hope we have good weather tomorrow.

- -

남 정말 신난다. 내일이 드디어 운동회 하는 날이야.

여 응, 하지만 나는 그것이 취소될 것이 걱정이 돼.

남 그게 왜 취소되겠어? 내일 비가 온대?

여 아니, 미세 먼지가 걱정스러워. 내일 그게 나쁠 수도 있다고 했거든.

남 하지만 우리는 여전히 체육관에서 운동회를 할 수 있어.

여 김 선생님께서 미세먼지가 너무 나쁘면, 우리가 운동회 대신에 수업을 들을 거라고 하셨어.

남 절대 안 돼. 내일 날씨가 좋으면 좋겠다.

19 ①

M Excuse me. I'd like to buy these pants.

W Okay. They are $30 each.

M Well, these are a little short for me. I should let out the hems.

W If you purchase more than $50, we do that for free.

M That sounds great. How long does it take to have them done?

W You can get them back in an hour. How much do you want to lengthen them?

- -

남 실례합니다. 이 바지들을 사고 싶은데요.

여 그래요. 그것들은 각각 30달러입니다.

남 음, 이것들은 제게 약간 짧아요. 단을 늘려야겠어요.

여 손님이 50달러 이상 구매하시면 그것은 저희가 무료로 해 드려요.

남 잘됐네요. 그것을 하는 데 얼마나 걸려요?

여 1시간 후에 찾아가실 수 있으세요. 바지를 얼마나 늘리고 싶으세요?

20 ⑤

W Michael and Sandra went to a tea shop. They were supposed to buy tea for themselves, and also for their mother. However, Michael forgot what his mother wanted to drink. It was either iced milk tea or iced black tea. Before he asks his mother on the phone, he wants to ask Sandra if she remembers which one it was. In this situation, what would Michael most likely to say to Sandra?

- -

여 Michael과 그의 여동생 Sandra는 차 판매점에 갔다. 그들은 그들 자신, 그리고 그들의 어머니를 위해 차를 살 예정이었다. 하지만, Michael은 그의 어머니께서 마시고 싶어 하셨던 것이 무엇인지 잊었다. 그것은 아이스 밀크티 또는 아이스 홍차 중 하나였다. 그가 그의 어머니께 전화로 여쭙기 전에, 그는 그것이 어느 것이었는지 Sandra가 기억하는지 물어보고 싶다. 이런 상황에, Michael은 Sandra에게 무엇이라고 말할 것 같은가?

01 ⑤   02 ④   03 ③   04 ②   05 ②   06 ①   07 ④   08 ⑤
09 ②   10 ①   11 ④   12 ③   13 ④   14 ②   15 ⑤   16 ③
17 ⑤   18 ②   19 ⑤   20 ①

Dictation Test

01 peel, pineapple sticks, canned, transparent container   **02** am worried that, while skating, in the park, bring your gloves   **03** not at the theater, go get, sold out, already bought   **04** plenty of time, The clock hands, drive, takes about   **05** take your temperature, Take, this porridge   **06** flowing out, might get wet, fortunate, covered with   **07** smell something burning, boiled, all burnt, the burnt smell   **08** awards, highly recommended, as a very hard-working   **09** push, pull each other, iron plates, tightly sticks   **10** mind closing, the main entrance, trim, sticky feet   **11** hot chocolate, homeroom teacher, played soccer, the shelf, wash my hands   **12** except, during the weekdays, the first week, haven't tried   **13** where I sat, at the back, the first row, sat by   **14** happened, grow taller, come to think, gained, should have exercised   **15** your school nurse, threatening, often as possible, catches the virus   **16** carry them in, It's better to, have them delivered   **17** The actors performed, like cats, not yet, compared to   **18** all off, the power is out, light up, without electricity   **19** envy, martial arts films, myself, invite   **20** do her hair, cut short, looked fine with, get her hair permed

---

01 ⑤

W   Let's buy some pineapples.

M   We have to peel them if we want to eat them. I have no idea how to do it.

W   I don't mean to buy a whole pineapple.

M   Okay, then do you want pineapple sticks?

W   They are too little. Why don't we buy that canned pineapple?

M   We don't need to. There're fresh pineapples. Let's buy the sliced pineapple in the transparent container.

W   Okay. That would be best.

- - -

여   파인애플을 좀 사자.

남   우리가 그것을 먹고 싶을 때 껍질을 벗겨야 하잖아. 나는 어떻게 하는지 몰라.

여   내 말은 파인애플을 통째로 사자는 뜻이 아니야.

남   그래, 그럼 너는 파인애플 스틱을 원해?

여   그건 너무 양이 적어. 저 파인애플 통조림을 사는 게 어때?

남   그럴 필요 없어. 저기 신선한 파인애플이 있잖아. 얇게 썰어서 투명한 용기에 담은 파인애플을 사자.

여   그래. 그게 가장 좋겠다.

---

02 ④

M   Why don't you go skating this weekend?

W   I don't know how to skate. Can you skate?

M   Yes. It's easy. I'll show you how.

W   I am worried that I'll fall down on the ice too much.

M   Don't worry. I'll hold your hands while skating.

W   Okay, then I'll try skating. Which ice rink are we going to?

M   A new ice rink just opened in the park. Let's go there.

W   Sounds perfect. How about meeting on Saturday at 10 a.m.?

M   Fine. Don't forget to bring your gloves.

- - -

남   이번 주말에 스케이트 타러 가지 않을래?

여   나는 스케이트를 못 타. 너는 스케이트를 탈 수 있니?

남   응. 쉬워. 내가 네게 방법을 알려 줄게.

여   나는 내가 얼음 위에서 너무 많이 넘어질 것이 걱정돼.

남   걱정하지 마. 네가 스케이트 타는 동안 내가 네 손을 잡아 줄게.

여   그래, 그럼 해 볼게. 우리는 어느 아이스 링크에 갈 거야?

남   공원 안에 새 아이스 링크가 열렸어. 거기 가자.

여   좋아. 토요일 오전 10시에 만나는 거 어때?

남   좋아. 네 장갑 가져오는 거 잊지 마.

---

03 ③

[Cellphone rings.]

M   Hello, Hana. Where are you? I'm in front of the ticket booth.

W   Brian. I'm sorry, but I'm not at the theater yet. I have no idea where I am.

M   Tell me what you see. I'll go get you.

W   That's okay. I took a taxi. I called you because I'm worried that the tickets might be sold out. Why don't you buy tickets now?

M   Don't worry, I already bought two.

W Thank you. I think I'll be there in 5 minutes.

M Okay. I'll be waiting for you buying some snacks.

[휴대 전화가 울린다.]

남 여보세요, 하나야. 너 어디니? 나는 매표소 앞에 있어.

여 Brian. 미안하지만, 나는 아직 극장에 못 갔어. 내가 어디에 있는지 전혀 모르겠어.

남 네게 보이는 것을 내게 말해 봐. 내가 너를 데리러 갈게.

여 괜찮아. 나 택시 탔어. 나는 표가 매진될 수도 있을 것 같아서 걱정이 되어서 전화했어. 네가 지금 표를 사는 게 어때?

남 걱정하지 마. 벌써 두 장 샀어.

여 고마워. 5분 후에는 거기 도착할 것 같아.

남 그래. 간식을 좀 사면서 너를 기다릴게.

---

04 ②

W Hurry up. You'll be late for school.

M Don't worry. It's only 7:20. I'll go out at 8 o'clock. We have plenty of time.

W What's wrong with the clock? It's 7:50 now.

M What? Oh, you're right. The clock hands are not moving at all.

W I think the battery is dead. I'll drive you to school today. What time do you have to get to school by?

M By 8:30.

W It takes about 15 minutes to get to school, so get in the car by 8:10.

M Okay. Thank you.

여 서둘러. 너 학교에 늦겠어.

남 걱정하지 마세요. 이제 겨우 7시 20분이에요. 저는 8시 정각에 나갈 거예요. 제게는 시간이 많아요.

여 시계가 무슨 문제가 있는 거니? 지금은 7시 50분이야.

남 네? 아, 그러네요. 시곗바늘이 전혀 움직이지 않아요.

여 건전지가 다 된 것 같다. 오늘은 내가 너를 학교에 차로 태워다 줄게. 너는 학교에 몇 시까지 도착해야 하니?

남 8시 30분까지요.

여 학교에 도착하는 데 15분 정도 걸리니까, 8시 10분까지 차에 타렴.

남 네. 고맙습니다.

---

05 ②

① M I have a headache. I think I have a fever, too.

  W Let's take your temperature.

② M Can you bring me the pills? It is time to take them.

  W Here you are. Take them with water.

③ M Are you okay? You look bad.

  W I think I'm too tired.

④ M I want to have some apples.

  W Okay. I'm going to peel one for you.

⑤ M Do you want to try this porridge?

  W Thank you. I was very hungry.

---

① 남 저는 머리가 아파요. 저 열이 있는 것 같아요.

  여 열을 재 보자.

② 남 제게 그 약을 갖다주실래요? 그것을 먹을 시간이에요.

  여 여기 있어. 물이랑 함께 먹으렴.

③ 남 너 괜찮니? 너 안 좋아 보인다.

  여 나는 너무 피곤한 것 같아.

④ 남 저는 사과를 좀 먹고 싶어요.

  여 그래. 너를 위해 내가 하나 깎아 줄게.

⑤ 남 이 죽 좀 먹을래?

  여 고마워요. 저는 매우 배가 고팠어요.

---

06 ①

M Mom, can you please come and help me?

W What's the matter? I have to go back to the kitchen again.

M The water's flowing out of the pot. Maybe I watered the plant too much.

W I think we should move the pot to the bathroom.

M But this is too heavy. I'm wiping the water from the floor, but the bed might get wet.

W Well, it seems that the water has stopped. It'll be okay soon.

M Whew. It is fortunate that the pot is not in the living room, where the floor is covered with carpet.

W I shouldn't have put the pot near the bed. I'll move it to the garden later.

남 엄마, 오셔서 저 좀 도와주실 수 있어요?

여 무슨 일이니? 나는 다시 부엌에 가 봐야 되는데.

남 화분에서 물이 흘러나오고 있어요. 아마 제가 나무에 물을 너무 많이 줬나 봐요.

여 내 생각에는 우리가 화분을 화장실로 옮겨야 할 것 같다.

남 하지만 이것은 너무 무거워요. 제가 바닥에서 물을 닦고 있지만, 침대가 젖을 수도 있겠어요.

여 음, 물이 멈춘 것 같아. 곧 괜찮을 거야.

남 휴. 화분이 거실에 있지 않아서 다행이에요. 거기는 카펫이 깔려 있잖아요.

여 내가 그 화분을 침대 근처에 두지 않았어야 했는데. 나중에 내가 그것을 정원으로 옮길게.

07 ④

W David, can't you smell something burning?

M Oh my! I forgot I boiled some sweet potatoes.

W That's okay. I turned off the stove.

M Thank you. They must be all burnt.

W I already checked them, and actually they looked quite delicious.

M That's fortunate. Then let's have them. I'll take out some plates.

W I'll do that. Can you please open the windows to get rid of the burnt smell?

M Sure. I will.

여 David, 뭔가 타는 냄새가 나지 않니?

남 세상에! 내가 고구마를 삶는다는 걸 잊어버렸어.

여 괜찮아. 내가 가스레인지를 껐어.

남 고마워. 그것들은 분명 다 타 버렸을 거야.

여 내가 이미 확인해 봤는데, 사실은 그것들이 꽤 맛있어 보였어.

남 그거 다행이다. 그럼 그것들을 먹자. 내가 접시를 꺼낼게.

여 그건 내가 할게. 너는 탄 냄새를 없애기 위해 창문을 좀 열어 줄래?

남 그래. 그럴게.

08 ⑤

M This year, Woodbridge High School gladly awards the Good Citizenship Award to Mark Thomson. He has been highly recommended by students and teachers. They said he has a positive attitude, and he studies very hard and actively volunteers. I also know him as a very hard-working student. I hope he will be a good role model for everyone. Please give a big hand to Mark, everyone.

남 올해, Woodbridge 고등학교는 훌륭한 시민상을 Mark Thomson에게 수여하는 것을 기쁘게 생각합니다. 그는 학생들과 교사들에 의해 적극적으로 추천받았습니다. 그들은 그가 긍정적인 태도를 지녔고, 그가 매우 열심히 공부하며 적극적으로 봉사한다고 말했습니다. 저 역시도 그를 아주 근면한 학생으로 알고 있습니다. 나는 그가 모든 이에게 좋은 롤모델이 되기를 희망합니다. Mark에게 크게 박수쳐 주시기 바랍니다, 여러분.

09 ②

W You may have seen this in your science class. This has two poles, the North pole and the South pole. Two North poles push each other away, and so do two South poles. However, the North pole and the South pole pull each other. You can put a note, using this, on iron plates like blackboards and refrigerator doors because this tightly sticks to them. However, this doesn't stick to plastic or rubber.

여 여러분은 아마 이것을 여러분의 과학 수업에서 봤을지도 모릅니다. 이것은 두 개의 극, N극과 S극이 있습니다. 두 개의 N극은 서로를 밀어내고, 두 개의 S극도 마찬가지입니다. 하지만, N극과 S극은 서로를 당깁니다. 여러분은 이것을 사용해서 칠판이나 냉장고 문과 같은 철판에 쪽지를 붙일 수 있는데, 그 이유는 이것이 그것들에 단단히 달라붙기 때문입니다. 하지만, 이것은 플라스틱이나 고무에는 붙지 않습니다.

10 ①

① W Do you mind closing the door?

M Of course. I'll do it for you.

② W Let me introduce my younger sister to you. This is Hana.

M Nice to meet you. I'm Jason.

③ W Where shall we meet tomorrow?

M See you at the main entrance of the museum.

④ W How would you like your hair done?

M Just trim it a little bit, please.

⑤ W How can a lizard not fall down from the ceiling?

M People say it has sticky feet.

---

① 여 문 좀 닫아 주지 않겠니?

남 아니. 내가 너를 위해 그것을 해 줄게.

② 여 내 여동생을 소개할게. 이쪽은 하나야.

남 만나서 반가워. 나는 Jason이야.

③ 여 우리 내일 어디서 만날까?

남 박물관 정문에서 봐.

④ 여 손님의 머리를 어떻게 하고 싶으세요?

남 그냥 조금만 다듬어 주세요.

⑤ 여 도마뱀은 어떻게 천장에서 떨어지지 않을 수 있어?

남 사람들 말로는 그것은 발이 끈적끈적하대.

11 ④

M Mom, I'm home. Oh, it's so cold outside.

W Do you want some hot chocolate?

M That would be great. Thank you.

W How was school today?

M My homeroom teacher seems very nice. I also made some friends already. We played soccer together after lunch.

W Sounds great. Can you take out the cookie jar from the shelf?

M Okay. Here you are. I'll wash my hands before I eat.

W Good idea.

남 엄마, 저 집에 왔어요. 아, 바깥이 정말 추워요.

여 핫초콜릿을 좀 마시고 싶니?

남 그러면 정말 좋겠어요. 고맙습니다.

여 오늘 학교는 어땠어?

남 담임 선생님은 아주 좋아 보이세요. 저는 벌써 친구들도 사귀었어요. 우리는 점심을 먹고 나서 같이 축구를 했어요.

여 잘했구나. 너 선반에서 쿠키 통 좀 꺼내 주겠니?

남 네. 여기 있어요. 먹기 전에 손 씻고 올게요.

여 좋은 생각이야.

12 ③

W What are you going to do this winter?

M Nothing special, except that I will play a lot of sports.

W What sports are you going to play?

M Well, first of all, I'm going to go swimming every morning during the weekdays. I'll also take skating lessons in the afternoon during the first week.

W Wow. That sounds like quite a lot.

M There's more. During every weekend, my family is going to go skiing.

W Will you go snowboarding, too?

M No, I haven't tried that yet. I would like to try that and curling someday.

여 너는 이번 겨울에 무엇을 할 거니?

남 운동을 많이 할 거라는 거 빼면 특별히 할 게 없어.

여 무슨 운동을 할 건데?

남 음, 우선 나는 주중에는 매일 아침 수영을 하러 갈 거야. 첫 주 동안에는 오후에 스케이트 수업도 들을 거야.

여 와, 그거 좀 많은 것 같은데.

남 더 있어. 주말마다 내 가족은 스키를 타러 갈 거야.

여 스노보드도 타러 갈 거니?

남 아니, 그건 아직 안 해 봤어. 나는 그것과 컬링을 언젠가 해 보고 싶어.

13 ④

M Good morning, Jina. What are you doing?

W I'm looking for my wallet. I think I left it in a desk yesterday, but I don't remember where I sat.

M I remember you sat at the back in your last class.

W I checked the back seats, but I couldn't find it there.

M Wait. Didn't you move to the first row later?

W Oh you're right. Now I remember, I sat by the front door. It's here. Thank you very much.

남 안녕, 지나야. 너 뭐 하고 있니?

여 나는 내 지갑을 찾고 있어. 내가 그것을 어제 책상 안에 둔 것 같은데, 내가 어디 앉았는지 기억이 안 나.

남 네가 마지막 수업에서 뒤쪽에 앉았던 걸로 기억하는데.

여 뒤쪽 자리들을 확인했는데, 거기서 그것을 찾을 수 없었어.

남 잠깐만. 너 나중에 첫 줄로 옮기지 않았니?

여 아, 맞아. 이제 내가 앞문 옆에 앉았던 게 기억난다. 여기 있어. 정말 고마워.

14 ②

W Sangho, you grew very tall. What happened to you during vacation?

M I don't know. I didn't do anything special to grow taller.

W Maybe you drank a lot of milk.

M Actually, I don't like milk, but come to think of it, I did eat a lot. I also gained a lot of weight.

W Yeah, I guess you should buy a new jacket.

M Right. I should have exercised at least a little. I should go on a diet now.

W You don't have to. You look pretty good now.

여 상호야, 너 키가 많이 컸다. 방학 동안에 네게 무슨 일이 일어난 거야?

남 모르겠어. 키가 더 크려고 특별히 한 건 아무 것도 없었어.

여 아마 네가 우유를 많이 마셨겠지.

남 사실 나는 우유는 안 좋아하는데, 그러고 보니 정말 많이 먹기는 했어. 나는 체중도 많이 늘었어.

여 그래, 너 새 재킷을 사야 할 것 같다.

남 맞아. 적어도 약간은 운동을 했어야 하는데. 나는 이제 다이어트를 해야겠어.

여 너는 그럴 필요 없어. 지금 아주 좋아 보여.

15 ⑤

W Hello, students! This is your school nurse Janet Brown. Recently, a scary virus has been threatening our health. Please wear masks all the time, and wash your hands as often as possible. You can buy masks, soap, and hand sanitizers at the school store. When you feel sick, please visit my office on the first floor. I hope nobody in this school catches the virus and everyone stays safe and healthy.

여 안녕하세요, 학생 여러분! 저는 여러분의 학교 보건 교사 Janet Brown입니다. 최근에 무서운 바이러스가 우리의 건강을 위협하고 있습니다. 항상 마스크를 착용하시고, 가능한 한 자주 손을 씻으세요. 여러분은 마스크, 비누, 그리고 손 소독제를 학교 매점에서 살 수 있습니다. 여러분이 몸이 안 좋으면, 1층의 제 사무실에 들르세요. 이 학교에서 아무도 바이러스에 걸리지 않고 모두가 안전하고 건강하기를 바랍니다.

16 ③

M Excuse me. How much are this calendar and this sketchbook?

W The calendar is $10, and the sketchbook is $3.

M Then I'll buy two calendars and three sketchbooks.

W That will be $29. Do you need a bag to carry them in? It's $1.

M These look too heavy to carry. It's better to have them delivered. Do you offer a delivery service?

W Yes. But you have to pay $3 if you purchase under $40.

M Okay. Then I'll pay $3 more and have them delivered.

남 실례합니다. 이 달력과 이 스케치북이 얼마인가요?

여 달력은 10달러이고 스케치북은 3달러입니다.

남 그러면 저는 달력 2개와 스케치북 3개를 살게요.

여 그러면 29달러입니다. 담아 갈 가방이 필요하신가요? 그것은 1달러입니다.

남 이것들은 들고 가기는 너무 무거워 보여요. 이것을 배달시키는 것이 낫겠어요. 배달 서비스를 하시나요?

여 네. 하지만 구매 금액이 40달러 이하이면 3달러를 지불하셔야 합니다.

남 그래요. 그러면 3달러를 더 지불하고 그것들을 배달시키겠습니다.

17 ⑤

W Did you watch the musical *Cats*?

M Yes, I watched it twice. I like it very much. The actors performed really well.

W I know. I watched it too. They move just like cats. I really liked the songs, too.

M Then did you also watch the movie *Cats*?

W Well, not yet. Did you watch it?

M Yes, I watched it with my family last weekend.

W Then how did you like it compared to the musical?

여 너 뮤지컬 〈캣츠〉 봤니?

남 응. 나는 그것을 두 번 봤어. 나는 그 작품을 정말 좋아해. 배우들이 정말 연기를 잘해.

여 맞아. 나도 그것을 봤어. 그들은 고양이들처럼 움직여. 나는 그 노래들도 정말 좋아해.

남 그럼 너는 영화 〈캣츠〉도 봤어?

여 음, 아직. 너는 그것을 봤니?

남 응. 나는 지난 주말에 가족들과 함께 그것을 봤어.

여 그럼 뮤지컬과 비교해서 너는 그것이 어땠어?

18 ②

M Oh my god. It suddenly got so dark. What happened?

W The lights are all off. Let's look out the window.

M The whole apartment complex is dark. I guess the power is out.

W You're right. What should we do now?

M We have to finish dinner. I'll light up the candles.

W Now I can see my food. But the candlelight is hot.

M We can't turn on the air conditioner without electricity. I can give you some ice instead if you want.

남 세상에. 갑자기 너무 어두워졌다. 무슨 일이 일어난 거지?

여 등이 모두 꺼졌어. 창밖을 보자.

남 아파트 단지 전체가 어두워. 아마도 정전이 됐나 봐.

여 맞아. 우리 이제 어떻게 하지?

남 우리는 저녁 식사를 마쳐야 해. 내가 초를 켤게.

여 이제 음식이 보인다. 하지만 촛불이 뜨거워.

남 전기가 없어서 에어컨을 켤 수는 없어. 그 대신 네가 원하면 얼음을 좀 줄 수는 있어.

남 Tom은 미용사이다. 어느 날, Anne이 머리를 손질하러 그의 미용실에 방문했다. 그녀는 그녀의 긴 머리를 짧게 자르기를 원해서, 그녀가 짧은 머리가 어울릴지 Tom에게 물었다. Tom은 긴 머리가 그녀에게 잘 어울린다고 대답했다. 그래서, 그녀는 마음을 바꾸었고 그녀의 머리에 파마를 해야 할지 그에게 묻고 싶다. 이런 상황에, Anne은 Tom에게 무엇이라고 말하겠는가?

19 ⑤

M Have you been to China?

W Yes. My grandparents live in China. I've been there many times.

M I envy you. I really want to travel to China.

W Why? Do you like Chinese food?

M No, I like Chinese martial arts films. I saw the huge mountains of China in those movies. I want to see them myself.

W You're right. I'll ask my grandparents to invite me one more time. Do you want to go with me?

- -

남 너는 중국에 가 봤니?

여 응. 내 조부모님들이 중국에 사셔. 나는 그곳에 여러 번 가 봤어.

남 네가 부럽다. 나는 정말 중국을 여행하고 싶어.

여 왜? 너는 중국 음식 좋아하니?

남 아니, 나는 중국 무술 영화들을 좋아해. 나는 그 영화들에서 중국의 거대한 산들을 보았어. 그것들을 직접 보고 싶어.

여 네 말이 맞아. 내가 조부모님께 나를 한 번 더 초대해 달라고 부탁드려야겠다. 너 나랑 같이 갈래?

20 ①

M Tom is a hair designer. One day, Anne visited his hair shop to do her hair. She wanted to have her long hair cut short, so she asked Tom if she would look good with short hair. Tom answered she looked fine with long hair. So, she changed her mind and wants to ask him if she should get her hair permed. In this situation, what would Anne most likely say to Tom?

01 ① 02 ⑤ 03 ③ 04 ④ 05 ④ 06 ④ 07 ③ 08 ⑤
09 ④ 10 ④ 11 ① 12 ⑤ 13 ③ 14 ③ 15 ③ 16 ⑤
17 ⑤ 18 ① 19 ⑤ 20 ③

Dictation Test

01 a square one, dots, with the heart pattern **02** some information, an entire week, The travel agent **03** the organization appreciated, your support, a big donation **04** how long, have to discuss, that presentation **05** used to, not allowed to, the receipt **06** quite everything, if you want, look comfortable, awesome **07** oil painting, before sunrise, the collection **08** the security line, a sealed clear, be taken out, screened separately **09** No problem, falls short of, do you prefer **10** enrolled, a conversation course, group project, can introduce you **11** comes up, have to install, print it out, one copy **12** for the exams, 50th anniversary, one more day **13** which program, right after that, if it's better, a lot more opportunities **14** already nine, why don't we, Let's go out **15** the school canceled, a severe thunderstorm, rescheduled **16** these red roses, dollars, dozen roses **17** can't be fixed, get replacement parts **18** look pale, you have a fever, shouldn't ignore, keep bothering **19** been waiting for, Help yourself, onion soup **20** have something, every time they meet, something different

---

01 ①

M May I help you?

W Yes, I need to buy a cushion for my sofa.

M Which do you prefer, a round one or a square one?

W I prefer the square one to the round one.

M Okay. Which do you like better, the one with dots or the one with hearts?

W I like the one with the heart pattern better. I'll take it.

M Good. Here it is.

남 무엇을 도와드릴까요?

여 네, 소파에 쓸 쿠션을 사려고 합니다.

남 둥근 것과 네모난 것 중에 뭐가 더 좋으신가요?

여 저는 둥근 것보다 네모난 것이 더 좋아요.

남 알겠습니다. 그럼 점 무늬가 있는 것과 하트 무늬가 있는 것 중에 뭐가 더 좋으신가요?

여 저는 하트 무늬가 있는 게 더 좋아요. 그것으로 할게요.

남 좋습니다. 여기 있습니다.

---

02 ⑤

W I got some information for our trip to Jejudo. If we buy a package tour, our hotel will only cost 200,000 won.

M That's for an entire week at the hotel? Wow, where is it?

W It's in the town center, so it's not close to the beach. Here are some pictures.

M It seems fine, but a little old. It will probably have poor air conditioning.

W Don't worry. The travel agent said the air conditioner works well.

M Good. Well, is there a swimming pool?

W Yes. There are also a gym and a business center.

여 내가 우리 제주도 여행을 위한 정보를 얻었어. 우리가 패키지 관광을 하면 우리 호텔 비용은 20만원밖에 안 해.

남 그것으로 호텔에서 일주일 동안 있을 수 있다고? 와, 어디야?

여 그것은 시내 중심부에 있어서 해변과 가깝지 않아. 여기 사진 몇 장이 있어.

남 괜찮아 보이지만, 좀 오래됐네. 아마 냉방이 잘 안 될 거야.

여 걱정하지 마. 여행사 직원이 에어컨이 잘 작동한다고 말했어.

남 좋아. 음, 거기 수영장이 있니?

여 응. 체육관과 비즈니스 센터도 있어.

---

03 ③

[Telephone rings.]

M Hello.

W Mr. James? This is Kate from the Hope Society.

M Yes, I know about the Hope Society. I volunteered there last Christmas.

W Oh, I'm sure everyone at the organization appreciated your help.

M It was my pleasure.

W We are trying to help feed hungry children, and your support will be a great help to them.

M Hmm... I can't afford to make a big donation, but I guess I can give you $30.

W Oh, thank you.

[전화벨이 울린다.]

남 여보세요.

여 James씨? 저는 Hope Society의 Kate입니다.

남 네, 저는 Hope Society에 관해 알고 있습니다. 저는 지난 크리스마스에 그곳에서 자원봉사를 했습니다.

여 오, 단체의 모든 사람들이 선생님의 도움에 감사했을 거라고 생각합니다.

남 천만에요.

여 우리는 굶주린 아이들에게 음식을 제공하는 데 도움이 되기 위해 노력하고 있고, 선생님의 지원이 그들에게 큰 도움이 될 거예요.

남 음... 제가 거액을 기부할 수는 없지만, 30달러는 드릴 수 있을 것 같아요.

여 오, 감사합니다.

04 ④

M Is the schedule for the 2 o'clock meeting ready?

W Yes. What do you want to know?

M I just want to know how long it will take.

W Well, we're supposed to review the new policies for 10 minutes.

M We also have to discuss the holiday season project, right?

W Yes, that will take 20 minutes.

M Lisa prepared a 15-minute presentation, too.

W Actually, I asked her to give that presentation next week.

M Great. Then, it will be a short meeting.

남 2시 회의의 일정이 다 준비되었나요?

여 네. 무엇을 알고 싶습니까?

남 저는 그것이 얼마나 걸릴지 알고 싶어요.

여 음. 우리는 새로운 정책을 10분 동안 검토할 예정입니다.

남 우리는 휴가철 프로젝트도 논의해야 하고요, 그렇죠?

여 네, 그것은 20분 걸릴 거예요.

남 Lisa도 15분간의 발표를 준비했어요.

여 사실, 그 발표를 다음 주에 하라고 그녀에게 요청했어요.

남 좋아요. 그럼 짧은 회의가 되겠군요.

05 ④

① M What are you doing?

　W I'm drawing people in the park.

② M Where are you in the picture?

　W I'm the person in the middle. I used to have long hair.

③ M Is it okay to bring food in here?

　W No, you are not allowed to do that in the museum.

④ M Can I exchange it for a different color?

　W Sure. Do you have the receipt?

⑤ M Excuse me! Can you take a picture of us?

　W Sure. Strike a pose!

① 남 너는 뭐 하는 중이니?

　여 나는 공원에서 사람들을 그리고 있어.

② 남 너는 사진 속에서 어디에 있어?

　여 가운데 있는 사람이 나야. 나는 머리가 길었어.

③ 남 여기 음식 가지고 와도 돼요?

　여 아뇨, 박물관에서는 그렇게 할 수 없습니다.

④ 남 이것을 다른 색으로 교환할 수 있나요?

　여 물론이죠. 영수증을 가지고 계세요?

⑤ 남 실례합니다! 저희 사진 좀 찍어주실래요?

　여 물론이죠. 포즈를 취하세요!

06 ④

W Wow, it looks like everything is on sale!

M Well, not quite everything. Only the women's items are on sale.

W Why don't we look around?

M Okay, if you want to.

W Hmm, I don't know what I should buy for my cousin's wedding. Look at these white heels. If I wear my green dress, these shoes will be perfect.

M They don't look comfortable at all. How about the flat ones over there?

W I don't like those. But look at these cute summer sandals. And those boots are awesome!

M Well, I think you should choose just one pair.

여 와, 모든 게 세일인 것 같아!

남 글쎄, 전부 다 그렇지는 않아. 여성용 상품만 세일 중이야.

여 우리 둘러보는 게 어때?

남 그래, 네가 그러고 싶다면.

여 흠, 사촌 결혼식을 위해 내가 어떤 것을 사야 할지 모르겠어. 이 하얀색 힐을 봐. 내가 녹색 드레스를 입으면 이 하얀 구두가 잘 어울릴 거야.

남 그것은 전혀 편해 보이지 않아. 저기 낮은 것은 어때?

여 나는 그것은 별로야. 하지만 이 귀여운 여름 샌들을 봐. 그리고 저 부츠는 정말 멋져!

남 음, 나는 네가 딱 한 켤레만 골라야 한다고 생각해.

07 ③

W *The Starry Night* is an oil painting by the Dutch painter, Vincent van Gogh. It was painted in June, 1889, and it shows the view from the window of van Gogh's room just before sunrise. It has been in the collection of the Museum of Modern Art in New York City since 1941. It is one of the most famous paintings in the history of Western culture.

여 〈The Starry Night〉는 네덜란드 화가 Vincent van Gogh가 그린 유화입니다. 그것은 1889년 6월에 그렸고, 그것은 해 뜨기 직전에 van Gogh의 방의 창문에서 보이는 경치를 보여줍니다. 그 작품은 1941년 이후 뉴욕 현대미술관에 소장되어 왔습니다. 그것은 서양 문화사에서 가장 유명한 그림들 중 하나입니다.

08 ⑤

M To all our passengers. You can help us keep the security line moving faster by following these rules. First, make sure that any liquids you're carrying are in bottles that are 100 ml or less in volume. Anything larger than that isn't allowed on the plane. Second, store all of your 100 ml containers in a sealed clear plastic bag. This bag should be taken out of your luggage and placed in the security bin to be screened separately. Do not leave any liquids inside your luggage. Thank you for your cooperation.

남 승객 여러분께 알립니다. 여러분이 다음 규칙을 잘 따라 주시면 저희가 보안 검색을 위해 선 줄이 더 빨리 움직이도록 유지하는 데 도움이 될 수 있습니다. 우선, 여러분이 소지한 액체는 100밀리리터 이하의 병에 담겨 있도록 해 주세요. 그보다 더 큰 것은 비행기에서 허용되지 않습니다. 둘째, 여러분의 100밀리리터 용기는 모두 밀봉된 투명 비닐봉투에 보관하세요. 이 봉투는 여러분의 짐에서 꺼내 보안 검색용 바구니에 담겨져서 별도로 검색되도록 해야 합니다. 어느 액체도 여러분의 짐 안에 남기지 마세요. 협조해 주셔서 감사합니다.

09 ④

① **M** Could you drive me home?
　W No problem.

② **M** Why don't we go out and watch a movie?
　W I wish I could, but I have an assignment to do.

③ **M** How do you like your new school?
　W It falls short of my expectation.

④ **M** How come you're late for the interview?
　W I came here by taxi. I am ready for the interview.

⑤ **M** Which color do you prefer, purple or red?
　W Neither. I like green.

---

① **남** 저를 집까지 태워다 주시겠어요?
　여 문제없어요.

② **남** 우리 나가서 영화 보는 게 어때?
　여 나도 그러고 싶은데 나는 해야 할 일이 있어.

③ **남** 네 새 학교는 어떠니?
　여 내 기대에는 못 미쳐.

④ **남** 당신은 어째서 면접에 늦었나요?
　여 저는 택시를 타고 여기에 왔어요. 저는 면접 볼 준비가 되었어요.

⑤ **남** 보라색과 빨간색 중에 어느 색을 더 좋아하나요?
　여 둘 다 별로예요. 저는 초록색을 좋아해요.

10 ④

M Hi, Kate. Are you taking a language class here?
W Yes, I enrolled in basic Spanish. How about you, Kevin?
M I'm in a conversation course now. How do you like it?
W I enjoy learning Spanish. But I'm worried about one thing.
M Oh, what's that?
W We have a group project coming up, but I don't know any of my classmates.
M Oh, my friend James is in that class, too. I can introduce you to him.
W Thank you!

남 안녕, Kate. 너는 여기서 어학 수업을 듣니?
여 응, 나는 기본 스페인어에 등록했어. 너는 어때, Kevin?
남 나는 지금 회화 과정을 듣고 있어. 수업은 어때?
여 나는 스페인어를 배우는 게 좋아. 하지만 한 가지 걱정이 있어.
남 오, 그게 뭐야?
여 우리에게는 곧 그룹 과제가 있는데, 나는 우리 반 친구들을 아무도 몰라.

남 오, 내 친구 James도 그 반에 있어. 내가 그에게 너를 소개해 줄 수 있어.

여 고마워!

11 ①

M What's wrong with my computer?

W What happened?

M I don't know. I tried to open this file, but this message comes up.

W Let me see. *[pause]* Ah, that's because your computer can't open that type of file.

M What should I do?

W You have to install a program first.

M Oh, I don't have that much time. I need to print it for a meeting in five minutes!

W I think my computer can open it. I can print it out if you send me the file.

M That's great! Could you just print one copy?

W Sure. Here is my USB drive.

남 내 컴퓨터에 무슨 문제가 있는 거지?

여 무슨 일이야?

남 모르겠어. 내가 이 파일을 열려고 했는데 이 메시지가 나타나.

여 어디 봐. *[잠시 후]* 아, 네 컴퓨터가 그 형식의 파일을 열 수 없기 때문이야.

남 내가 어떻게 해야 하지?

여 너는 우선 프로그램을 설치해야 해.

남 아, 내게는 시간이 별로 없어. 5분 후에 회의를 위해 그것을 인쇄해야 해!

여 내 컴퓨터가 그것을 열 수 있을 것 같아. 네가 그 파일을 내게 보내주면 내가 그것을 인쇄할 수 있어.

남 다행이다! 한 부만 인쇄해 주겠니?

여 물론이지. 여기 내 USB 드라이브가 있어.

12 ⑤

M Irene, are you studying for the exams on Thursday? It's already Monday.

W Didn't you know? This Thursday we don't have any exams.

M Really? How come?

W It's our school's 50th anniversary.

M Oh, I forgot. Then does it mean that I have one more day to study?

W You're right.

M Wow! How lucky!

남 Irene, 너는 목요일 시험을 위해 공부를 하고 있니? 벌써 월요일이야.

여 너 몰랐니? 이번 주 목요일에 우리는 시험이 없어.

남 정말? 어째서?

여 그날은 우리 학교 창립 50주년이야.

남 아, 내가 깜빡했네. 그러면 내게 공부할 날이 하루 더 있다는 의미인가?

여 네 말이 맞아.

남 와! 정말 운이 좋군!

13 ③

M Look at this! Erica, which program will you sign up for?

W I've already been to the U.S., so I want to try another country.

M When are you planning to leave?

W I'm going to finish my first year here in June, so I'd like to leave right after that.

M I see.

W But I can't decide if it's better to do a program with a homestay or with a dormitory.

M With a homestay, you would have a lot more opportunities to speak English.

W That's true. I guess I know what I'm going to do.

남 이것 좀 봐! Erica, 너는 어느 프로그램에 등록할 거야?

여 음, 나는 이미 미국에 가본 적이 있어서 나는 다른 나라에 가보고 싶어.

남 너는 언제 떠날 계획이니?

여 나는 6월에 여기서 첫 해를 마칠 거니까, 그 직후에 떠나고 싶어.

남 그렇구나.

여 하지만 나는 홈스테이 프로그램과 기숙사 프로그램 중에 어느 것이 더 좋은지 결정할 수가 없어.

남 홈스테이를 하면, 네가 영어를 말할 수 있는 기회가 훨씬 더 많아질 거야.

여 맞아. 내가 뭘 해야 할지 알 것 같아.

14 ③

M   Hey, aren't you hungry?

W   Yes, it's already nine. When did you eat dinner?

M   I had Chinese food at five.

W   I see. We still have a lot of work to do. So why don't we go out and eat something?

M   Sure. What would you like to eat?

W   How about doughnuts and coffee? There is an Uncle Doughnuts near here.

M   Great! Let's go out now

남   야, 너 배고프지 않니?

여   응, 벌써 9시야. 저녁은 언제 먹었니?

남   나는 5시에 중국 음식을 먹었어.

여   그렇구나. 우리는 아직 할 일이 많아. 그러니 나가서 뭐 좀 먹는 게 어때?

남   물론이지. 너는 무엇을 먹고 싶니?

여   도넛과 커피는 어때? 이 근처에 Uncle Doughnuts가 있어.

남   잘됐네. 지금 나가자.

15 ③

W   Good morning, students. I know many of you feel disappointed because the school canceled the football game last Saturday. I've received many emails asking me to explain why this decision was made. The reason was the weather. The Weather Service had issued a severe thunderstorm warning. This meant that there was a chance of dangerous lightning in the area. I'll let you know when the game is rescheduled. Thank you for your understanding.

남   학생 여러분, 안녕하세요. 학교가 지난 토요일의 축구 경기를 취소해서 여러분 중 다수가 실망한 것을 저는 압니다. 저는 이 결정이 내려졌던 이유를 설명해 줄 것을 제게 요청하는 이메일을 많이 받았습니다. 이유는 날씨였습니다. 기상청이 심한 뇌우경보를 발령했습니다. 이것은 그 지역에 위험한 번개가 칠 가능성이 있다는 것을 의미했습니다. 경기 일정이 다시 정해지면 여러분에게 알리겠습니다. 이해해 주셔서 감사합니다.

16 ⑤

W   Hello. I really like these tulips. How much are they?

M   They're one dollar each, or six dollars for seven.

W   Hmm. How about these red roses?

M   They're also a dollar each. But a dozen only costs nine dollars.

W   Okay. And what about these lilies?

M   They're a little cheaper. I can give you a dozen for five dollars.

W   Great. Then I'd like seven tulips and a dozen roses.

M   Okay.

여   안녕하세요. 저는 이 튤립을 정말 좋아해요. 그것은 가격이 얼마죠?

남   그것들은 각각 1달러이고, 7송이에 6달러입니다.

여   음. 이 빨간 장미는 어떤가요?

남   장미도 각각 1달러입니다. 하지만 12송이는 9달러밖에 안 해요.

여   알겠습니다. 이 백합들은요?

남   그것은 좀 더 저렴합니다. 5달러에 12송이를 드릴 수 있어요.

여   좋아요. 그럼 튤립 7송이와 장미 12송이를 사겠어요.

남   물론이죠.

17 ⑤

W   Has the repairman fixed the heater yet?

M   Unfortunately, he said it can't be fixed.

W   What? But he said he could fix it last week.

M   The heater company was unable to get replacement parts because it is an old model.

W   That's terrible news! We don't have enough money.

M   I know. What should we do?

W   I think my parents have one they're not using right now.

M   Oh, great! We could use that heater until we buy a new one.

여   수리공이 벌써 히터를 고쳤니?

남   불행히도, 그는 그것은 수리가 안 된다고 했어.

여   뭐? 하지만 그 사람이 지난주에 그것을 고칠 수 있다고 말했어.

남 그 히터 회사는 그것이 구형 모델이라서 그 교체 부품을 구할 수가 없대.

여 정말 안 좋은 소식이군! 우리는 충분한 돈이 없어.

남 알아. 우리 어떻게 하지?

여 음, 내 생각에는 우리 부모님께서 지금은 사용하지 않는 것을 가지고 계신 것 같아.

남 오, 좋아! 우리는 새 히터를 살 때까지 그 히터를 사용할 수 있겠어.

---

18 ①

M Lisa, why are you wearing winter clothes? It's not that cold out today.

W Really? I feel a little cold.

M Hmm…. You look pale. You might be getting sick.

W No. I didn't sleep well last night. That's all.

M Are you sure? You look like you have a fever, too. Let me check.

W I'm okay, Tommy. It's just because of lack of sleep.

M It might be more than you think. You shouldn't ignore the signs your body is sending to you.

W All right, all right. Why do you keep bothering me?

남 Lisa, 너는 왜 겨울옷을 입고 있니? 오늘은 그렇게 춥지 않아.

여 정말? 조금 쌀쌀해.

남 흠…. 너 창백해 보여. 너는 몸이 안 좋아질 수도 있겠어.

여 아니, 어젯밤에 잠을 잘 못 잤어. 그게 다야.

남 정말이야? 너는 열도 있는 것 같구나. 확인해 볼게.

여 나는 괜찮아, Tommy. 그것은 단지 수면 부족 때문이야.

남 네 생각 이상의 뭔가가 있을 수도 있어. 너는 네 몸이 보내는 신호를 무시해서는 안 돼.

여 알았어. 알았어. 너는 왜 나를 귀찮게 하니?

---

19 ⑤

M Thanks for inviting me, Suji.

W Welcome to my house, Andy! We've been waiting for you. I cooked roast beef. I'm sure you'll like it.

M Hmm…. It looks good, but is there anything else?

W We also have some meatballs. I made them myself this morning. Help yourself.

M I'm sorry. But actually, I'm a vegetarian. I don't eat meat.

W Oh my! I didn't know that. I didn't make anything without meat except for the onion soup.

M Don't worry about it. I'll just have some soup.

남 수지야, 초대 해줘서 고마워.

여 우리 집에 온 것을 환영해, Andy! 우리는 너를 기다리고 있었어. 나는 구운 쇠고기를 요리했어. 틀림없이 네 마음에 들 거야.

남 흠…. 보기 좋긴 한데, 다른 것은 없니?

여 우리는 미트볼도 있어. 오늘 아침에 내가 직접 만들었어. 많이 먹어.

남 미안해. 하지만, 나는 사실 채식주의자야. 나는 고기를 안 먹어.

여 세상에! 나는 몰랐어. 나는 양파 수프 말고는 고기가 들어간 것만 만들었어.

남 그것은 걱정하지 마. 나는 그냥 수프를 먹을게.

---

20 ③

M Amy and her boyfriend watched a movie at the theater. Afterwards, they were hungry, so they decided to have something to eat at a nice restaurant. Amy's boyfriend suggested an Italian restaurant because he knows that Amy likes pasta and pizza. But they go to an Italian restaurant every time they meet. So Amy wants to have something different today. She is in the mood for Korean food. However, she is not sure if her boyfriend likes Korean food. In this situation, what would Amy most likely say to her boyfriend?

남 Amy와 그녀의 남자친구는 극장에서 영화를 봤다. 그 후, 그들은 배가 고파서 멋진 식당에서 뭔가 먹기로 했다. Amy의 남자친구는 Amy가 파스타와 피자를 좋아하는 것을 알고 있기 때문에 이탈리아 식당을 제안했다. 하지만 그들은 만날 때마다 이탈리아 식당에 간다. 그래서 Amy는 오늘 뭔가 다른 것을 먹고 싶다. 그녀는 한국 음식을 먹고 싶은 생각이 든다. 하지만, 그녀는 그녀의 남자친구가 한국 음식을 좋아하는지 확신하지 못한다. 이런 상황에서 Amy는 남자친구에게 뭐라고 말할 것인가?

01 ①	02 ④	03 ②	04 ⑤	05 ②	06 ②	07 ③	08 ④
09 ①	10 ⑤	11 ①	12 ⑤	13 ③	14 ⑤	15 ⑤	16 ③
17 ③	18 ①	19 ④	20 ⑤				

Dictation Test

01 looking for, to carry one, You can pay **02** rice noodles, walking a lot, The prices, cheap **03** possible to cancel, started cooking, deliver the food **04** shakes while I'm driving, a close inspection, How long **05** by express, pay in cash, wrap this box **06** don't blame, a quick shower, I'm starving, can eat it **07** biggest worry, those who worry about, less teens who **08** fundraising event, take place, a flea market, go to charity **09** the most common, during the winter season, protect our ears **10** volunteer work, a nursing home, helped them take a walk **11** never been, any thoughts about, ride a bike **12** the very back row, the full screen, at least once, Which side, prefer **13** wedding anniversary, the date today, still have time **14** something happened, disappeared, drop by anywhere, go and check **15** an announcement, passengers, due to bad weather, new departure time **16** Each box includes, the total comes, reasonable price **17** to return this cap, the receipt, give you a refund, exchange **18** made an appointment, supposed to see, a business trip, instead **19** an impressive speech, must have practiced, get a good result **20** lose some weight, has no energy, ruining her health

01 ①

M How can I help you?

W I'm looking for a wallet. Where are they?

M They are in the corner over there.

W I can see only long ones. Do you have shorter ones, too? I want to carry one in my bag.

M The short ones are on the shelf right next to you.

W Oh, there are many cute wallets. I like this black one with white dots.

M OK. You can pay at the counter.

남 무엇을 도와 드릴까요?

여 저는 지갑을 찾고 있어요. 그건 어디에 있나요?

남 그것은 저쪽에 모퉁이에 있어요.

여 저는 긴 것밖에 안 보이네요. 더 짧은 것들도 있나요? 저는 제 가방에 넣고 다닐 것을 원해요.

남 짧은 것들은 손님 바로 옆에 있는 선반 위에 있어요.

여 오, 귀여운 지갑들이 많이 있네요. 저는 이 흰색 점 무늬가 있는 검은 지갑이 좋아요.

남 네. 카운터에서 계산하시면 됩니다.

02 ④

M Jina, how was your trip to Vietnam?

W It was fantastic. The beach was so beautiful and the sand was very soft.

M How was the food? Did you eat Vietnamese rice noodles?

W Of course I did. I loved it, but my parents didn't like it because of the smell.

M I see. How did you get around there? Did you take a taxi?

W I was thinking of walking a lot, but I couldn't. There were so many motorcycles on the street. I usually took a taxi.

M Sounds like you had a wonderful time there. I want to go there some day.

W You should. The prices are very cheap and the people are nice. I'm already planning my next visit to Vietnam.

남 지나야, 네 베트남 여행은 어땠니?

여 환상적이었어. 해변이 너무 아름다웠고 모래가 굉장히 부드러웠어.

남 음식은 어땠니? 너는 베트남 쌀국수를 먹었니?

여 물론 먹었지. 나는 맛있었는데, 나의 부모님께서는 냄새 때문에 좋아하지 않으셨어.

남 그렇구나. 너는 거기를 어떻게 다녔니? 택시를 탔니?

여 나는 많이 걸을 생각이었는데 그럴 수가 없었어. 길거리에 오토바이가 너무 많았어. 주로 택시를 탔어.

남 너는 그곳에서 즐거운 시간을 보낸 것 같네. 나도 언젠가 거기에 가고 싶다.

여 너도 꼭 가 봐야 해. 물가도 싸고 사람들도 친절해. 나는 벌써 다음 베트남 방문을 계획하고 있어.

03 ②

[Telephone rings.]

W Uncle Jim's Hamburger Store. How may I help you?

M   Hello. This is Brian Milan. I ordered two hamburgers just before.

W   Yeah. You ordered a cheeseburger and a chicken burger. Is it right?

M   That's right. Is it possible to cancel the order? Something popped up.

W   I'm so sorry. But we already started cooking.

M   Okay. Then please deliver the food as I ordered.

W   It will take about 15 minutes. Is it okay?

M   No problem. Thank you.

[전화벨 소리가 울린다.]

여   Uncle Jim 햄버거 가게입니다. 무엇을 도와 드릴까요?

남   안녕하세요. 저는 Brian Milan입니다. 방금 전에 햄버거 두 개를 주문했습니다.

여   네. 치즈버거와 치킨버거를 주문하셨네요. 맞나요?

남   맞습니다. 주문을 취소하는 게 가능할까요? 갑자기 일이 생겨서요.

여   정말 죄송해요. 벌써 조리가 시작되었어요.

남   네, 그러면 제가 주문했던 대로 음식을 배달해 주세요.

여   15분 정도 걸릴 거예요. 괜찮나요?

남   문제없어요. 감사합니다.

04 ⑤

M   What seems to be the problem with your car?

W   The steering wheel shakes while I'm driving.

M   Oh, I see. Is there any other problem?

W   And sometimes it makes a noise when I start the engine.

M   Umm... I think I should take a close inspection of the car.

W   How long will it take?

M   It will take more than three hours.

W   Then, I'll come back tomorrow morning.

M   OK.

남   손님 차에 무슨 문제가 있나요?

여   제가 운전할 때 운전대가 흔들려요.

남   아, 그렇군요. 다른 문제도 있나요?

여   그리고 시동을 켤 때 가끔씩 소음이 나요.

남   음... 제 생각에는 차를 정밀 검사를 해야겠어요.

여   얼마나 걸릴까요?

남   3시간 이상 걸릴 거예요.

여   그러면, 내일 아침에 올게요.

남   알겠습니다.

05 ②

① W   Can you help me move this box?
   M   Of course I can.

② W   I'd like to send this package by express.
   M   OK. Place it on the scale.

③ W   How much is it all together?
   M   It's 10,000 won.

④ W   Will you pay in cash or by credit card?
   M   I'll pay in cash.

⑤ W   Can you wrap this box?
   M   I'm afraid I can't.

---

① 여   제가 이 상자 옮기는 것을 도와줄 수 있나요?
   남   물론 가능합니다.

② 여   저는 이 소포를 속달로 보내고 싶어요.
   남   알겠습니다. 그것을 저울에 올려 주세요.

③ 여   모두 해서 얼마인가요?
   남   만원입니다.

④ 여   현금으로 내시겠어요, 아니면 카드로 내시겠어요?
   남   현금으로 낼게요.

⑤ 여   이 상자를 포장해 주시겠어요?
   남   미안하지만 안 됩니다.

06 ②

M   Oh, no! It's already 7:30! I'm going to be late.

W   I tried to wake you up, but you kept sleeping. So, don't blame me.

M   No, I won't. I'll take a quick shower and leave for school.

W   Aren't you hungry? You skipped dinner yesterday.

M   Actually, I'm starving. But I don't have time for breakfast.

W   That's too bad.

M   Mom. Can you make a sandwich while I'm taking a shower? I think I can eat it on my way to school.

W   OK, I can do that.

M   I love you, Mom.

남   오, 안 돼! 벌써 7시 30분이네! 늦겠어.

여   너를 깨우려고 노력했는데 너는 계속 자더구나. 그러니, 나를 원망하지 마라.

남   네, 안 할게요. 빨리 샤워하고 학교에 가야겠어요.

여   배고프지 않니? 너는 어제 저녁을 걸렀잖니.

남 사실 저는 너무 배고파요. 하지만 아침 먹을 시간은 없어요.

여 그거 참 안됐구나.

남 엄마. 제가 샤워하는 동안 샌드위치를 만들어 주시겠어요? 학교 가는 길에 그것을 먹을 수 있을 거 같아요.

여 그래. 그렇게 할게.

남 사랑해요, 엄마.

07 ③

① **M** Teens' biggest worry is their grades.

② **M** Friends are the second biggest worry for teens.

③ **M** There are more teens who worry about their future than those who worry about their friends.

④ **M** The fourth top ranked problem for teens is money.

⑤ **M** There are less teens who have family problems than those who have money problems.

① **남** 십 대들의 가장 큰 고민은 그들의 성적이다.

② **남** 친구가 십 대들에게 두 번째로 큰 고민이다.

③ **남** 장래에 대해 고민하는 십 대들이 친구에 대해 고민하는 십 대들보다 더 많다.

④ **남** 상위 네 번째인 십 대들의 고민은 돈이다.

⑤ **남** 가족 문제를 가진 십 대들은 돈 걱정을 하는 십 대들보다 더 적다.

08 ④

W Hello, I'm Park Mina, the president of the student council. Our school is holding a fundraising event for people in need. It will take place in the Community Center, on Saturday, May 9th. For the event, we are planning a flea market, food booths, and a concert. There's no entrance fee for the flea market and food booths, but you need to pay ten dollars for the concert. The profits from this event will go to charity. Thank you.

여 안녕하세요. 저는 학생회 회장인 박미나입니다. 우리 학교는 도움이 필요한 사람들을 위한 기금 마련 행사를 개최할 예정입니다. 그것은 시민회관에서 5월 9일 토요일에 개최될 것입니다. 이 행사를 위해 우리는 벼룩시장과 음식 부스, 그리고 콘서트를 계획하고 있습니다. 벼룩시장과 음식 부스에 대해서는 입장료가 없지만 콘서트에 입장하려면 여러분은 10달러를 내셔야 합니다. 이 행사의 수익금은 자선단체로 보낼 것입니다. 감사합니다.

09 ①

M These are one of the most common winter accessories. These are a pair of small pieces of material like fur with a strap that goes over the head. Little children wear these items during the winter season. But these days, we can see women wearing these for their fashion. With these items, we can protect our ears from the cold.

남 이것은 가장 흔한 겨울철 액세서리들 중 하나이다. 머리 위에 띠는 띠로 연결된 털 같은 재질의 작은 한 쌍의 조각이다. 어린아이들이 겨울철에 이것을 착용한다. 하지만 요즘에는 패션을 위해 이것을 착용한 여성들을 볼 수 있다. 이 물건으로 우리는 귀를 추위로부터 보호할 수 있다.

10 ⑤

M What did you do during the weekend?

W Nothing special. I just read books at home. What about you?

M I did volunteer work.

W Where did you go?

M I went to a nursing home.

W You went there before. Did you clean their room this time, too?

M No, this time I talked with the elderly people and helped them take a walk in the garden.

W How was it?

M It was very rewarding. They looked happy.

남 너는 주말 동안 뭐 했니?

여 특별한 일은 없었어. 나는 집에서 책을 읽었어. 너는 어때?

남 나는 자원봉사를 했어.

여 너는 어디에 갔니?

남 나는 양로원에 갔어.

여 너는 전에도 거기 갔었지. 이번에도 그분들의 방을 청소했니?

남 아니, 이번에는 어르신들과 이야기를 하고 그분들이 정원을 산책하시는 것을 도와 드렸어.

여 그것은 어땠니?

남 그것은 무척 보람 있었어. 그분들이 행복해 보였어.

11 ①

① **W** How have you been?

　 M I've never been there.

② W You have a long face. What's wrong?

M My pet dog is very sick.

③ W How often do you eat out?

M About once a month.

④ W Do you have any thoughts about our talent show?

M How about dancing together?

⑤ W How do you go to school?

M I ride a bike.

---

① 여 너는 어떻게 지냈니?

남 나는 그곳에 가 본 적이 없어.

② 여 너 우울해 보인다. 무슨 일이야?

남 내 애완견이 매우 아파.

③ 여 너는 얼마나 자주 외식을 하니?

남 한 달에 한 번 정도.

④ 여 우리의 장기 자랑에 관해 아이디어가 있니?

남 함께 춤을 추는 건 어때?

⑤ 여 너는 학교에 어떻게 가니?

남 나는 자전거를 타고 가.

12 ⑤

W Let's choose where to sit in the theater.

M I usually sit in the middle of the very back row.

W Is there any reason?

M I can enjoy the full screen there.

W But it's difficult to get out of the seat if we sit there. I have to visit the restroom at least once while the movie is showing.

M Then let's sit on the back seat of the corner. I can still enjoy the full screen there.

W Thanks. Which side do you prefer? Right or left?

M I prefer the right one near the exit.

여 극장에서 어디에 앉을지 고르자.

남 나는 보통 맨 뒷줄의 가운데에 앉아.

여 무슨 이유가 있니?

남 그곳에서 스크린 전체를 볼 수 있어.

여 하지만 우리가 거기에 앉으면 자리에서 나오기가 힘들잖아. 나는 영화가 상영되는 동안 적어도 한번은 화장실에 가야 해.

남 그러면 구석 뒤쪽 자리에 앉자. 거기에서도 스크린 전체를 볼 수 있거든.

여 고마워. 어느 쪽이 좋아? 오른쪽 아니면 왼쪽?

남 출구에 가까운 오른쪽이 더 좋아.

13 ③

M You know what? Our parents' wedding anniversary is coming.

W You're right. It's on November 30th.

M Yeah. What shall we do for them? Last year, we bought some flowers and a bottle of wine for them.

W Yeah, they loved our present. I remember. Oh, wait! What's the date today?

M It's November 12th. Why?

W Oh my god! Their anniversary is tomorrow.

M Oh, you're right. It is November 13th, not 30th.

W We still have time. Let's think about what to do for them.

남 그거 알아? 부모님의 결혼기념일이 다가오고 있어.

여 네 말이 맞아. 11월 30일이야.

남 응. 우리는 부모님을 위해 무엇을 할까? 작년에는 꽃과 와인 한 병을 사 드렸잖아.

여 응, 부모님께서 우리 선물을 좋아하셨어. 기억 나. 오, 잠깐만! 오늘이 며칠이지?

남 11월 12일이야. 왜?

여 오, 이런! 결혼기념일은 내일이야.

남 아, 네 말이 맞다. 11월 30일이 아니라 13일이야.

여 우리에겐 아직 시간이 있어. 부모님을 위해 무엇을 할지 생각해 보자.

14 ⑤

W What took you so long, Jake? Did the class finish late?

M No, the English class finished on time. But something happened on my way home.

W What is it?

M My cellphone disappeared. I looked for it everywhere, but I couldn't find it. So I couldn't contact you, either.

W I see. Where did you look for it?

M I went back to the street again. And I searched the classroom, too.

W Didn't you drop by anywhere on your way home?

M Oh, I stopped at the ice cream store! I didn't think about it.

W Maybe you dropped your phone there. Let's go and check together.

M Okay. Thanks, Mom.

여 너 왜 이렇게 늦었니, Jake? 영어 수업이 늦게 끝났니?

남 아니오, 영어 수업은 제때 끝났어요. 그런데 집에 오는 길에 일이 생겼어요.

여 그게 뭔데?

남 제 휴대전화가 사라졌어요. 제가 모두 다 찾아봤는데 못 찾았어요. 그래서 엄마한테 연락도 못했고요.

여 그렇구나. 어디서 그것을 찾아봤니?

남 길거리로 다시 되돌아갔어요. 그리고 교실도 찾아봤고요.

여 집에 오는 길에 어딘가에 들르지 않았니?

남 아, 아이스크림 가게에 들렸어요! 그 생각은 못했네요.

여 아마도 그곳에 전화기를 떨어뜨린 것 같은데. 같이 가서 확인해 보자.

남 네. 감사해요, 엄마.

---

15 ⑤

W This is an announcement for passengers on flight 123 to Helsinki, with a stop in Istanbul. The flight has been delayed due to bad weather conditions. The flight crew has arrived at the gate, but the ground crew is still de-icing the wings of the aircraft in preparation for departure. Our new departure time is 10:50 a.m. Thank you for your patience.

여 이스탄불을 거쳐 헬싱키로 가는 123 항공편 탑승객들을 위한 안내 방송입니다. 궂은 날씨로 인해 비행이 지연되었습니다. 비행 승무원들은 게이트에 도착했으나, 지상 근무원들이 출발 준비를 위해 비행기 날개의 제빙 작업을 하는 중입니다. 새로운 출발 시각은 오전 10시 50분입니다. 기다려 주셔서 감사합니다.

---

16 ③

M Excuse me, I want to buy those postcards.

W They're 5 dollars per box.

M Five dollars? How many cards are there in the box?

W Each box includes 10 different cards. And if you buy more than 10 boxes, you can get a ten percent discount.

M Hmm... If I buy ten boxes, the total comes to 50 dollars. Then I can get a ten percent discount on it. Am I right?

W Yeah. You're right.

M Then it's a reasonable price. I'll take ten boxes.

W Thanks a lot.

남 실례합니다, 저는 저 엽서를 사고 싶어요.

여 한 상자에 5달러입니다.

남 5달러요? 한 상자에 엽서가 몇 장 들어있나요?

여 각 상자에 10개의 다른 엽서가 들어 있어요. 그리고 손님께서 열 상자 이상 사시면 10퍼센트 할인도 받으실 수 있어요.

남 음... 제가 10상자를 사면 총액이 50달러가 되는군요. 거기에서 10퍼센트 할인을 받을 수 있는 거네요. 맞나요?

여 네. 맞습니다.

남 그렇다면 합리적인 가격이네요. 열 상자 살게요.

여 매우 감사합니다..

---

17 ③

W How may I help you?

M I want to return this cap. Is it possible?

W Let me see. It's our product. Do you have the receipt?

M No, I don't. Actually, I got it as a gift.

W I'm afraid we can't give you a refund if you don't have the receipt.

M I see. Then, can I exchange it for something else?

W Of course you can. What you do want to exchange it for?

여 무엇을 도와 드릴까요?

남 이 모자를 환불하고 싶어요. 가능한가요?

여 볼게요. 이것은 저희 상품이 맞네요. 영수증이 있으신가요?

남 아니요. 사실은 선물로 받은 거예요.

여 죄송하지만, 영수증이 없으면 환불해 드릴 수 없습니다.

남 그렇군요. 그러면 다른 것으로 교환할 수 있나요?

여 물론 하실 수 있습니다. 무엇으로 교환하고 싶으세요?

---

18 ①

[Telephone rings.]

W Doctor Lee's dental clinic. What can I do for you?

M Hello. I made an appointment for this Wednesday, but I want to change it.

W OK. Can I have your name?

M   It's John Brown.

W   Yes, you're supposed to see the doctor at 2 p.m. this Wednesday. How do you want to change it?

M   I have a business trip on that day. Can I come on Thursday instead?

W   Sure. What time is convenient for you?

[전화벨이 울린다.]

여   Doctor Lee 치과입니다. 무엇을 도와 드릴까요?

남   저는 이번 주 수요일에 예약했지만, 그것을 바꾸고 싶어요.

여   네. 성함을 알려 주시겠어요?

남   John Brown입니다.

여   네, 손님은 이번 주 수요일 오후 2시에 진찰 받으시기로 되어 있네요. 어떻게 바꾸고 싶으세요?

남   저는 그날 출장이 있어요. 대신 목요일에 가도 될까요?

여   물론입니다. 몇 시가 편하세요?

19 ④

M   Mina, that was an impressive speech. I didn't know you were so good at English.

W   Thanks. I was very nervous, but at least I didn't forget my lines.

M   You must have practiced hard.

W   Yes, I've been practicing for this speech contest for more than two months.

M   I'm sure you will get a good result. By the way, how come your pronunciation is so perfect? How long have you been speaking English?

남   미나야, 그것은 정말 인상적인 연설이었어. 나는 네가 영어를 그렇게 잘하는지 몰랐어.

여   고마워. 나는 너무 긴장했는데, 적어도 나는 내 원고를 잊지는 않았어.

남   너는 분명히 열심히 연습했겠구나.

여   응, 이 말하기 대회를 위해 두 달 넘게 연습해 왔어.

남   나는 네가 꼭 좋은 결과를 얻을 거라 믿어. 그런데, 네 발음은 어쩜 그렇게 완벽해? 너는 얼마나 오랫동안 영어를 말해 왔니?

20 ⑤

M   Minsu's friend Jisu thinks she is too fat. She decided to lose some weight and stopped eating. She looks pale and has no energy. Minsu is worried that Jisu is ruining her health. He thinks it is much better to have a good diet and do some exercise than to go hungry. In this situation, what would Minsu most likely say to his friend, Jisu?

남   민수의 친구인 지수는 자신이 너무 뚱뚱하다고 생각한다. 그녀는 체중을 좀 줄이기로 결심하고 먹는 것을 중단했다. 그녀는 창백해 보이고 힘이 없다. 민수는 지수가 그녀의 건강을 해치고 있는 것을 걱정한다. 그는 굶는 것보다 좋은 식습관을 가지고 운동을 좀 하는 것이 훨씬 더 낫다고 생각한다. 이런 상황에서 민수는 친구인 지수에게 뭐라고 말할 것인가?

01 ⑤   02 ④   03 ②   04 ③   05 ③   06 ④   07 ⑤   08 ④

09 ①   10 ①   11 ②   12 ⑤   13 ③   14 ①   15 ⑤   16 ④

17 ④   18 ⑤   19 ⑤   20 ⑤

Dictation Test

01 into the universe, no handle, need a handle **02** to wear, work out, selling well, on sale   **03** a tea break, turning, store, want me to send   **04** permed naturally, recommend giving, dye your hair, would damage   **05** holding it, afraid not, get on   **06** ask you a favor, not sure if, are closed   **07** our school festival, our auditorium, amazing performances **08** directed by, the gap between, The running time, not boring   **09** but invisible, eye, exist on earth, very concerned about   **10** she has been, forgot to write, the stationery store   **11** mind if, What day, The more, the better, ever been to   **12** Which do you prefer, Either is fine, much more exciting   **13** a swimming lesson, You'll be hungry, A quarter past   **14** sprained my ankle, a big deal, really hurts   **15** make an announcement, a clearance sale, a discount, range from   **16** it costs, sweet and cheap, Here they are **17** bought a printer, for the inconvenience, find the form   **18** messed up, something wrong, try to memorize   **19** can't park here, the handicapped, The ground floor **20** is full of, shake his legs, concentrates on, decides to ask

---

01 ⑤

W   Wow! There are so many cups! Where did they come from?

M   My classmates and I made them in our art class.

W   That's amazing. Where's yours?

M   Why don't you find it yourself?

W   Umm. You're into the universe. So maybe that one with the stars?

M   That was close. But mine is that one with the moon and the stars.

W   Oh, there's no handle.

M   No, I don't need a handle. Actually, I made it to use as a pen holder.

···

여   와! 컵이 정말 많다! 이것들은 다 어디서 난 거야?

남   우리 반 친구들과 내가 그것을 미술 시간에 만들었어.

여   놀랍다. 네 것은 어디에 있니?

남   네가 직접 찾아보는 게 어때?

여   음. 너는 우주에 관심이 많지. 그러니까 아마도 별들이 있는 저것?

남   비슷했어. 하지만 내 것은 저기 달과 별이 있는 거야.

여   오, 손잡이가 없네.

남   응, 나는 손잡이가 필요 없어. 사실은, 나는 그것을 연필꽂이로 쓰려고 만들었어.

02 ④

W   How may I help you?

M   I'm looking for a pair of sneakers.

W   Are they for you?

M   Yes, I'm going to wear them when I work out at the gym.

W   What's your size?

M   I wear a size ten.

W   Would you try these on? They're selling well.

M   These are very light. How much are they?

W   They're on sale now. They are 40 dollars now.

M   That's a good price. I'll take them.

···

여   무엇을 도와 드릴까요?

남   저는 운동화 한 켤레를 찾고 있어요.

여   손님께서 신으실 건가요?

남   네, 제가 체육관에서 운동할 때 신을 거예요.

여   사이즈가 어떻게 되시나요?

남   저는 10 사이즈를 신습니다.

여   이것을 신어 보실래요? 이것이 잘 팔립니다.

남   이것은 정말 가볍네요. 얼마죠?

여   그것은 지금 할인 판매 중이에요. 40달러입니다.

남   좋은 가격이네요. 이걸로 살게요.

03 ②

[Telephone rings.]

M   Hello, honey. It's me. Are you busy now?

W   No, I'm not. I was just having a tea break. What's up?

M   I left an important file on my computer. Can you send it to me?

W   Ok. Please wait. I'm turning on the computer. Where did you store it?

M   It's in my document file folder. And the name is Annual Report 2019.

W I found it. Do you want me to send it to your email?

M Yes. Thanks.

[전화벨 소리가 울린다.]

남 여보세요, 여보. 나예요. 당신 지금 바빠요?

여 아니요. 차를 마시면서 쉬고 있었어요. 무슨 일이에요?

남 내 컴퓨터에 중요한 파일을 놓고 왔어요. 그것을 저에게 보내 줄 수 있어요?

여 네. 기다려요. 지금 컴퓨터를 켜고 있어요. 그것을 어디에 저장했어요?

남 그것은 내 문서 파일 폴더에 있어요. 그리고 이름은 Annual Report 2019예요.

여 찾았어요. 당신 이메일로 보낼까요?

남 네. 고마워요.

---

04 ③

M How would you like your hair done?

W I want it trimmed a little and permed naturally.

M Oh, I see. But before the perm, I strongly recommend giving some nutrition to your hair. Your hair is very dry now.

W Okay. And is it possible to change the hair color, too?

M It would be better to dye your hair later. Having the two procedures at the same time would damage your hair.

W Then I'll follow your advice. I don't want my hair damaged.

M All right. I'll wash your hair first. Follow me this way.

남 머리를 어떻게 해드릴까요?

여 약간 다듬고 자연스럽게 파마를 하고 싶어요.

남 오, 알겠습니다. 하지만 파마를 하기 전에, 저는 손님의 머리카락에 영양분을 줄 것을 강력히 추천합니다. 손님의 머리카락은 지금 매우 건조해요.

여 알겠어요. 그리고 머리카락 색을 바꾸는 것도 가능한가요?

남 손님의 머리를 염색하는 것은 나중에 하는 것이 나을 겁니다. 동시에 두 가지 시술을 하면 머리카락이 손상될 수 있어요.

여 그러면 당신의 충고를 따를게요. 제 머리카락이 상하는 것은 원하지 않아요.

남 좋습니다. 머리를 먼저 감겨 드릴게요. 이쪽으로 따라오세요.

---

05 ③

① **W** How do you usually go to school?
   M I take the bus.

② **W** I can't find my transportation card.
   M But you're holding it now.

③ **W** Does this bus go to the City Hall?
   M I'm afraid not. Take the green bus.

④ **W** Here comes the bus.
   M Let's get on it!

⑤ **W** How long does it take to get there by bus?
   M It takes only ten minutes.

---

① **여** 너는 학교에 주로 어떻게 가니?
   남 나는 버스를 타.

② **여** 내 교통카드가 안 보여.
   남 네가 손에 들고 있잖아.

③ **여** 이 버스는 시청에 가나요?
   남 유감이지만 안 갑니다. 초록색 버스를 타세요.

④ **여** 여기 버스가 왔네.
   남 타자!

⑤ **여** 버스로 거기 가는 데 시간이 얼마나 걸리죠?
   남 10분밖에 안 걸려요.

---

06 ④

[Cellphone rings.]

M Mina, it's me, Minsu. Are you still at school?

W Yes, I'm reading a book in the library.

M Can I ask you a favor?

W Tell me. What is it?

M I left the classroom last, but I'm not sure if I closed the windows.

W But you can close them tomorrow morning.

M It's going to rain tonight, so the windows should be closed.

W Oh, I see. Then, I will go to the classroom and make sure the windows are closed before I go home. Don't worry.

M Thanks a lot, Mina.

[휴대전화가 울린다.]

남 미나야, 나야 민수. 너 아직 학교에 있니?

여 응, 나는 도서관에서 책을 읽고 있어.

남 내가 부탁 좀 해도 될까?

여 말해 봐. 뭔데?

남 내가 마지막으로 교실에서 떠났는데, 내가 창문을 닫았는지 잘 모르겠어.

여 하지만 내일 아침에 닫으면 되잖아.

남 오늘 밤에 비가 올 거라서, 창문이 닫혀 있어야 해.

여 아, 그렇구나. 그러면, 내가 집에 가기 전에 교실에 가서 창문이 닫혔는지 확인할게. 걱정하지 마.

남 정말 고마워, 미나야.

07 ⑤

W Hello, everyone. This is your student leader Lee Yuna. I'm happy to tell you about our school festival. It is going to be held next Friday, November 6th. It will begin at 4 p.m., so please come to our auditorium by 3:40. There will be amazing performances by the school band and the dance group. Also, there will be a prize lottery with various kinds of gifts. Don't miss this exciting event!

여 여러분, 안녕하세요. 저는 학생회장인 이유나입니다. 우리 학교 축제에 대해 여러분께 알리게 되어 기쁩니다. 그것은 다음 주 금요일인 11월 6일에 열릴 예정입니다. 축제는 오후 4시에 시작할 것이니, 강당으로 3시 40분까지 오세요. 학교 밴드와 댄스 팀의 멋진 공연이 있을 예정입니다. 또한, 다양한 종류의 선물들과 함께 경품 추첨이 있을 것입니다. 이 신나는 행사를 놓치지 마세요!

08 ④

W Did you see the famous movie directed by Mr. Bong?

M Are you talking about the movie that won the best movie award last week?

W That's right.

M Unfortunately, I didn't see the movie yet. What's it about?

W It's about the gap between the rich and the poor.

M Oh, I see. Is it long?

W Kind of. The running time is about 130 minutes. But it's not boring at all.

M I think I should watch it.

여 너는 봉 감독이 연출한 그 유명한 영화를 봤니?

남 지난주에 최고 영화상을 받았던 그 영화에 관해 말하는 거니?

여 맞아.

남 불행히도, 나는 아직 그 영화를 못 봤어. 그것은 무엇에 대한 영화니?

여 그것은 빈부 격차에 관한 거야.

남 오, 그렇구나. 그 영화가 길어?

여 그런 편이야. 상영 시간이 대략 130분이야. 하지만 전혀 지루하지 않아.

남 나도 그 영화를 봐야겠다.

09 ①

M This is everywhere but invisible to the human eye. Without this, no living thing can exist on earth. In the past, people didn't really care about the quality of this. These days, however, people are very concerned about the quality of this. There are applications to show the quality of this, and there are home appliances to purify this. What is this?

남 이것은 모든 곳에 있지만 사람 눈에 보이지 않는다. 이것이 없으면, 지구상에 어떤 생명체도 존재할 수 없다. 과거에 사람들은 이것의 질에 대해 별로 신경 쓰지 않았다. 하지만 요즘에는 사람들은 이것의 질에 대해 걱정한다. 이것의 질을 알려주는 어플리케이션이 있고, 이것을 정화시키는 가전제품이 있다. 이것은 무엇인가?

10 ①

M Mom, I think we're all set for the welcome home party for grandma.

W Great! She will be very surprised to see all of this.

M You know, she has been in the hospital for about a month. I really want to make her happy.

W Right. She will be very moved. The food is ready and we decorated the living room and the table.

M Oh, we forgot to write the card.

W You're right. Do we have a card at home?

M I don't think so. I will go to the stationery store and buy one. We still have some time.

W Okay. But please hurry.

남 엄마, 할머니를 위한 귀가 환영파티 준비가 다 된 것 같아요.
여 잘됐다! 할머니께서 이 모든 걸 보시면 정말 놀라실 거야.
남 할머니는 한 달 정도 병원에 계셨잖아요. 저는 정말 할머니를 행복하게 해 드리고 싶어요.
여 맞아. 할머니는 정말 감동 받으실 거야. 음식은 준비되었고, 거실과 탁자도 장식했어.
남 아, 우리가 카드 쓰는 것을 잊었어요.
여 네 말이 맞아. 집에 카드가 있나?
남 없을 거예요. 제가 문구점에 가서 하나 사 올게요. 아직 시간이 있어요.
여 그래. 하지만 서둘러.

11 ②

① W Do you mind if I open the windows?
　　M Please don't. There's yellow dust today.
② W What day will you be arriving from the trip?
　　M I'll be arriving at around 5 p.m.
③ W Can I bring Susan to your birthday party?
　　M Why not? The more, the better.
④ W Did you watch the soccer game yesterday?
　　M I missed it because of an important meeting.
⑤ W Have you ever been to Spain?
　　M Yes, I went there five years ago.

- -

① 여 제가 창문을 열어도 될까요?
　　남 그러지 마세요. 오늘은 황사가 있어요.
② 여 너는 여행에서 무슨 요일에 돌아오니?
　　남 나는 오후 5시쯤 돌아올 거야.
③ 여 네 생일파티에 Susan을 데려가도 될까?
　　남 왜 안 되겠어? 많을수록 더 좋아.
④ 여 너는 어제 축구 경기 봤니?
　　남 중요한 회의 때문에 나는 그것을 놓쳤어.
⑤ 여 너는 스페인에 가 봤니?
　　남 응, 5년 전에 가 봤어.

12 ⑤

W We have two movies showing now. One is *My Pet* and the other is *Spiderman*. Which do you prefer?
M I don't like animation movies. Let's watch *Spiderman*.
W Either is fine for me. Shall we watch the 2 o'clock movie?

M But it's 2D. I want to watch the 3D movie. It's a little expensive, but much more exciting.
W I've never watched a 3D movie. We still have two options.
M Let's watch the movie in the afternoon. How about meeting 30 minutes earlier in front of the theater?
W Okay.

- -

여 상영 중인 영화가 두 개 있어. 하나는 〈마이 펫〉이고, 다른 하나는 〈스파이더맨〉이야. 너는 어느 쪽이 더 좋아?
남 나는 애니메이션 영화는 좋아하지 않아. 〈스파이더맨〉을 보자.
여 나는 어느 쪽이든 좋아. 2시 영화를 볼까?
남 하지만 그것은 2D잖아. 나는 3D 영화를 보고 싶어. 그것이 조금 비싸지만, 훨씬 더 재미있거든.
여 나는 3D 영화를 본 적이 없어. 아직도 2가지 선택이 남았어.
남 오후에 상영하는 영화를 보자. 극장 앞에서 30분 전에 만나는 게 어때?
여 좋아.

13 ③

M Do you have any idea about our team project for science class? I think we should get started.
W You're right. Can we talk about this now?
M Sorry. I have to leave now. I have a swimming lesson.
W When does it finish?
M It starts at five and finishes at six.
W Hmm. You'll be hungry then. What about talking about the project over some snacks?
M Okay.
W Then, let's meet in front of the swimming pool.
M Good. Please give me fifteen more minutes to take a shower and change clothes.
W All right. A quarter past six then.

- -

남 너는 우리 과학 조별 과제에 대해 아이디어가 있니? 우리는 시작해야 할 것 같은데.
여 네 말이 맞아. 지금 이야기할까?
남 미안해. 나는 지금 가야 해. 수영 수업이 있거든.
여 그것은 언제 끝나?
남 그것은 5시에 시작해서 6시에 끝나.
여 흠. 그때쯤이면 네가 배고플 텐데. 간단히 뭔가 먹으면서 과제에 관해 얘기하는 게 어때?
남 좋아.

여 그러면, 수영장 앞에서 보자.

남 좋아. 샤워하고 옷 갈아입게 내게 15분만 시간을 좀 줘.

여 그래. 그러면 6시 15분.

14 ①

M Jisu, you don't look well. Is anything wrong?

W Actually, I sprained my ankle while taking a walk yesterday.

M Did you go see a doctor?

W No, I thought it was not a big deal. So, I just put ice on it.

M Can I see it? [pause] Oh, it's swollen. I think you really need to go see a doctor.

W You're right. It really hurts now.

남 지수야, 너 안 좋아 보인다. 무슨 문제라도 있니?

여 사실은 어제 산책을 하는 중에 발목을 삐었어.

남 너 진찰 받았니?

여 아니, 나는 별거 아니라고 생각했어. 그래서 그 위에 얼음만 댔어.

남 내가 봐도 될까? [멈춤] 오, 부었네. 내 생각에는 너는 정말 병원에 가야 할 것 같아.

여 네 말이 맞아. 이제 아파.

15 ⑤

W Hello, shoppers. May I have your attention, please? We would like to make an announcement about a special offer. We will be having a clearance sale starting from tomorrow to next Monday. We will have a discount of up to 70% on some of the selected merchandise in our company. The products range from clothing to accessories. For more information, please visit our website, www.bestgoods.com. We hope you will enjoy your shopping. Thank you.

여 안녕하세요, 손님 여러분. 잠시 주목해 주시겠습니까? 저희는 특가 판매에 관한 안내를 드리려고 합니다. 내일부터 다음 주 월요일까지 저희는 재고 정리 할인을 할 예정입니다. 저희는 저희 회사의 엄선된 상품들에 대해 최고 70퍼센트까지 할인해 드릴 것입니다. 상품은 의류부터 액세서리까지 있습니다. 더 많은 정보를 원하시면, 저희 웹사이트인 www.bestgoods.com을 방문하세요. 즐거운 쇼핑을 하시기를 바랍니다. 감사합니다.

16 ④

M Excuse me, I want to buy some fruits.

W How about some apples? They're very fresh.

M How much are they?

W Two dollars for each one. But if you buy a bag of six apples, it costs ten dollars.

M Then I'll take a bag. And how much are those oranges? They look delicious.

W They are very sweet and cheap. Only one dollar for each one. How many do you want?

M I'd like five oranges.

W One bag of apples and five oranges. Here they are.

M Thank you.

남 실례합니다, 저는 과일을 좀 사고 싶습니다.

여 사과 어떠세요? 그것은 매우 신선해요.

남 그것은 얼마죠?

여 개당 2달러입니다. 하지만 6개 들은 한 봉지를 사시면 10달러입니다.

남 그럼 한 봉지를 살게요. 그리고 저 오렌지는 얼마죠? 맛있어 보이네요.

여 그것은 맛이 매우 달고 저렴합니다. 개당 겨우 1달러에요. 몇 개를 원하세요?

남 오렌지 5개를 주세요.

여 사과 한 봉지와 오렌지 다섯 개. 여기 있습니다.

남 감사합니다.

17 ④

M It's Ace Electronics service center. May I help you?

W I bought a printer from your online store last week, but there's a problem.

M What's the problem?

W The paper is constantly getting jammed.

M I'm so sorry for the inconvenience. If you fill out the service form, we will pick it up and repair it.

W Where can I find the form?

남 Ace 전자 서비스 센터입니다. 무엇을 도와 드릴까요?

여 지난주에 귀사의 온라인 스토어에서 프린터를 샀는데 문제가 있어요.

남 문제가 무엇인가요?

여 종이가 계속 낍니다.

남 불편을 끼쳐 드려서 죄송합니다. 서비스 양식을 기재하시면, 저희가 그것을 가져다 고치겠습니다.

여 양식을 어디서 찾을 수 있나요?

남 죄송합니다, 부인. 여기에 주차하시면 안 됩니다.

여 왜 그렇죠? 여기는 비었는데요.

남 표지판을 보세요. 이곳은 장애인을 위한 구역입니다.

여 오, 죄송해요. 제가 그것을 못 봤네요. 이 근처에 주차할 곳이 있나요?

남 1층은 지금 다 찼지만, 지하 주차장에는 자리가 좀 있어요.

여 감사합니다. 지하 주차장에는 제가 어떻게 내려가죠?

18 ⑤

W How was your test today?

M I did pretty well on math, but I messed up the history test.

W I'm sorry to hear that. You studied hard for the history test.

M That's what I'm saying. Maybe there's something wrong with my study methods.

W Tell me. How do you study history?

M I just try to memorize all the important information.

W Umm... I don't think that's a good way to study history.

M Then how should I study?

여 오늘 시험 어땠어?

남 나는 수학은 꽤 잘 봤는데 역사 시험을 완전히 망쳤어.

여 그랬다니 안됐다. 너는 역시 시험을 위해 공부 열심히 했잖아.

남 내 말이 그 말이야. 아마도 내 공부 방법에 문제가 있나봐.

여 말해 봐. 너는 역사를 어떻게 공부하니?

남 나는 그냥 중요한 정보를 다 외우려고 노력해.

여 음... 내 생각에는 그것은 역사를 공부하는 좋은 방법은 아닌 것 같아.

남 그러면 내가 어떻게 공부해야 해?

20 ⑤

W Mira is studying at the library. The final exam is tomorrow and the library is full of students. Soon, a boy comes and sits right next to her. He starts to shake his legs. Mira tries to ignore it and concentrates on her studies. But his shaking doesn't stop. To make it worse, now he starts to tap his pen. Finally, Mira decides to ask him to stop distracting her concentration. In this situation, what would Mira most likely say to the boy?

여 미라는 도서관에서 공부를 하고 있다. 기말고사가 내일이라 도서관은 학생들로 가득하다. 곧, 한 남자가 와서 그녀 옆자리에 앉는다. 그는 자신의 다리를 떨기 시작한다. 미라는 이를 무시하고 자신의 공부에 집중하려고 애쓴다. 하지만 그의 다리 떨기는 멈추지 않는다. 설상가상으로, 그는 펜을 똑딱거리기 시작한다. 결국 미라는 그에게 그녀의 집중력을 분산시키는 것을 멈추라고 요청하기로 결심한다. 이런 상황에서 미라는 남자에게 뭐라고 말할 것인가?

19 ⑤

M Excuse me, ma'am. You can't park here.

W Why is that? It's empty.

M Look at the sign. It's for the handicapped.

W Oh, I'm so sorry. I didn't see that. Is there anywhere to park around here?

M The ground floor is full now, but there is some space in the underground parking lot.

W Thank you. How can I get down to the underground parking lot?